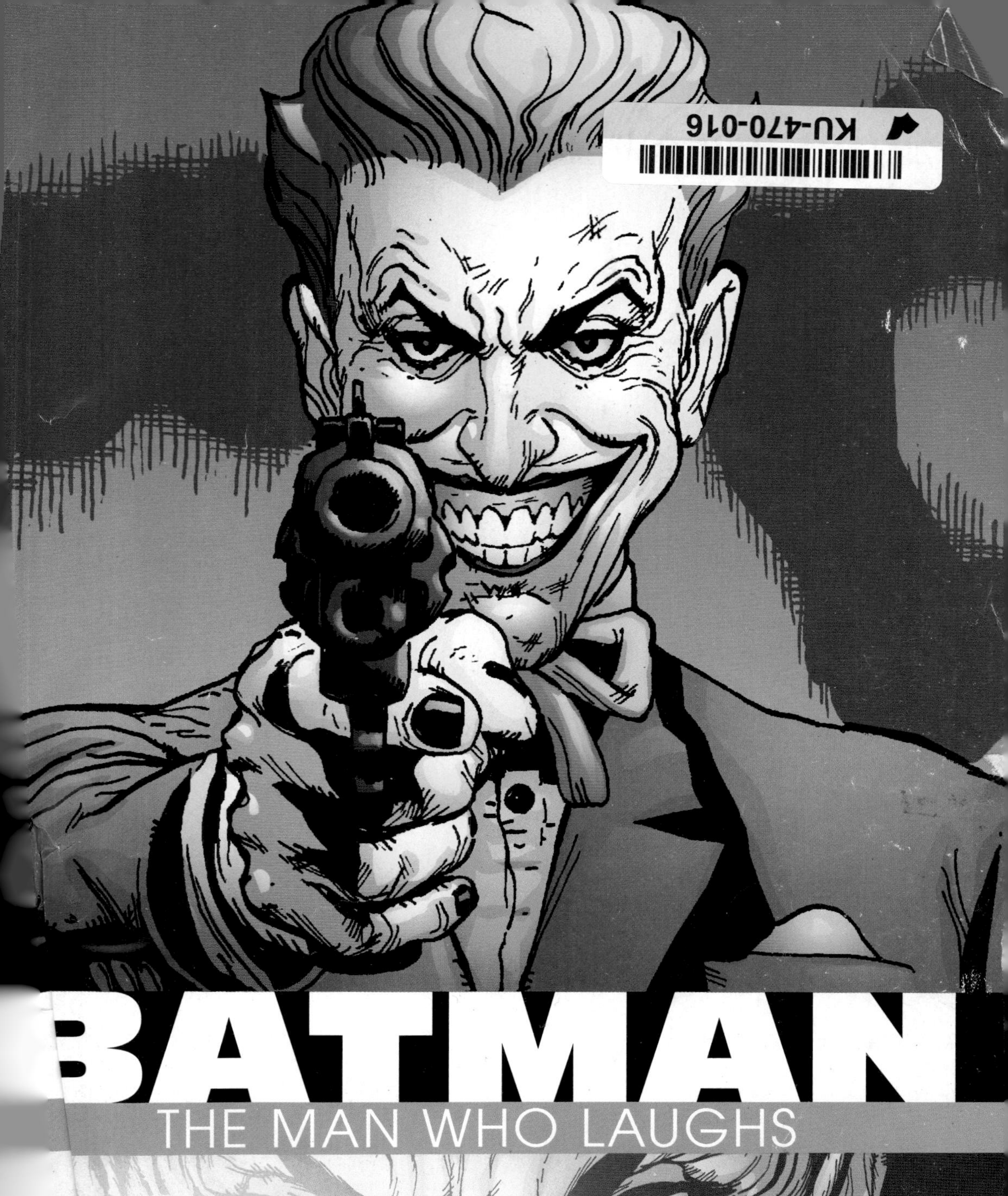

BATMAN
THE MAN WHO LAUGHS

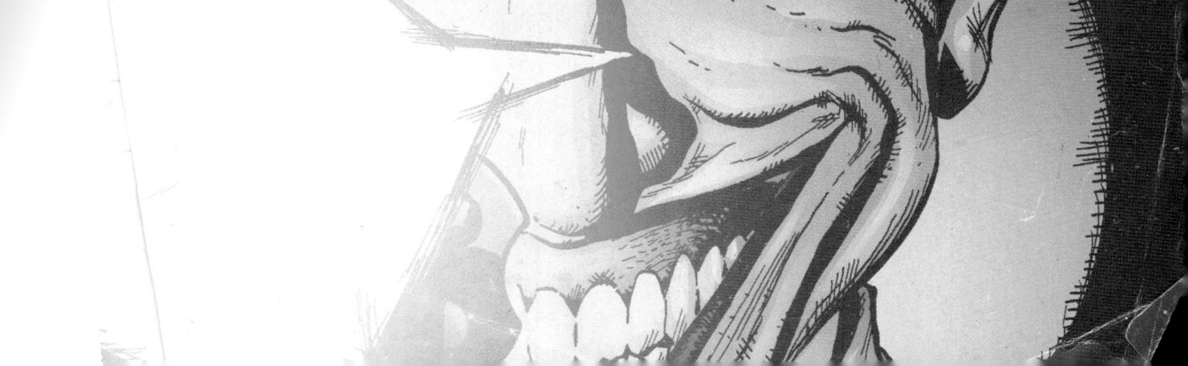

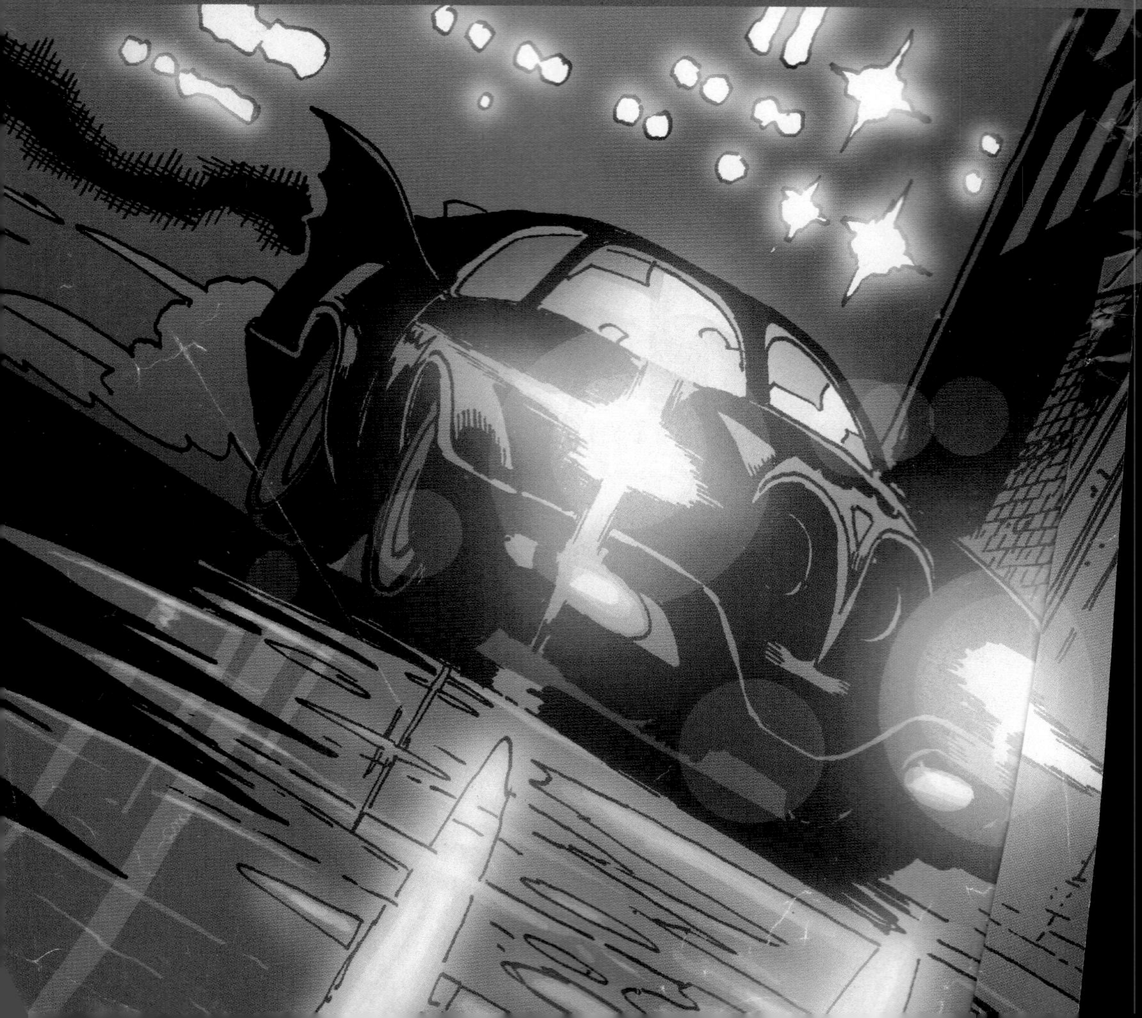

BATMAN
THE MAN WHO LAUGHS

Ed Brubaker Writer

Doug Mahnke / Patrick Zircher Pencillers

Doug Mahnke / Aaron Sowd / Steve Bird Inkers

David Baron / Jason Wright Colorists

Rob Leigh / Todd Klein Letterers

Doug Mahnke / Tim Sale Original Series Covers

Batman created by Bob Kane

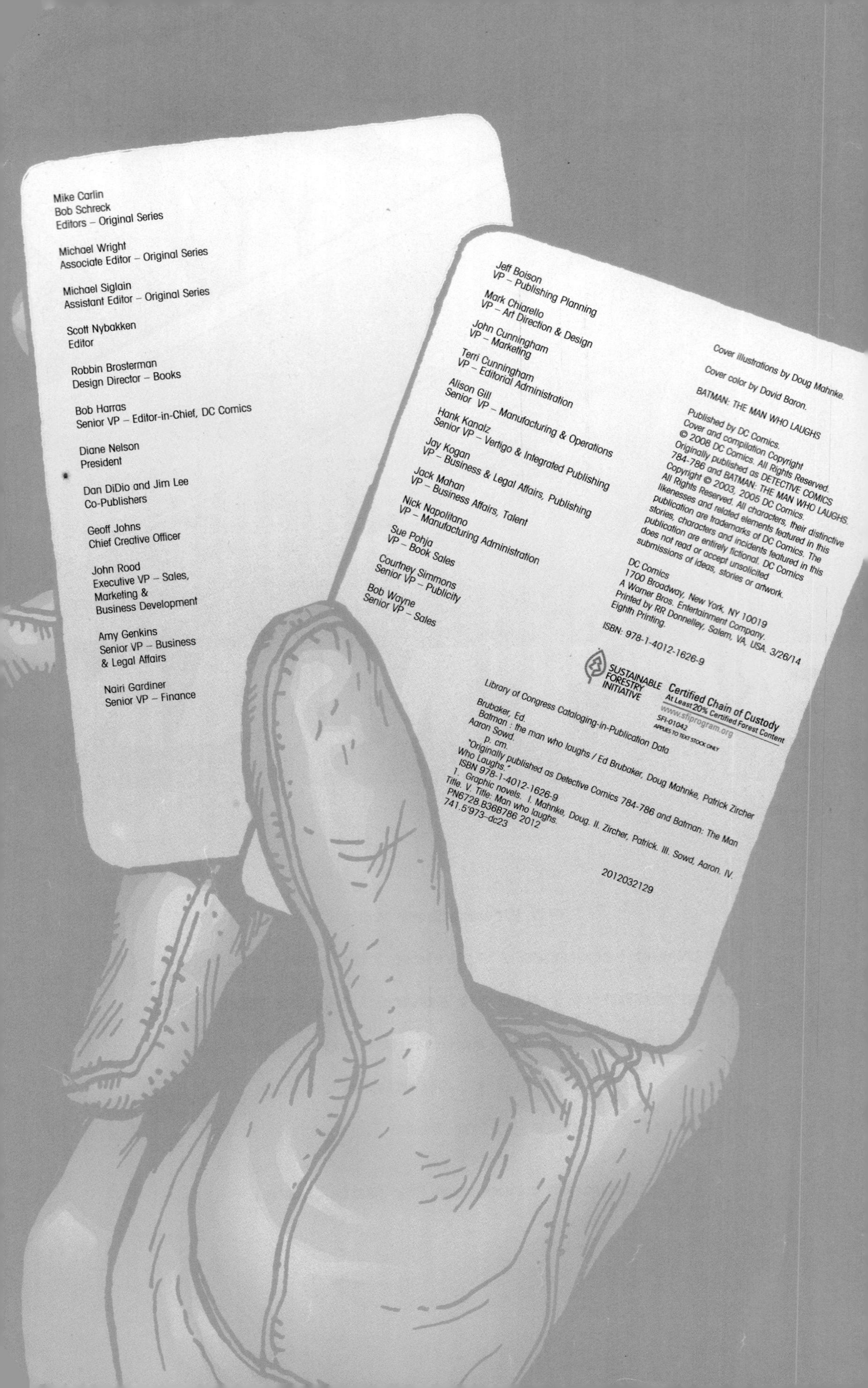

Cover illustrations by Doug Mahnke.

Cover color by David Baron.

BATMAN: THE MAN WHO LAUGHS

Published by DC Comics. Cover and compilation Copyright
© 2008 DC Comics. All Rights Reserved.
Originally published as DETECTIVE COMICS
784-786 and BATMAN: THE MAN WHO LAUGHS.
Copyright © 2003, 2005 DC Comics.
All Rights Reserved. All characters, their distinctive
likenesses and related elements featured in this
publication are trademarks of DC Comics. The
stories, characters and incidents featured in this
publication are entirely fictional. DC Comics
does not read or accept unsolicited
submissions of ideas, stories or artwork.

DC Comics
1700 Broadway, New York, NY 10019
A Warner Bros. Entertainment Company.
Printed by RR Donnelley, Salem, VA, USA. 3/26/14
Eighth Printing.

ISBN: 978-1-4012-1626-9

SUSTAINABLE
FORESTRY
INITIATIVE
Certified Chain of Custody
At Least 20% Certified Forest Content
www.sfiprogram.org
SFI-01042
APPLIES TO TEXT STOCK ONLY

Library of Congress Cataloging-in-Publication Data

Brubaker, Ed.
Batman : the man who laughs / Ed Brubaker, Doug Mahnke, Patrick Zircher,
Aaron Sowd.
p. cm.
"Originally published as Detective Comics 784-786 and Batman: The Man
Who Laughs."
ISBN 978-1-4012-1626-9
1. Graphic novels. I. Mahnke, Doug. II. Zircher, Patrick. III. Sowd, Aaron. IV.
Title. V. Title: Man who laughs.
PN6728.B368B786 2012
741.5'973--dc23

2012032129

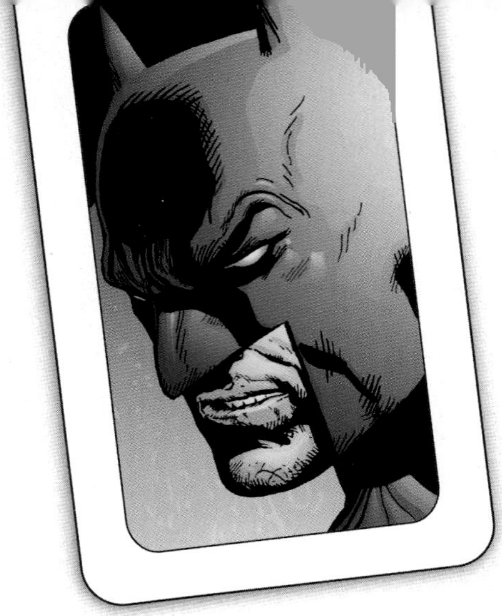

Contents

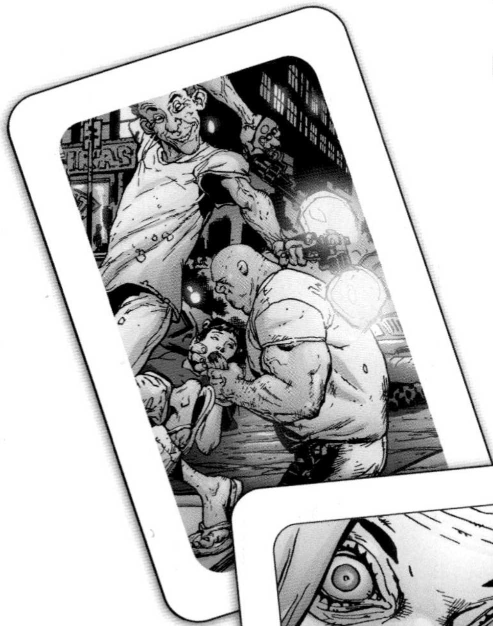

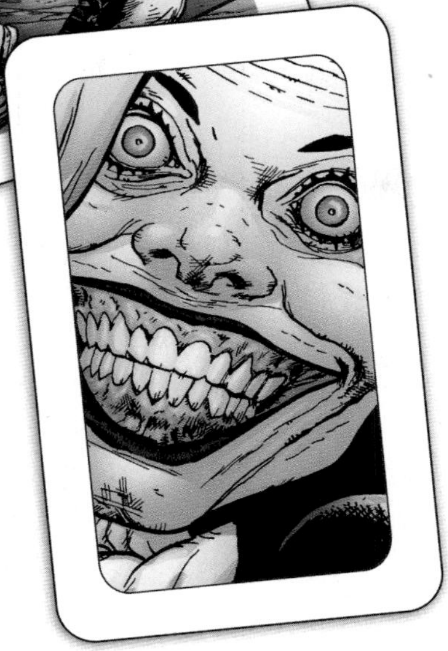

THE MAN WHO LAUGHS

Art by Doug Mahnke
Color By David Baron
Lettering by Rob Leigh

With thanks to Shawn Moll

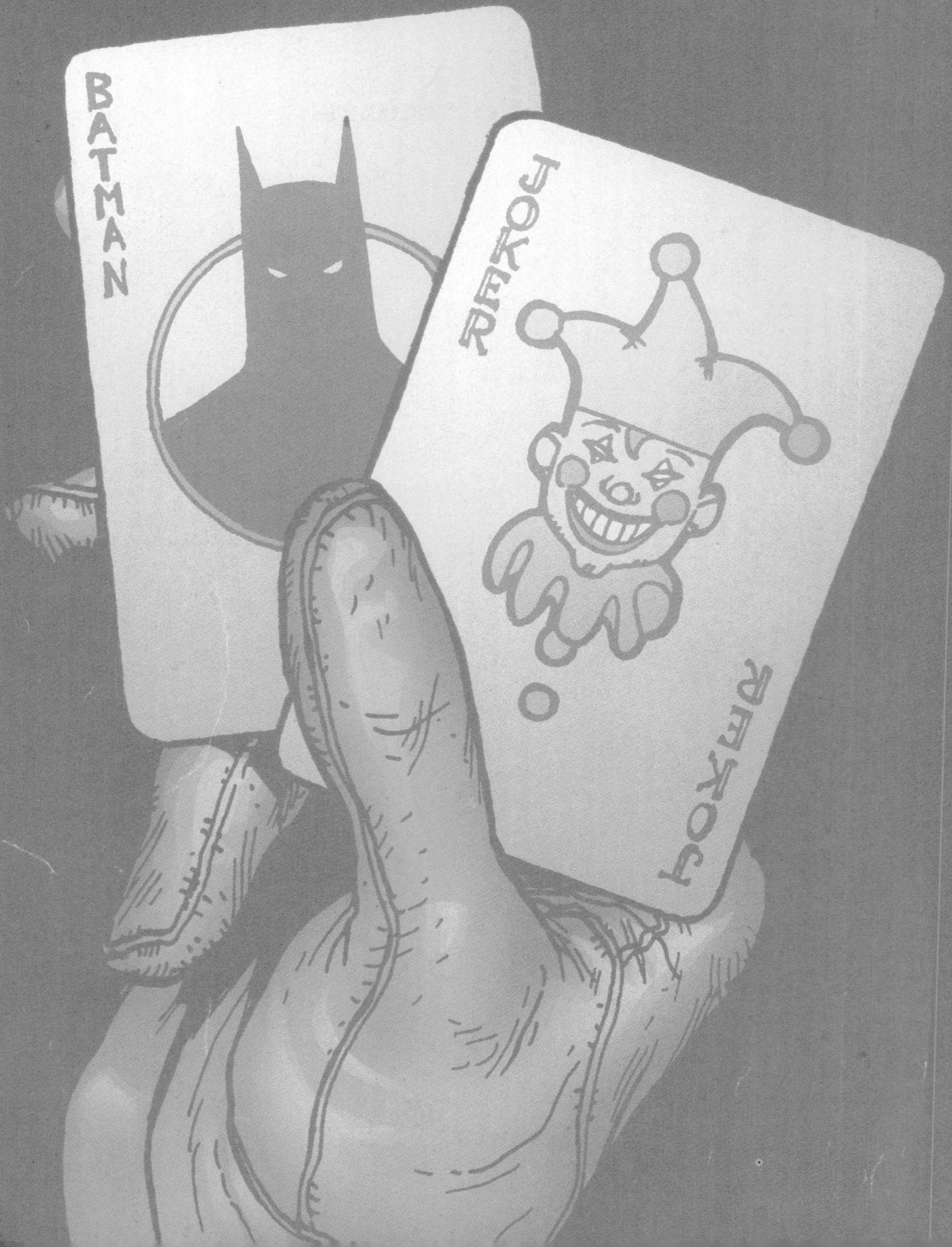
BATMAN
JOKER
JOKER

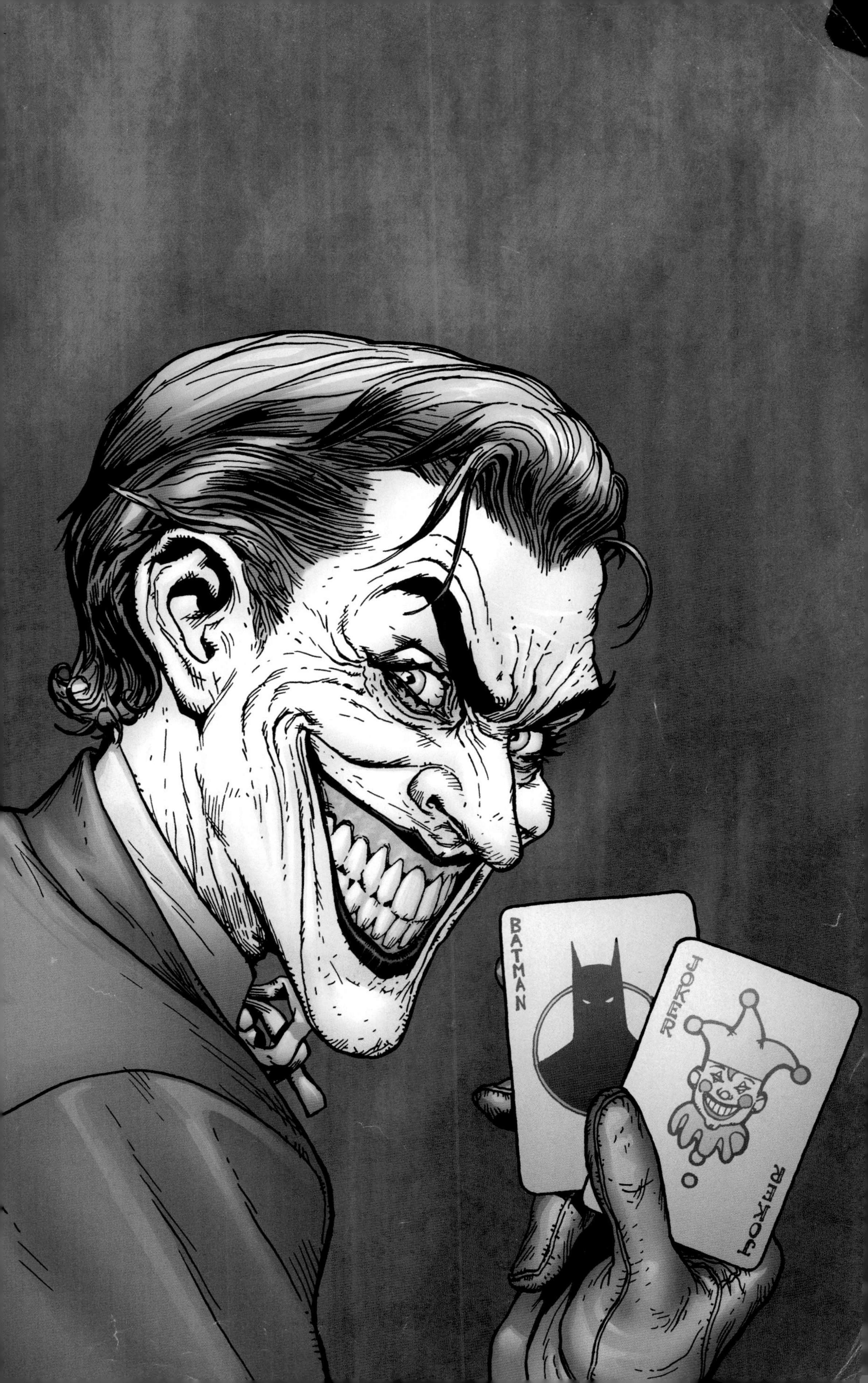
BATMAN
JOKER

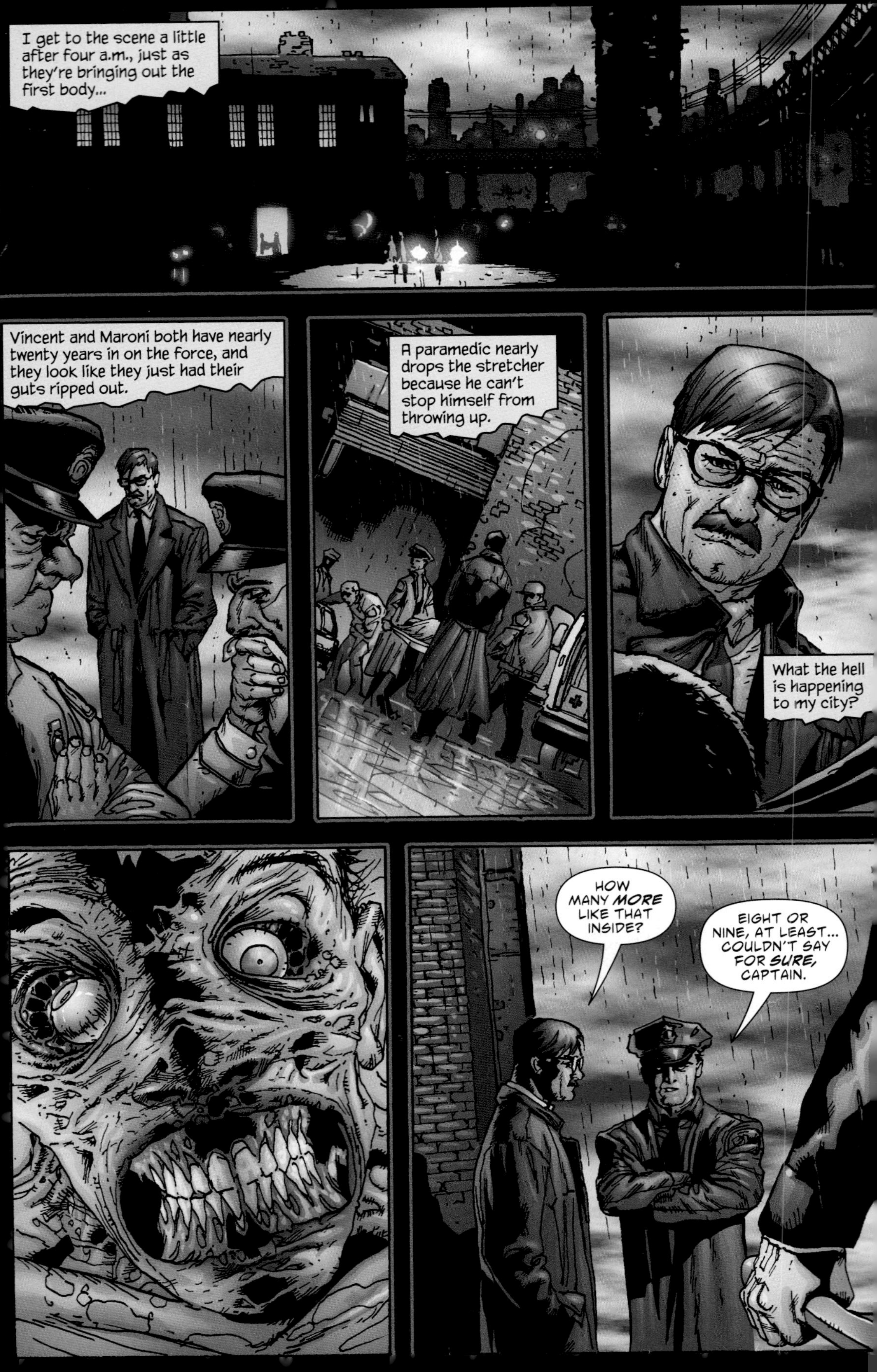
I get to the scene a little after four a.m., just as they're bringing out the first body...
Vincent and Maroni both have nearly twenty years in on the force, and they look like they just had their guts ripped out.
A paramedic nearly drops the stretcher because he can't stop himself from throwing up.
What the hell is happening to my city?
HOW MANY MORE LIKE THAT INSIDE?
EIGHT OR NINE, AT LEAST... COULDN'T SAY FOR SURE, CAPTAIN.

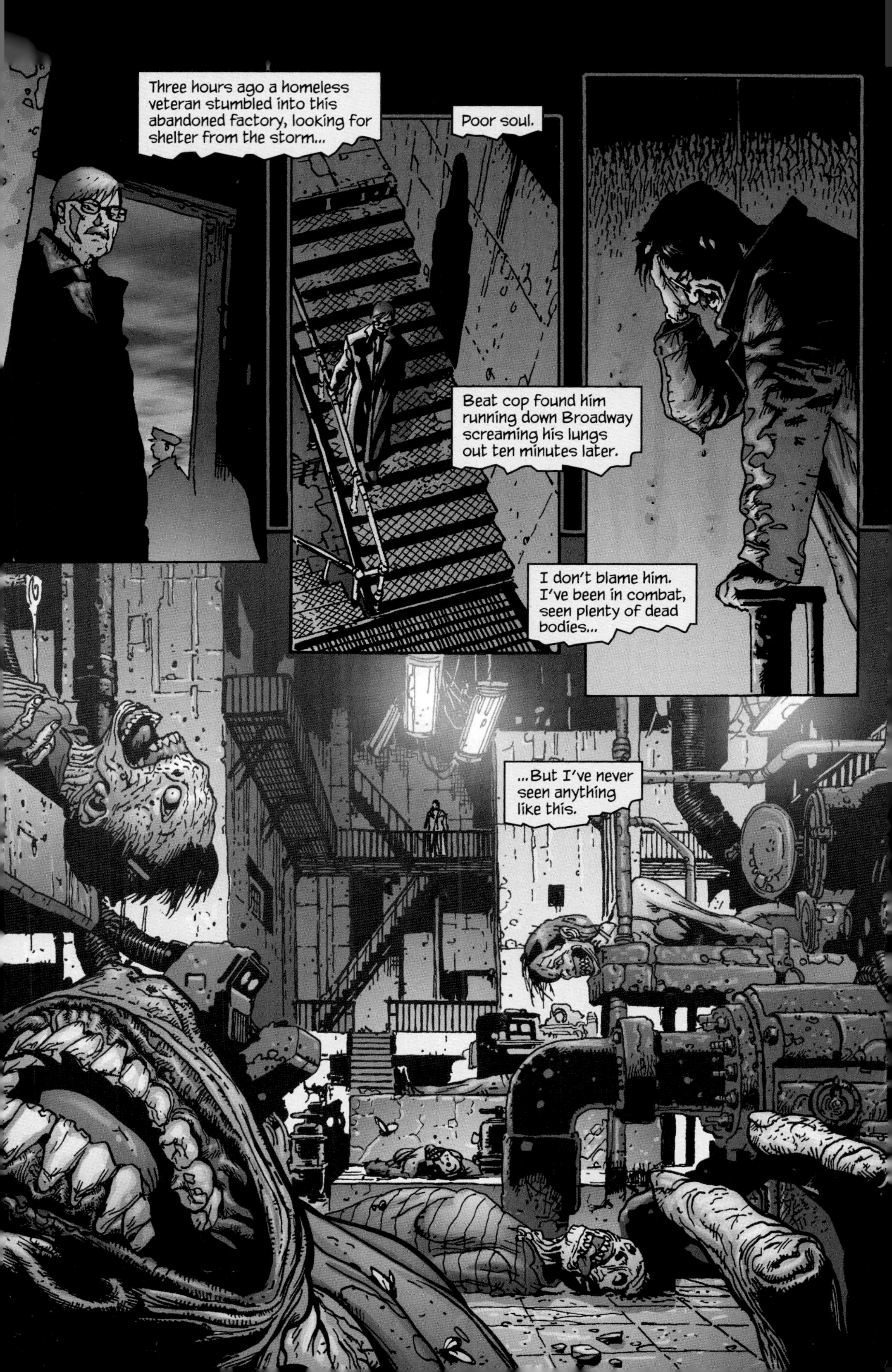
Three hours ago a homeless veteran stumbled into this abandoned factory, looking for shelter from the storm...
Poor soul.
Beat cop found him running down Broadway screaming his lungs out ten minutes later.
I don't blame him. I've been in combat, seen plenty of dead bodies...
...But I've never seen anything like this.

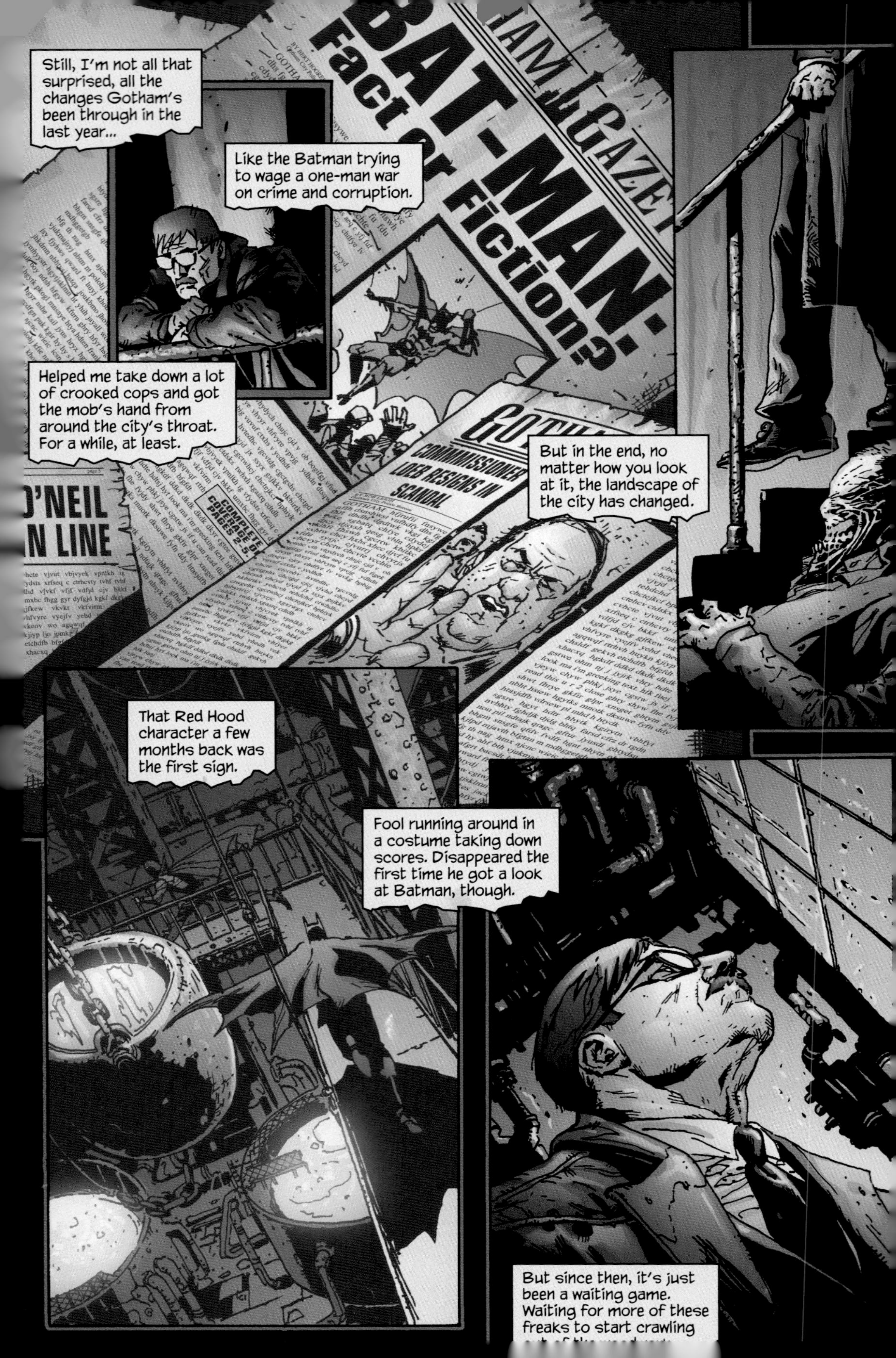

Still, I'm not all that surprised, all the changes Gotham's been through in the last year...
Like the Batman trying to wage a one-man war on crime and corruption.
BAT-MAN: Fact or Fiction?
Helped me take down a lot of crooked cops and got the mob's hand from around the city's throat. For a while, at least.
COMMISSIONER LOEB RESIGNS IN SCANDAL
COMPLETE COVERAGE PAGES 2-5
O'NEIL
N LINE
But in the end, no matter how you look at it, the landscape of the city has changed.
That Red Hood character a few months back was the first sign.
Fool running around in a costume taking down scores. Disappeared the first time he got a look at Batman, though.
But since then, it's just been a waiting game. Waiting for more of these freaks to start crawling

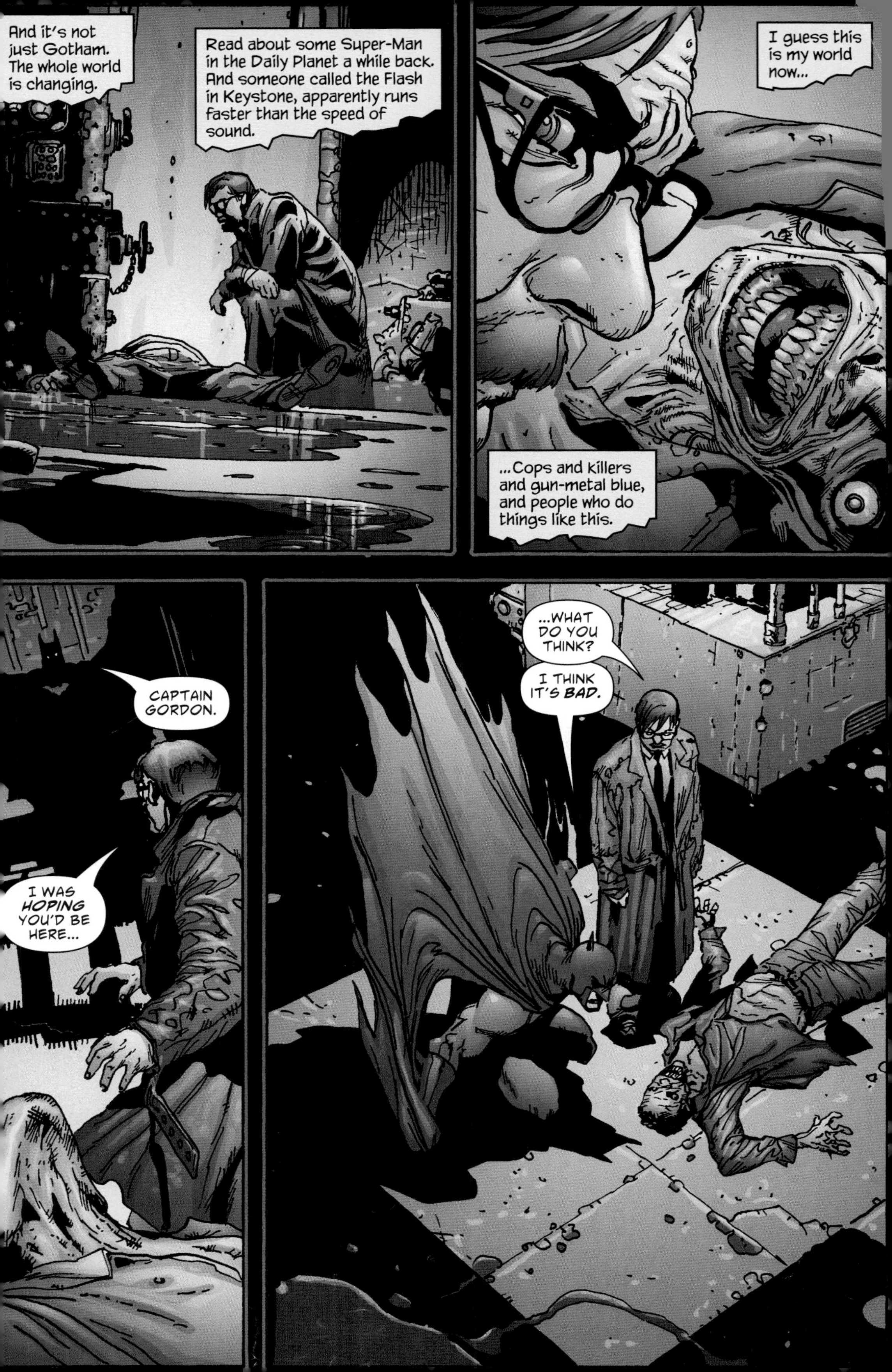
And it's not just Gotham. The whole world is changing.
Read about some Super-Man in the Daily Planet a while back. And someone called the Flash in Keystone, apparently runs faster than the speed of sound.
I guess this is my world now...
...Cops and killers and gun-metal blue, and people who do things like this.
CAPTAIN GORDON.
I WAS *HOPING* YOU'D BE HERE...
...WHAT DO YOU THINK?
I THINK IT'S *BAD*.

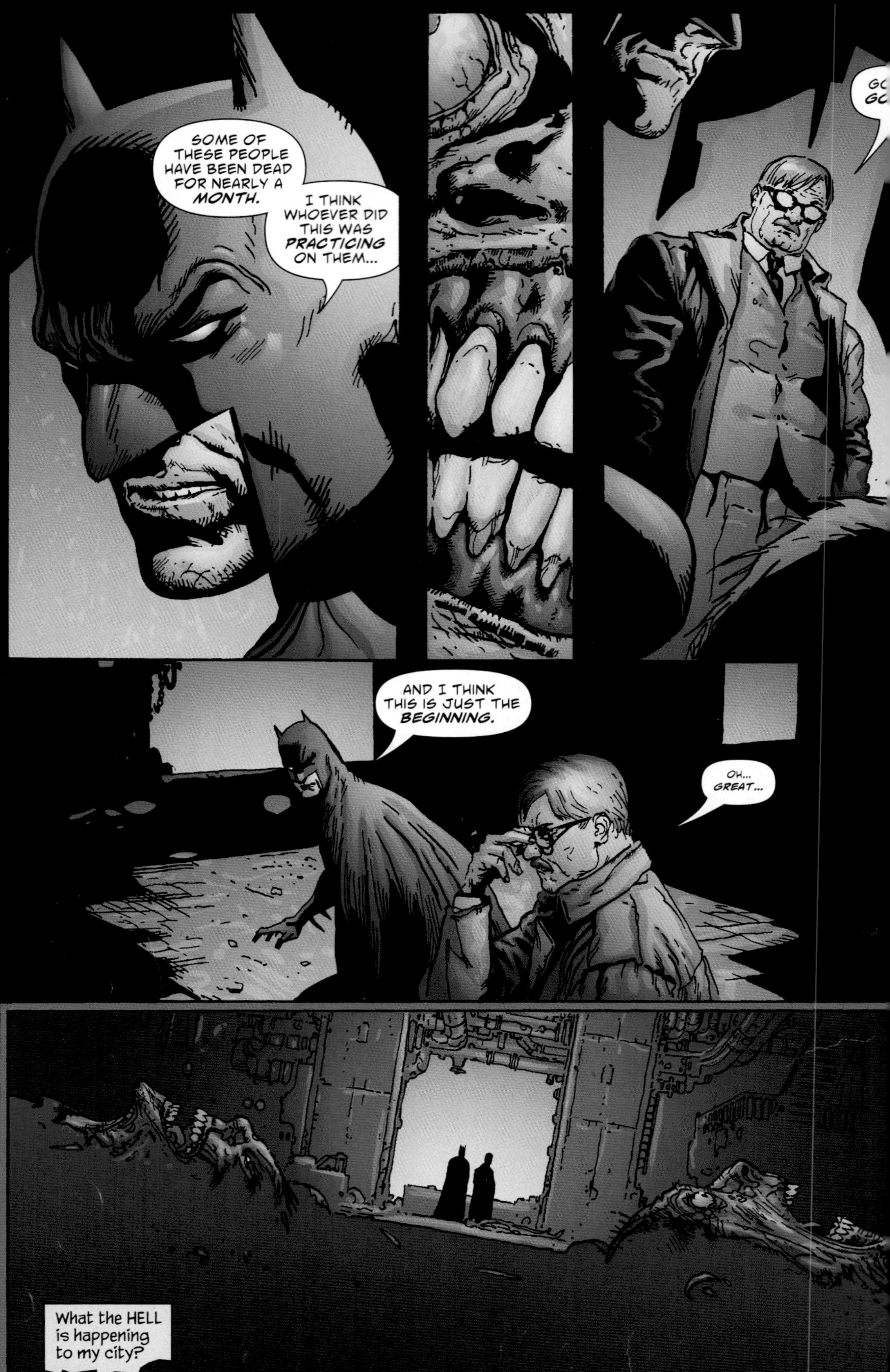
SOME OF THESE PEOPLE HAVE BEEN DEAD FOR NEARLY A MONTH.
I THINK WHOEVER DID THIS WAS PRACTICING ON THEM...
AND I THINK THIS IS JUST THE BEGINNING.
OH... GREAT...
What the HELL is happening to my city?

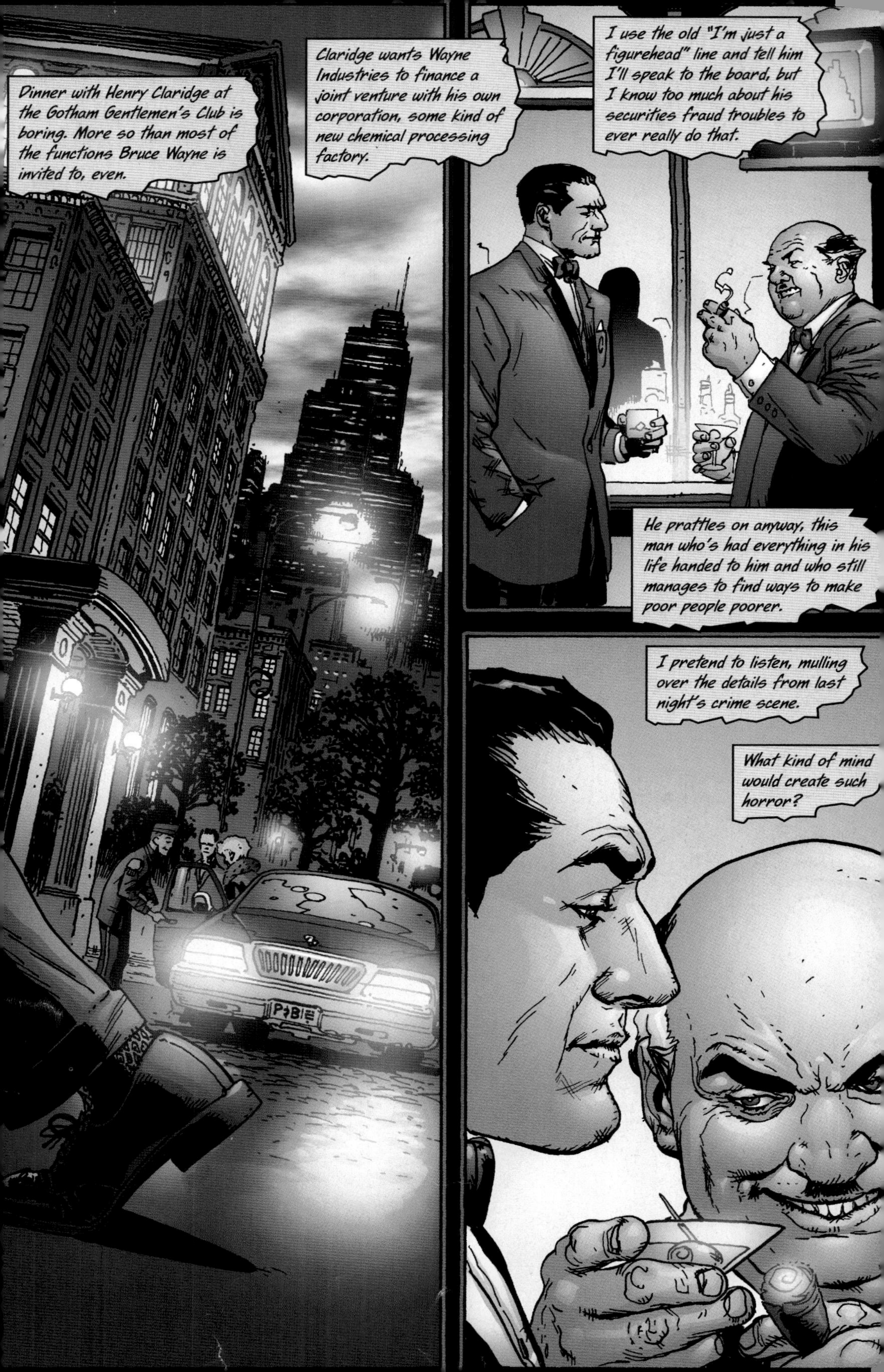

Dinner with Henry Claridge at the Gotham Gentlemen's Club is boring. More so than most of the functions Bruce Wayne is invited to, even.
Claridge wants Wayne Industries to finance a joint venture with his own corporation, some kind of new chemical processing factory.
I use the old "I'm just a figurehead" line and tell him I'll speak to the board, but I know too much about his securities fraud troubles to ever really do that.
He prattles on anyway, this man who's had everything in his life handed to him and who still manages to find ways to make poor people poorer.
I pretend to listen, mulling over the details from last night's crime scene.
What kind of mind would create such horror?

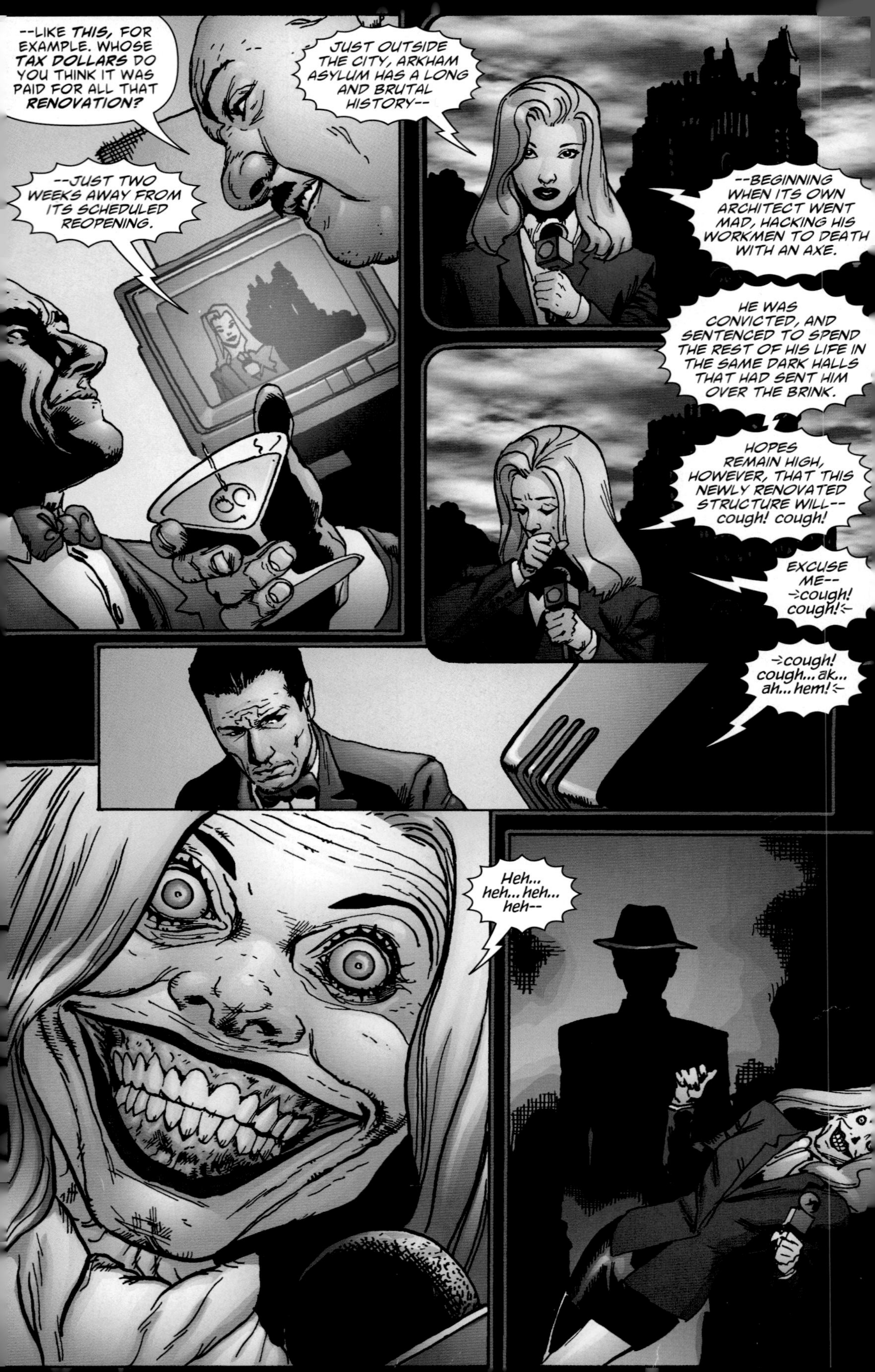
--LIKE THIS, FOR EXAMPLE. WHOSE TAX DOLLARS DO YOU THINK IT WAS PAID FOR ALL THAT RENOVATION?
--JUST TWO WEEKS AWAY FROM ITS SCHEDULED REOPENING.
JUST OUTSIDE THE CITY, ARKHAM ASYLUM HAS A LONG AND BRUTAL HISTORY--
--BEGINNING WHEN ITS OWN ARCHITECT WENT MAD, HACKING HIS WORKMEN TO DEATH WITH AN AXE.
HE WAS CONVICTED, AND SENTENCED TO SPEND THE REST OF HIS LIFE IN THE SAME DARK HALLS THAT HAD SENT HIM OVER THE BRINK.
HOPES REMAIN HIGH, HOWEVER, THAT THIS NEWLY RENOVATED STRUCTURE WILL-- cough! cough!
EXCUSE ME-- cough! cough!
cough! cough... ak... ah... hem!
Heh... heh... heh... heh--

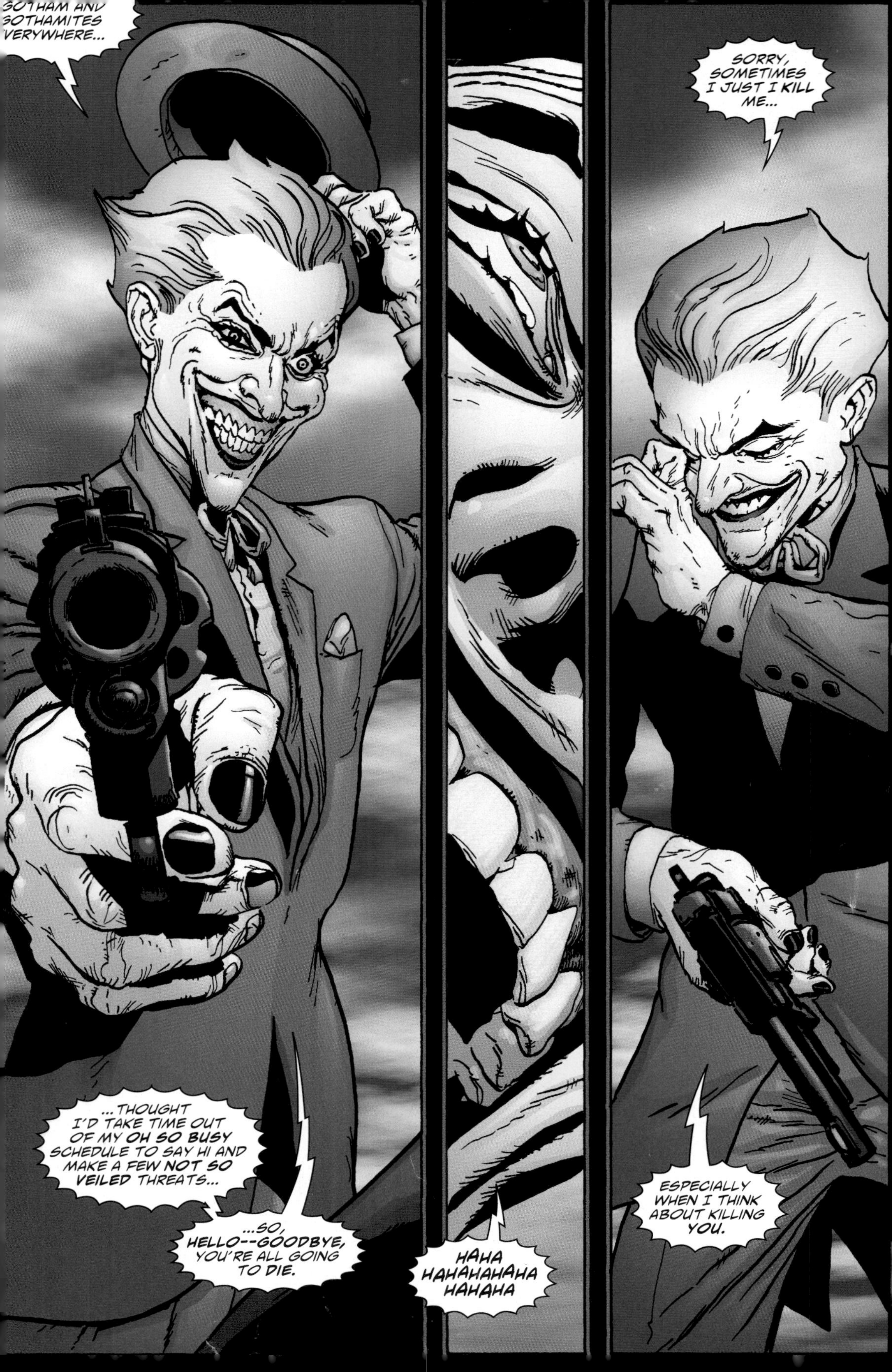
GOTHAM AND GOTHAMITES EVERYWHERE...
...THOUGHT I'D TAKE TIME OUT OF MY OH SO BUSY SCHEDULE TO SAY HI AND MAKE A FEW NOT SO VEILED THREATS...
...SO, HELLO--GOODBYE, YOU'RE ALL GOING TO DIE.
HAHA HAHAHAHAHA HAHAHA
SORRY, SOMETIMES I JUST I KILL ME...
ESPECIALLY WHEN I THINK ABOUT KILLING YOU.

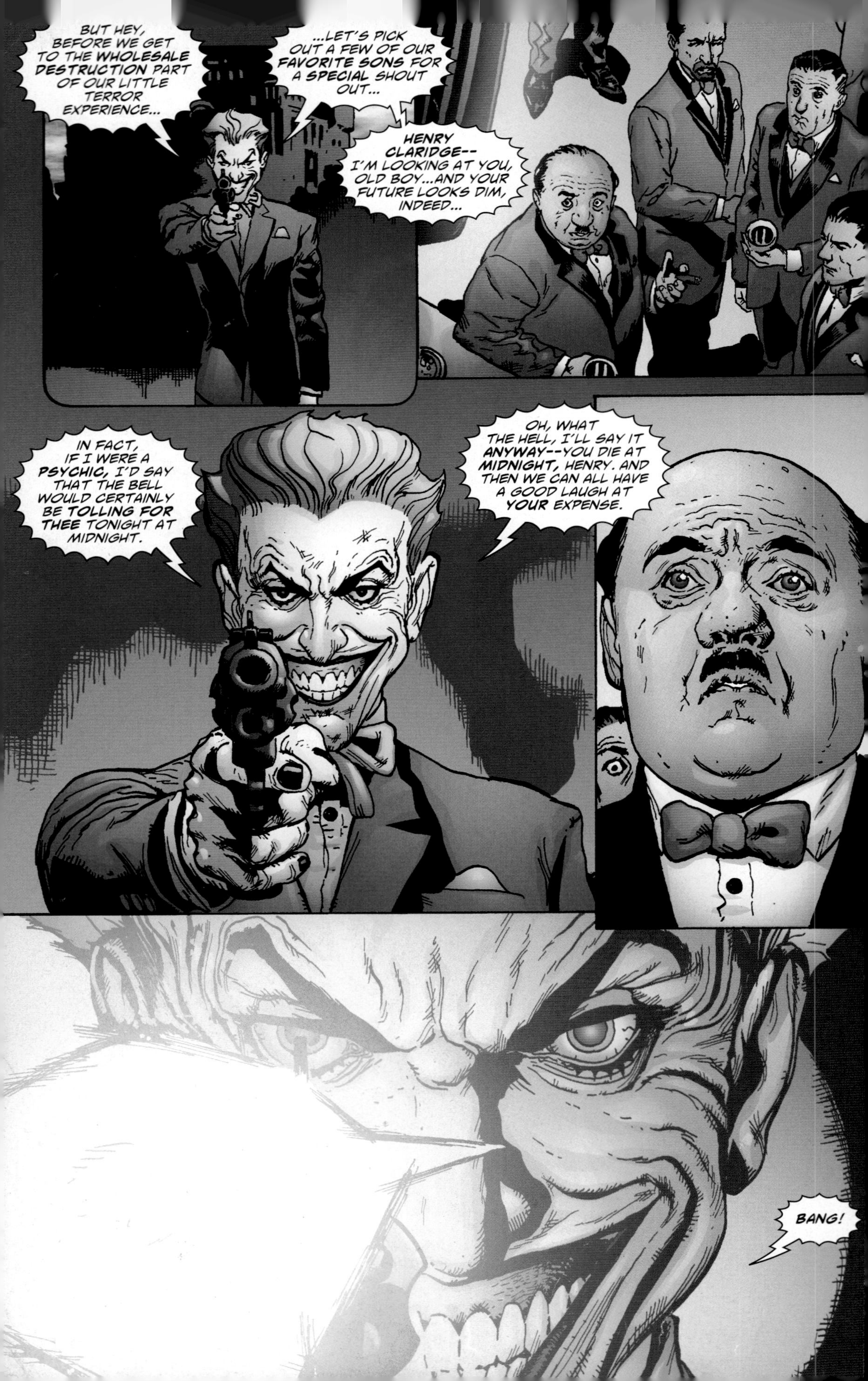
BUT HEY, BEFORE WE GET TO THE WHOLESALE DESTRUCTION PART OF OUR LITTLE TERROR EXPERIENCE...
...LET'S PICK OUT A FEW OF OUR FAVORITE SONS FOR A SPECIAL SHOUT OUT...
HENRY CLARIDGE-- I'M LOOKING AT YOU, OLD BOY...AND YOUR FUTURE LOOKS DIM, INDEED...
IN FACT, IF I WERE A PSYCHIC, I'D SAY THAT THE BELL WOULD CERTAINLY BE TOLLING FOR THEE TONIGHT AT MIDNIGHT.
OH, WHAT THE HELL, I'LL SAY IT ANYWAY--YOU DIE AT MIDNIGHT, HENRY. AND THEN WE CAN ALL HAVE A GOOD LAUGH AT YOUR EXPENSE.
BANG!

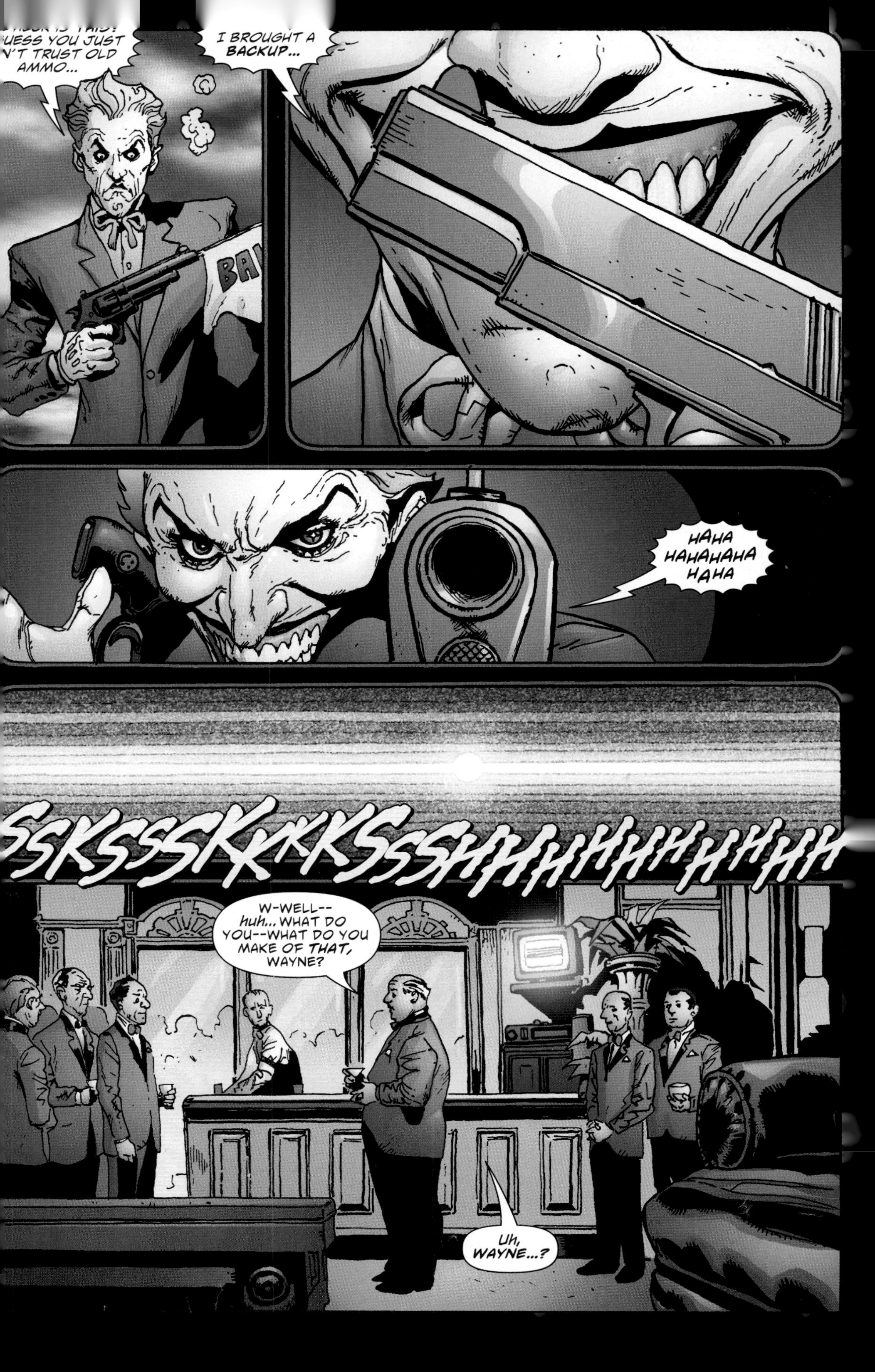
UESS YOU JUST N'T TRUST OLD AMMO...
I BROUGHT A BACKUP...
HAHA HAHAHAHA HAHA
SSKSSSKKKKSSSHHHHHHHHHHH
W-WELL-- huh... WHAT DO YOU--WHAT DO YOU MAKE OF THAT, WAYNE?
Uh, WAYNE...?

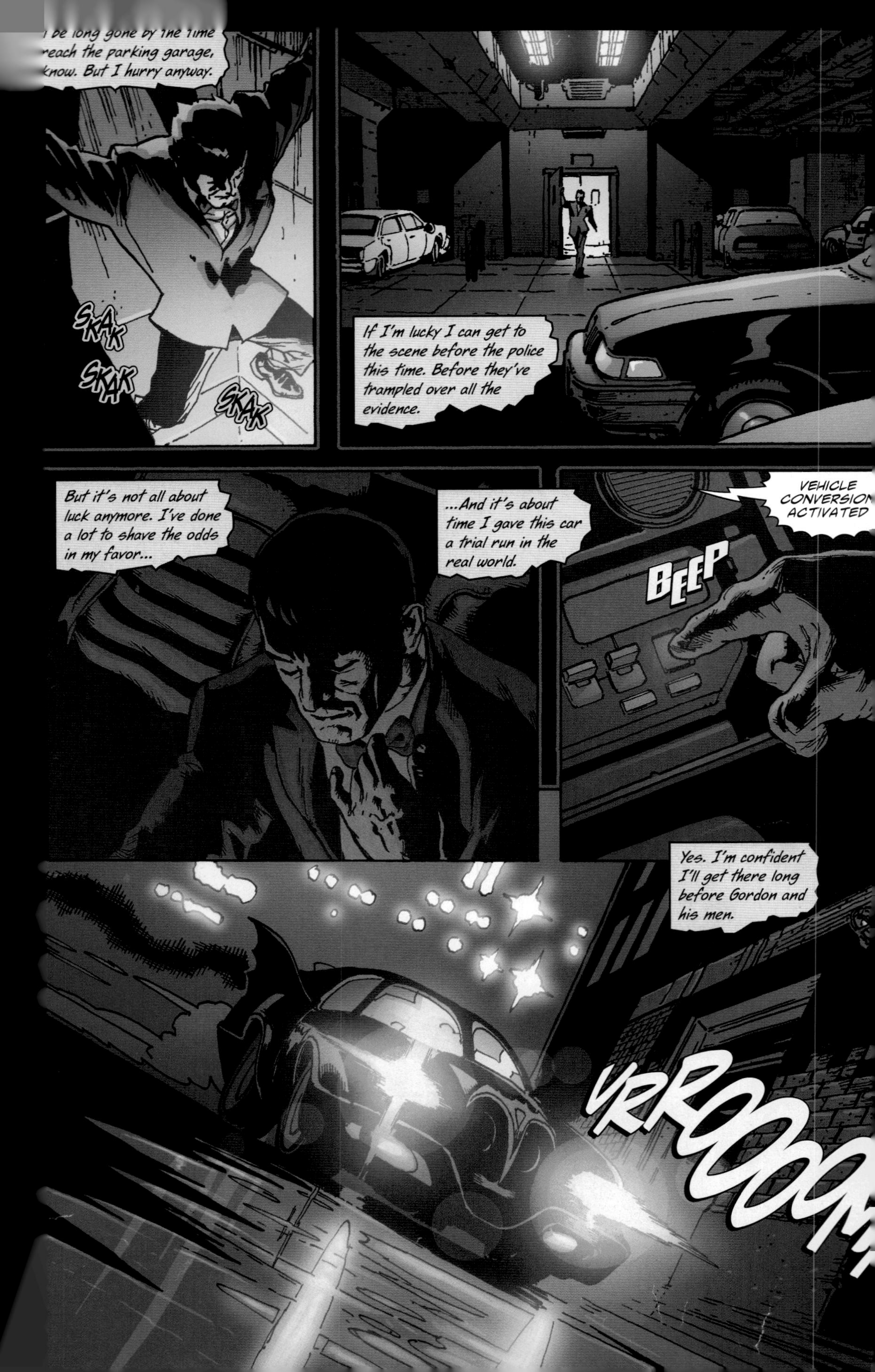

be long gone by the time
reach the parking garage,
know. But I hurry anyway.
SKAK
SKAK
SKAK
If I'm lucky I can get to the scene before the police this time. Before they've trampled over all the evidence.
But it's not all about luck anymore. I've done a lot to shave the odds in my favor...
...And it's about time I gave this car a trial run in the real world.
VEHICLE CONVERSION ACTIVATED
BEEP
Yes. I'm confident I'll get there long before Gordon and his men.
VRROOOM

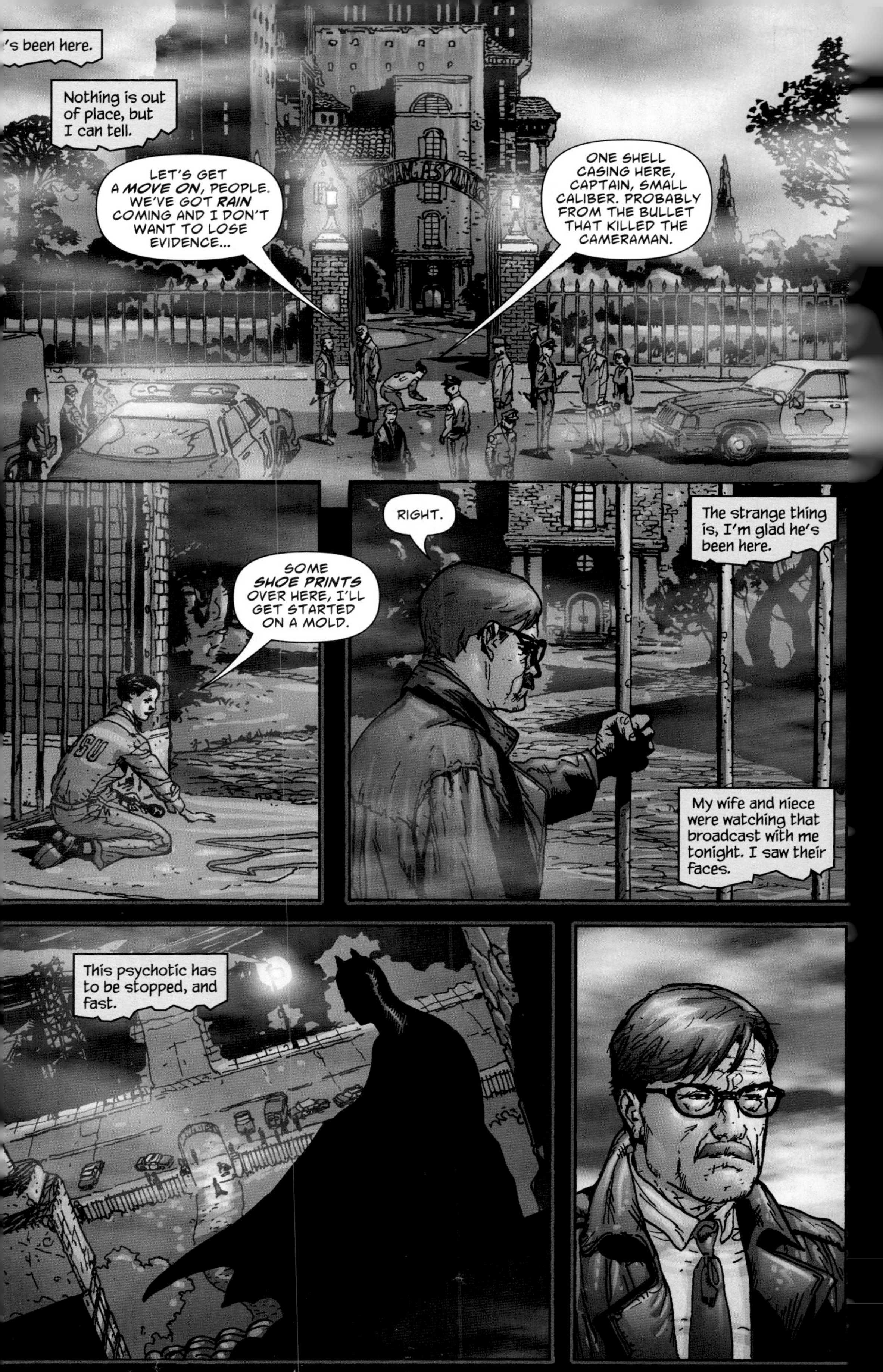

'S BEEN HERE.
Nothing is out of place, but I can tell.
LET'S GET A MOVE ON, PEOPLE. WE'VE GOT RAIN COMING AND I DON'T WANT TO LOSE EVIDENCE...
ONE SHELL CASING HERE, CAPTAIN, SMALL CALIBER. PROBABLY FROM THE BULLET THAT KILLED THE CAMERAMAN.
SOME SHOE PRINTS OVER HERE, I'LL GET STARTED ON A MOLD.
RIGHT.
The strange thing is, I'm glad he's been here.
My wife and niece were watching that broadcast with me tonight. I saw their faces.
This psychotic has to be stopped, and fast.

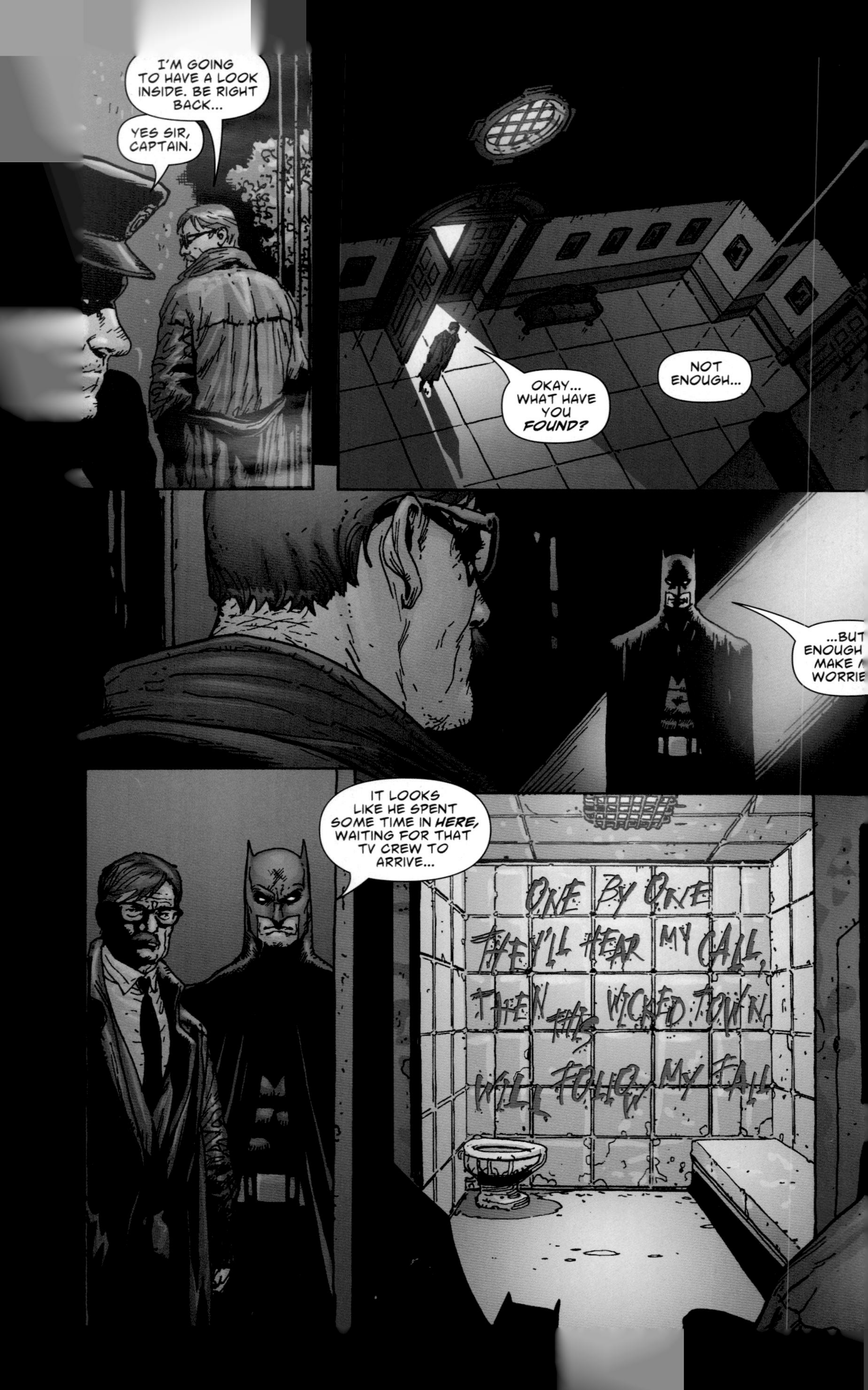

I'M GOING TO HAVE A LOOK INSIDE. BE RIGHT BACK...
YES SIR, CAPTAIN.
OKAY... WHAT HAVE YOU *FOUND?*
NOT ENOUGH...
IT LOOKS LIKE HE SPENT SOME TIME IN *HERE,* WAITING FOR THAT TV CREW TO ARRIVE...
ONE BY ONE
THEY'LL HEAR MY CALL,
THEN THIS WICKED TOWN
WILL FOLLOW MY FALL

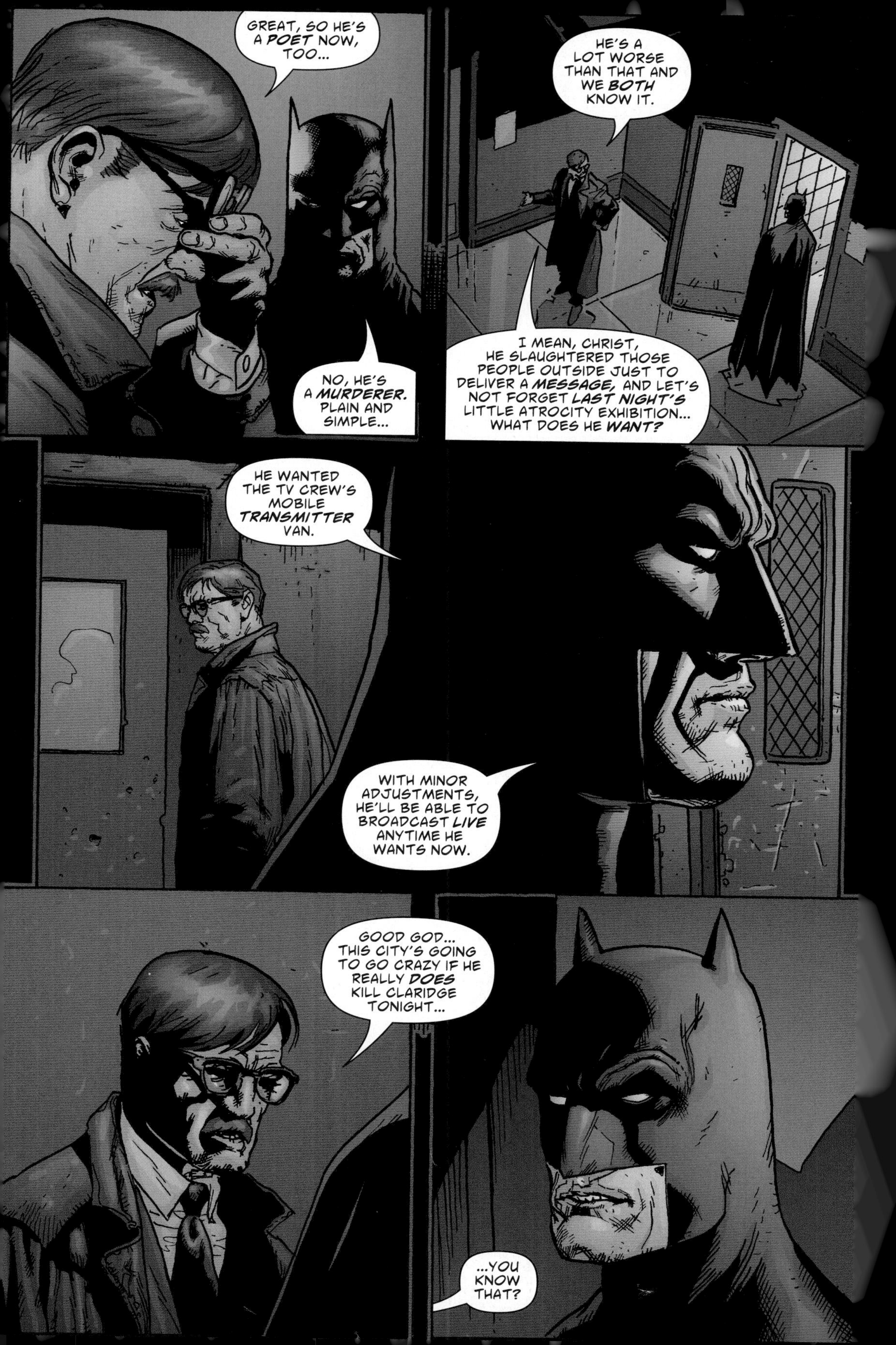
GREAT, SO HE'S A POET NOW, TOO...
NO, HE'S A MURDERER. PLAIN AND SIMPLE...
HE'S A LOT WORSE THAN THAT AND WE BOTH KNOW IT.
I MEAN, CHRIST, HE SLAUGHTERED THOSE PEOPLE OUTSIDE JUST TO DELIVER A MESSAGE, AND LET'S NOT FORGET LAST NIGHT'S LITTLE ATROCITY EXHIBITION... WHAT DOES HE WANT?
HE WANTED THE TV CREW'S MOBILE TRANSMITTER VAN.
WITH MINOR ADJUSTMENTS, HE'LL BE ABLE TO BROADCAST LIVE ANYTIME HE WANTS NOW.
GOOD GOD... THIS CITY'S GOING TO GO CRAZY IF HE REALLY DOES KILL CLARIDGE TONIGHT...
...YOU KNOW THAT?

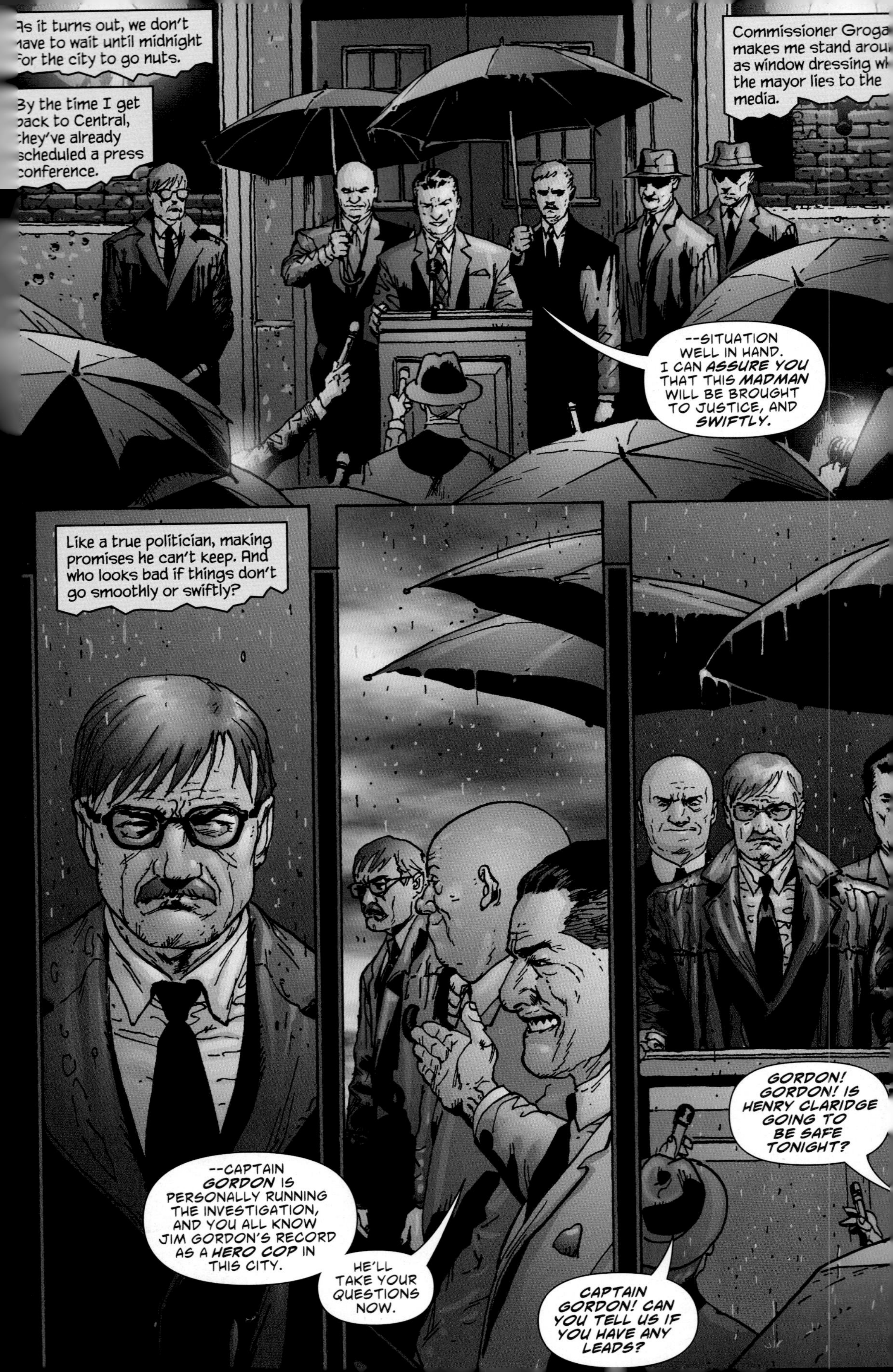

As it turns out, we don't have to wait until midnight for the city to go nuts.
By the time I get back to Central, they've already scheduled a press conference.
Commissioner Groga makes me stand arou as window dressing wh the mayor lies to the media.
--SITUATION WELL IN HAND. I CAN ASSURE YOU THAT THIS MADMAN WILL BE BROUGHT TO JUSTICE, AND SWIFTLY.
Like a true politician, making promises he can't keep. And who looks bad if things don't go smoothly or swiftly?
--CAPTAIN GORDON IS PERSONALLY RUNNING THE INVESTIGATION, AND YOU ALL KNOW JIM GORDON'S RECORD AS A HERO COP IN THIS CITY.
HE'LL TAKE YOUR QUESTIONS NOW.
GORDON! GORDON! IS HENRY CLARIDGE GOING TO BE SAFE TONIGHT?
CAPTAIN GORDON! CAN YOU TELL US IF YOU HAVE ANY LEADS?

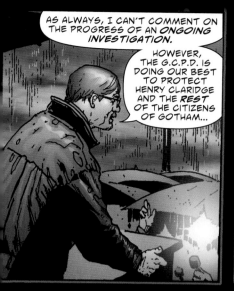

AS ALWAYS, I CAN'T COMMENT ON THE PROGRESS OF AN *ONGOING* INVESTIGATION.

HOWEVER, THE G.C.P.D. IS DOING OUR BEST TO PROTECT HENRY CLARIDGE AND THE *REST* OF THE CITIZENS OF GOTHAM...

SO THE G.C.P.D. *CAN'T GUARANTEE* CLARIDGE'S SAFETY?

THERE ARE *NO GUARANTEES* IN THIS LIFE. WE'LL DO OUR *BEST*.

IS IT TRUE POLICE HAVE *DUBBED* THIS FREAK THE JOKER?

I HADN'T *HEARD* THAT, BUT THE NAME *FITS*...

WHAT ABOUT THE *BAT*? IS HE INVOLVED IN THE JOKER CASE?

I'M SORRY, IF THERE ARE NO MORE *REAL* QUESTIONS, I'LL GET BACK TO WORK...

I'VE GOT A *KILLER* TO CATCH.

Grogan'll tear my head off later, but I don't care. I wasn't hired to play nice with the press. I'm a police.

And right now I've got to figure out how to keep Henry Claridge alive.

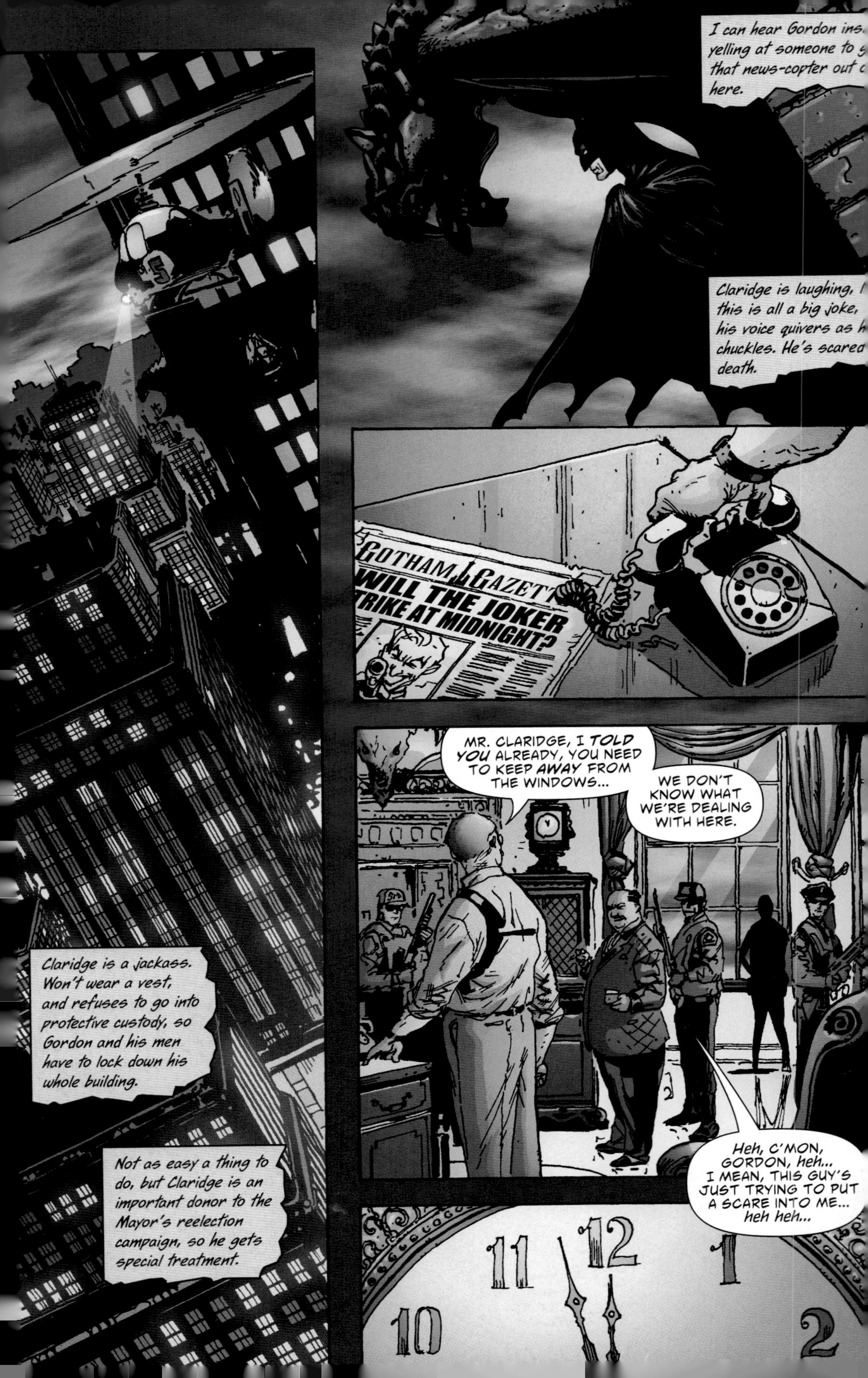
Claridge is a jackass. Won't wear a vest, and refuses to go into protective custody, so Gordon and his men have to lock down his whole building.
Not as easy a thing to do, but Claridge is an important donor to the Mayor's reelection campaign, so he gets special treatment.
I can hear Gordon ins yelling at someone to g that news-copter out o here.
Claridge is laughing, this is all a big joke, his voice quivers as h chuckles. He's scared death.
GOTHAM GAZETT
WILL THE JOKER
TRIKE AT MIDNIGHT?
MR. CLARIDGE, I TOLD YOU ALREADY, YOU NEED TO KEEP AWAY FROM THE WINDOWS...
WE DON'T KNOW WHAT WE'RE DEALING WITH HERE.
Heh, C'MON, GORDON, heh... I MEAN, THIS GUY'S JUST TRYING TO PUT A SCARE INTO ME... heh heh...

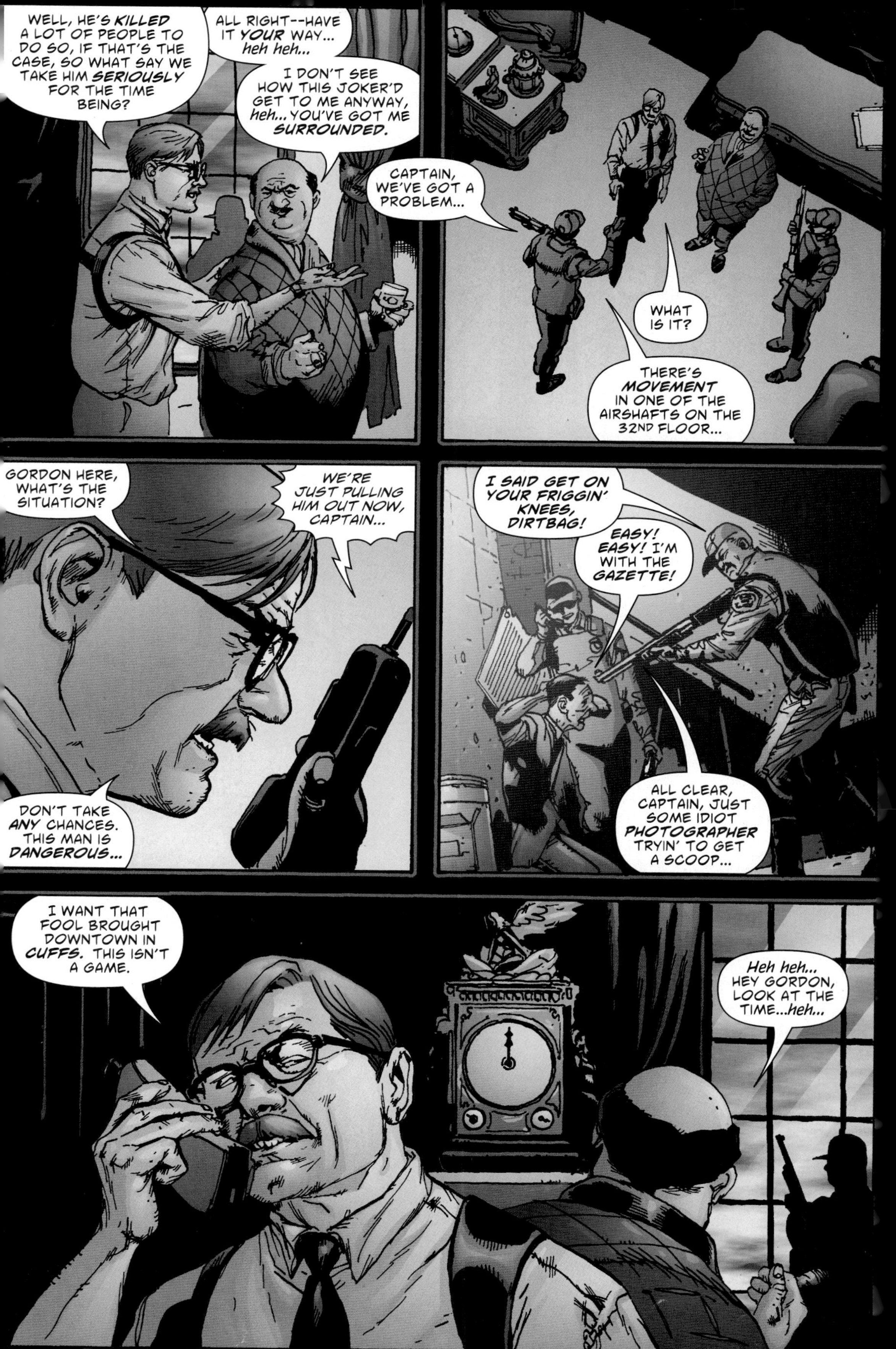
WELL, HE'S KILLED A LOT OF PEOPLE TO DO SO, IF THAT'S THE CASE, SO WHAT SAY WE TAKE HIM SERIOUSLY FOR THE TIME BEING?
ALL RIGHT--HAVE IT YOUR WAY... heh heh...
I DON'T SEE HOW THIS JOKER'D GET TO ME ANYWAY, heh... YOU'VE GOT ME SURROUNDED.
CAPTAIN, WE'VE GOT A PROBLEM...
WHAT IS IT?
THERE'S MOVEMENT IN ONE OF THE AIRSHAFTS ON THE 32ND FLOOR...
GORDON HERE, WHAT'S THE SITUATION?
WE'RE JUST PULLING HIM OUT NOW, CAPTAIN...
DON'T TAKE ANY CHANCES. THIS MAN IS DANGEROUS...
I SAID GET ON YOUR FRIGGIN' KNEES, DIRTBAG!
EASY! EASY! I'M WITH THE GAZETTE!
ALL CLEAR, CAPTAIN, JUST SOME IDIOT PHOTOGRAPHER TRYIN' TO GET A SCOOP...
I WANT THAT FOOL BROUGHT DOWNTOWN IN CUFFS. THIS ISN'T A GAME.
Heh heh... HEY GORDON, LOOK AT THE TIME...heh...

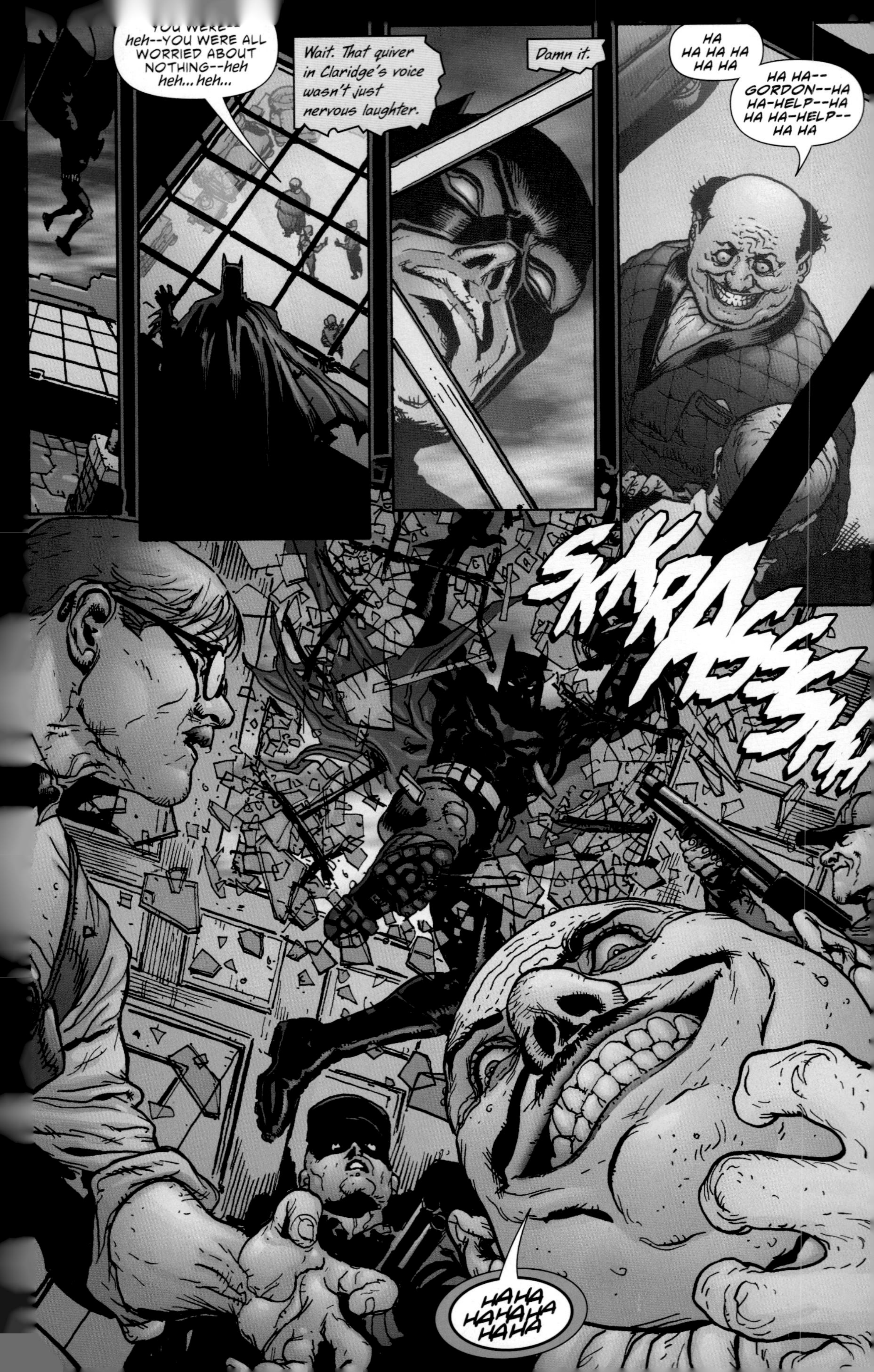
YOU WERE-- heh--YOU WERE ALL WORRIED ABOUT NOTHING--heh heh...heh...
Wait. That quiver in Claridge's voice wasn't just nervous laughter.
Damn it.
HA HA HA HA HA HA
HA HA-- GORDON--HA HA-HELP--HA HA HA-HELP-- HA HA
SKRASSH
HA HA HA HA HA HA HA

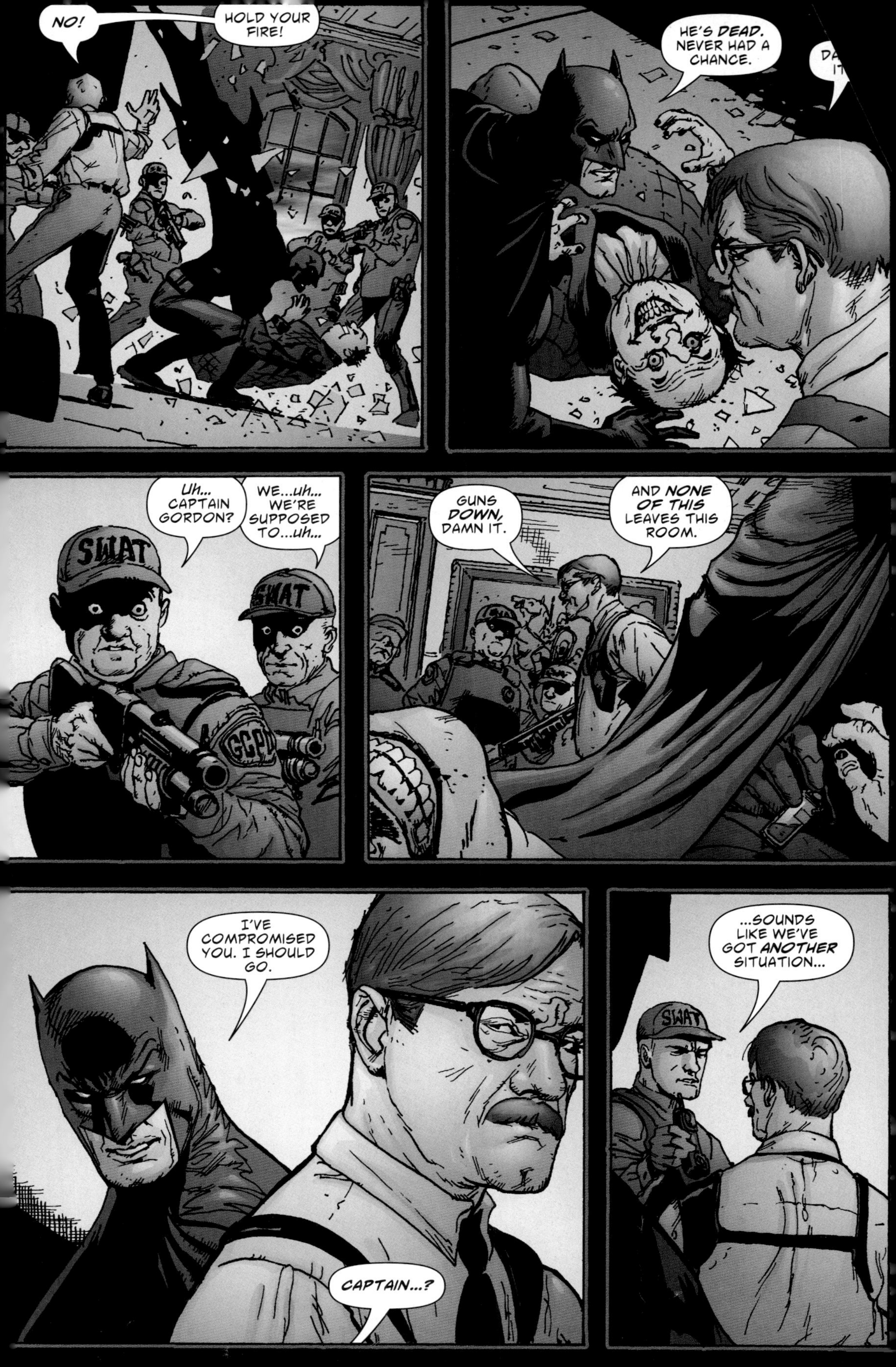
NO!
HOLD YOUR FIRE!
HE'S *DEAD.* NEVER HAD A CHANCE.
Uh... CAPTAIN GORDON?
WE...*uh...* WE'RE SUPPOSED TO...*uh...*
GUNS *DOWN,* DAMN IT.
AND *NONE OF THIS* LEAVES THIS ROOM.
I'VE COMPROMISED YOU. I SHOULD GO.
CAPTAIN...?
...SOUNDS LIKE WE'VE GOT *ANOTHER* SITUATION...
SWAT
SWAT
GCPD
SWAT

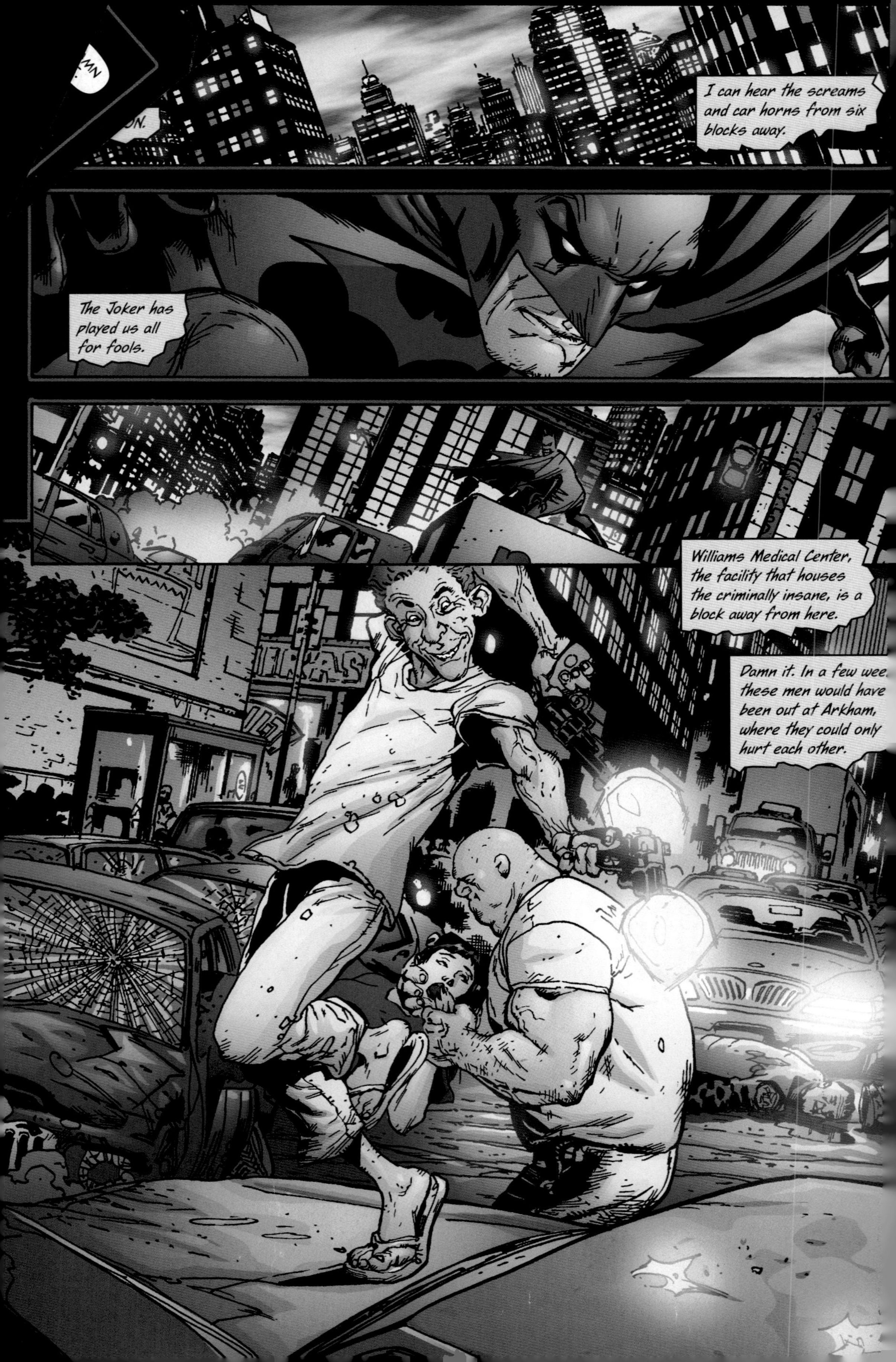
I can hear the screams and car horns from six blocks away.
The Joker has played us all for fools.
Williams Medical Center, the facility that houses the criminally insane, is a block away from here.
Damn it. In a few wee
these men would have been out at Arkham, where they could only hurt each other.

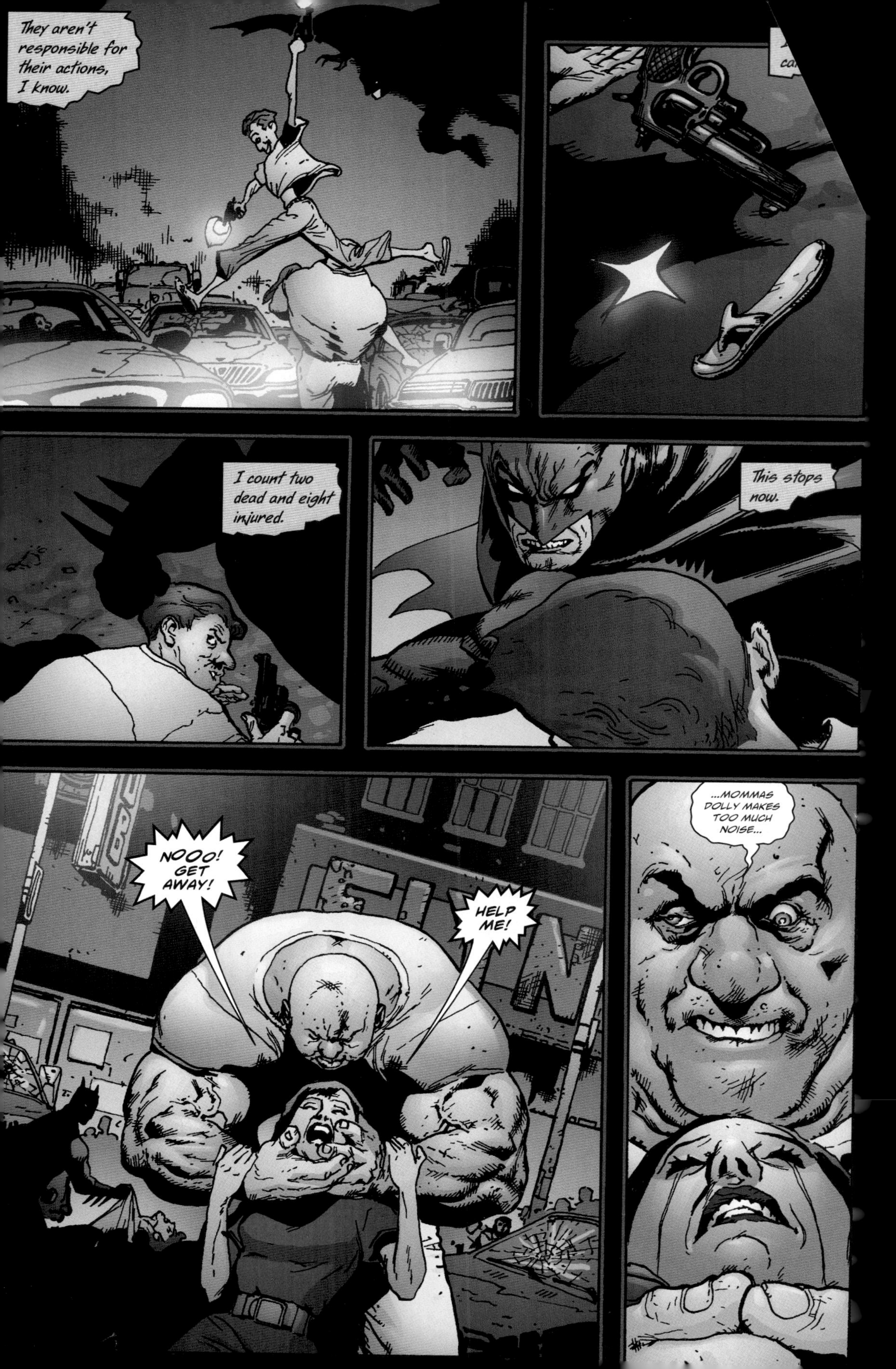
They aren't responsible for their actions, I know.
I count two dead and eight injured.
This stops now.
NOOO! GET AWAY!
HELP ME!
...MOMMAS DOLLY MAKES TOO MUCH NOISE...

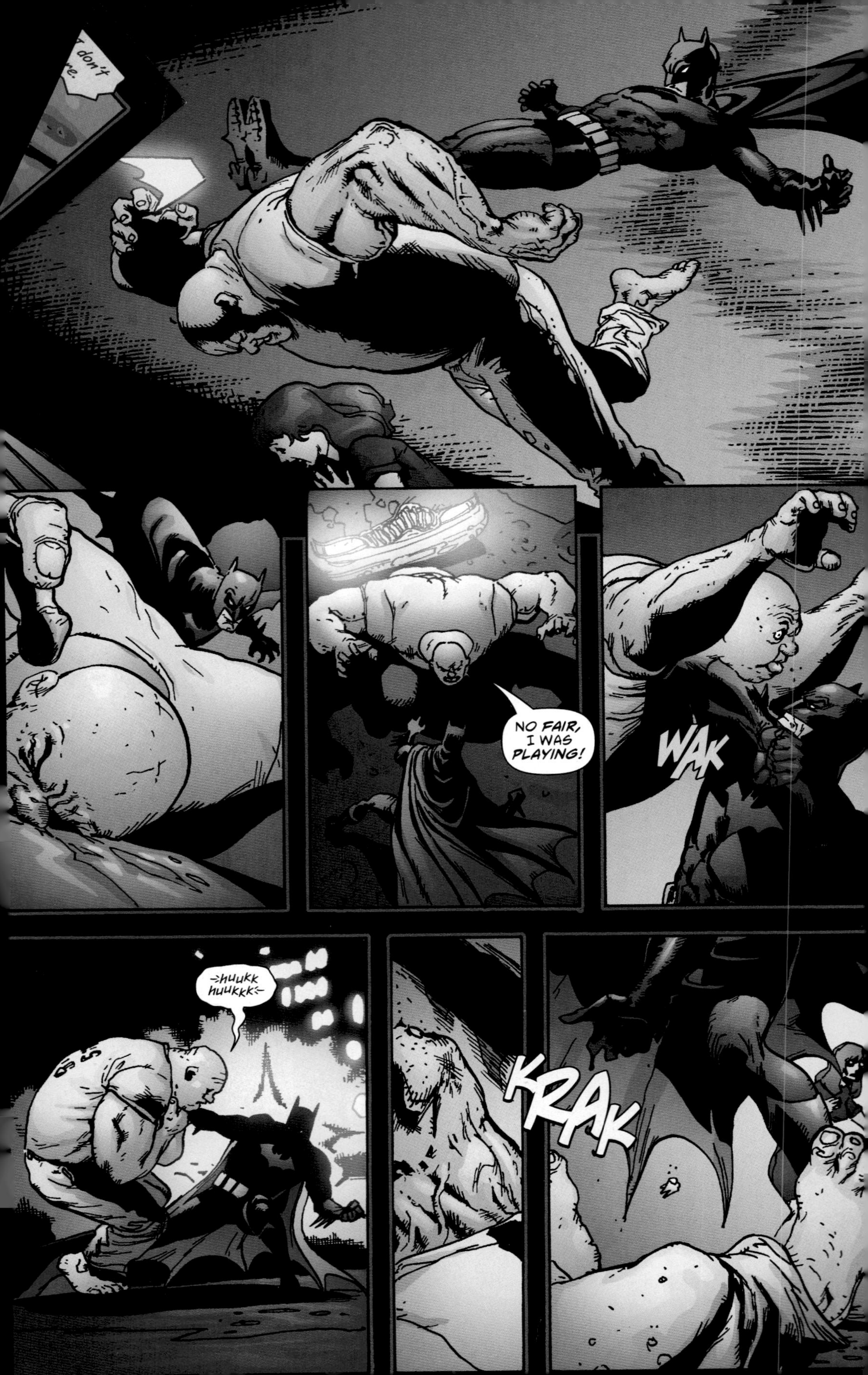

don't
re.
NO FAIR, I WAS PLAYING!
WAK
-huukk huukkk-
KRAK

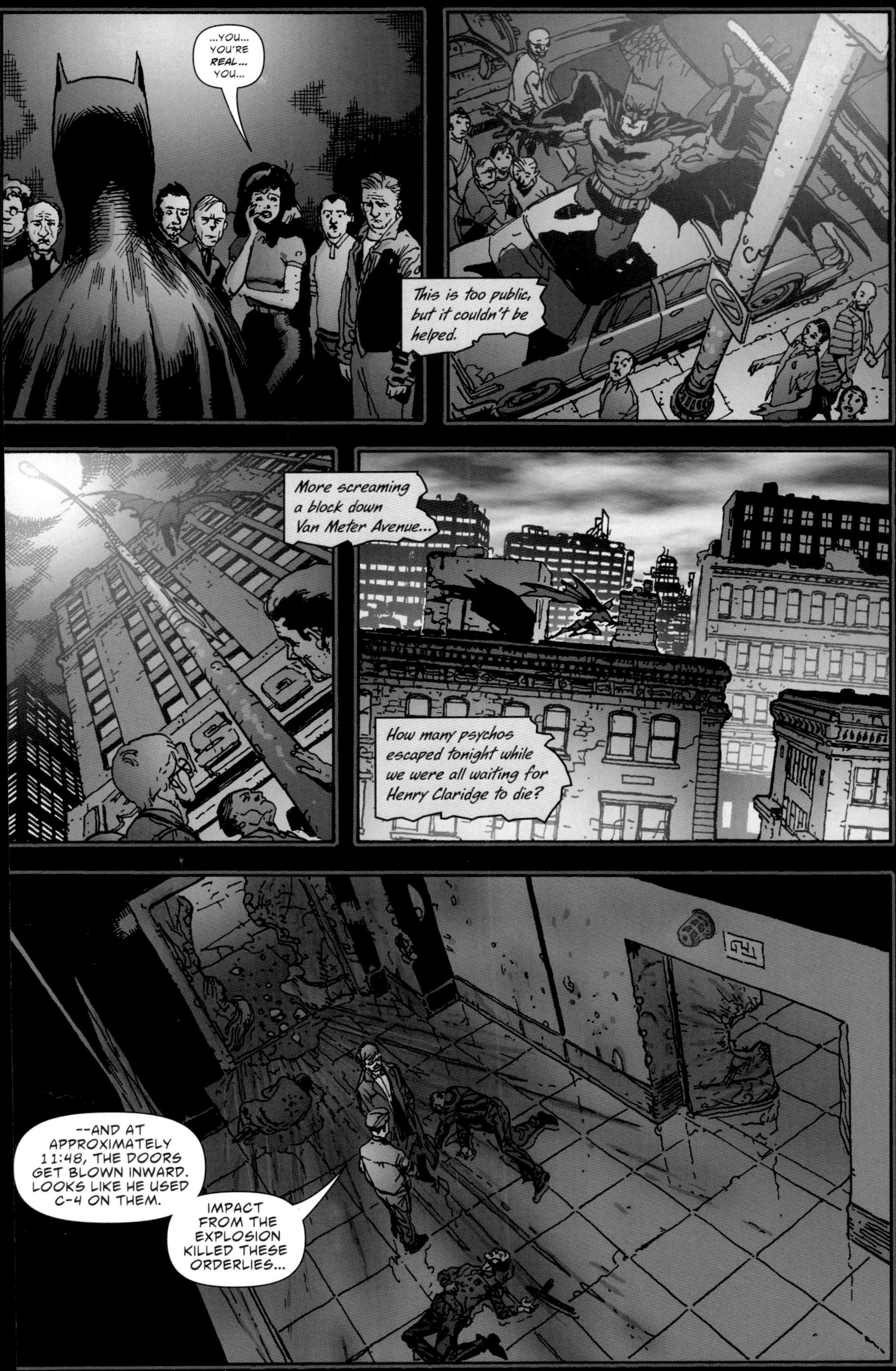
...YOU... YOU'RE REAL... YOU...
This is too public, but it couldn't be helped.
More screaming a block down Van Meter Avenue...
How many psychos escaped tonight while we were all waiting for Henry Claridge to die?
--AND AT APPROXIMATELY 11:48, THE DOORS GET BLOWN INWARD. LOOKS LIKE HE USED C-4 ON THEM.
IMPACT FROM THE EXPLOSION KILLED THESE ORDERLIES...

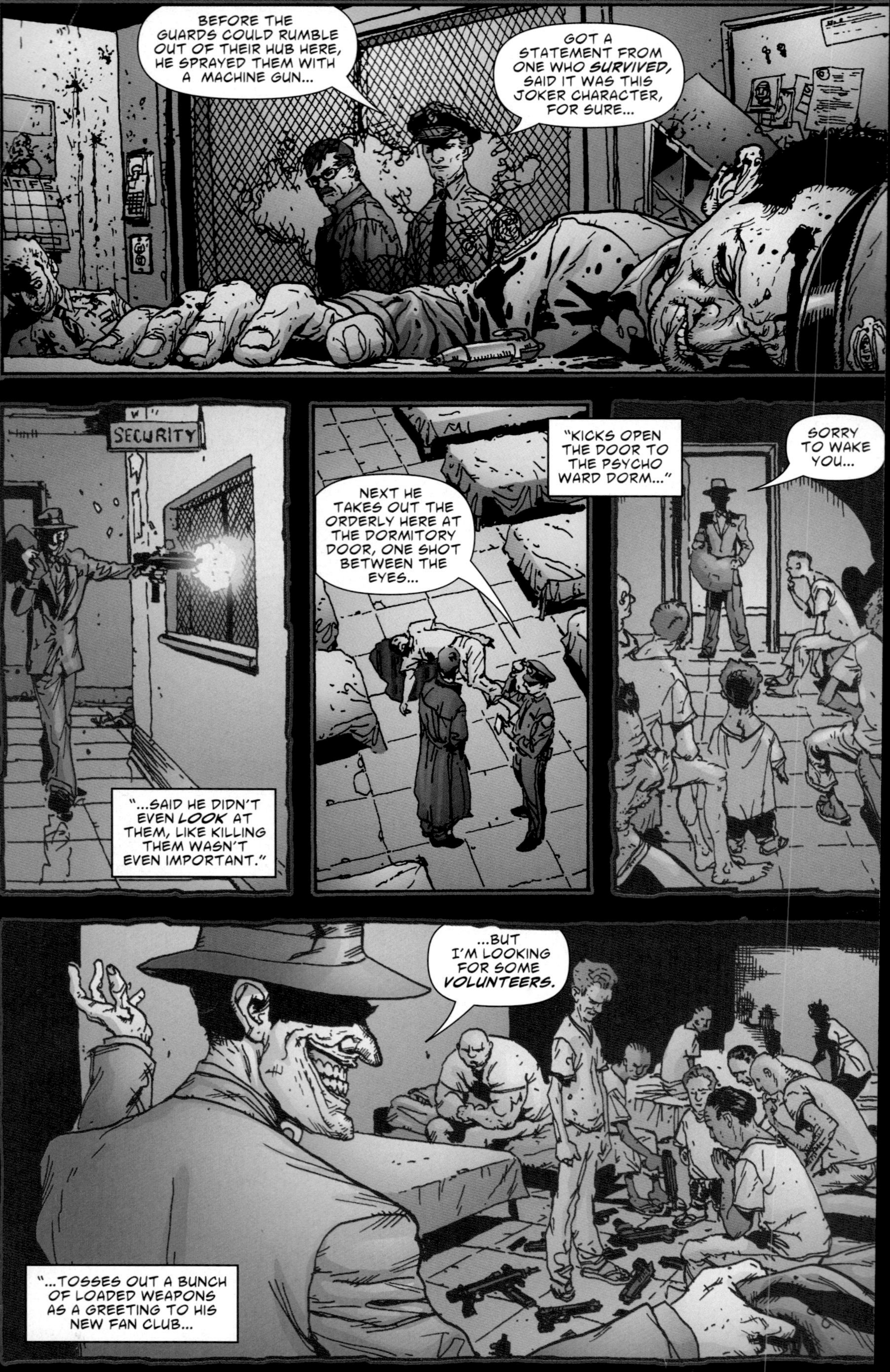
BEFORE THE GUARDS COULD RUMBLE OUT OF THEIR HUB HERE, HE SPRAYED THEM WITH A MACHINE GUN...
GOT A STATEMENT FROM ONE WHO SURVIVED, SAID IT WAS THIS JOKER CHARACTER, FOR SURE...
SECURITY
"...SAID HE DIDN'T EVEN LOOK AT THEM, LIKE KILLING THEM WASN'T EVEN IMPORTANT."
NEXT HE TAKES OUT THE ORDERLY HERE AT THE DORMITORY DOOR, ONE SHOT BETWEEN THE EYES...
"KICKS OPEN THE DOOR TO THE PSYCHO WARD DORM..."
SORRY TO WAKE YOU...
...BUT I'M LOOKING FOR SOME VOLUNTEERS.
"...TOSSES OUT A BUNCH OF LOADED WEAPONS AS A GREETING TO HIS NEW FAN CLUB...

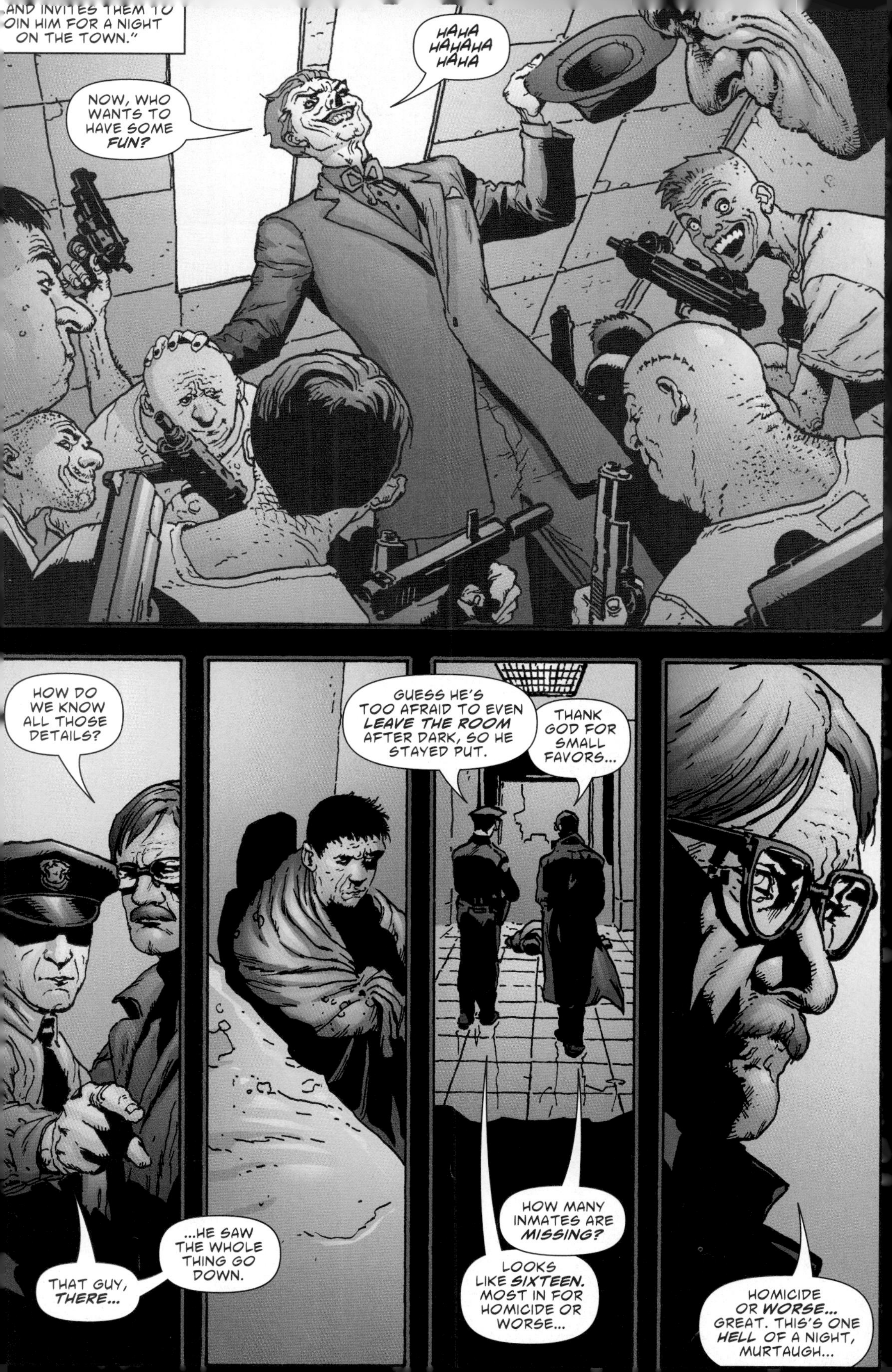
AND INVITES THEM TO OIN HIM FOR A NIGHT ON THE TOWN."
NOW, WHO WANTS TO HAVE SOME FUN?
HAHA HAHAHA HAHA
HOW DO WE KNOW ALL THOSE DETAILS?
THAT GUY, THERE...
...HE SAW THE WHOLE THING GO DOWN.
GUESS HE'S TOO AFRAID TO EVEN LEAVE THE ROOM AFTER DARK, SO HE STAYED PUT.
THANK GOD FOR SMALL FAVORS...
HOW MANY INMATES ARE MISSING?
LOOKS LIKE SIXTEEN. MOST IN FOR HOMICIDE OR WORSE...
HOMICIDE OR WORSE... GREAT. THIS'S ONE HELL OF A NIGHT, MURTAUGH...

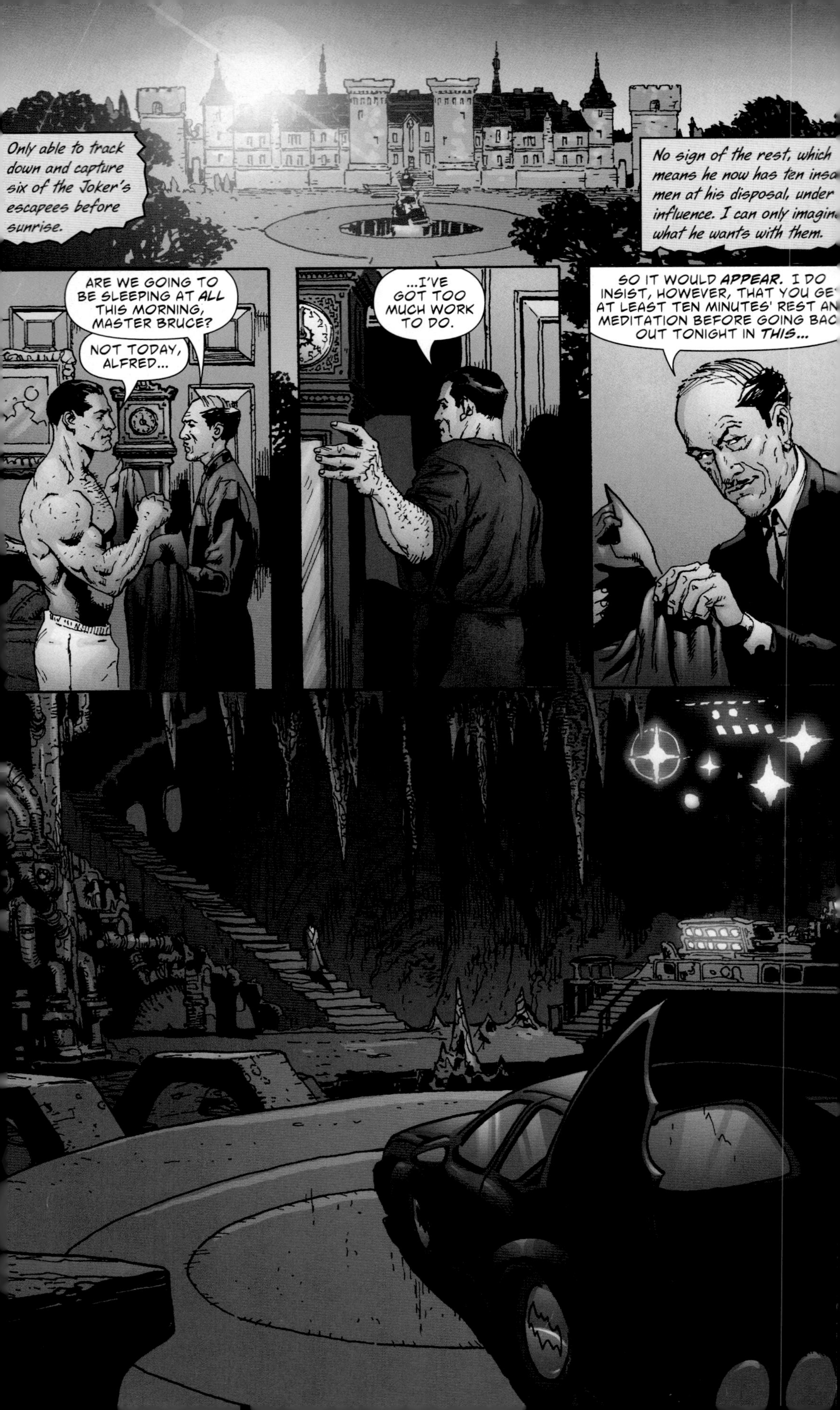
Only able to track down and capture six of the Joker's escapees before sunrise.
No sign of the rest, which means he now has ten insa men at his disposal, under influence. I can only imagin what he wants with them.
ARE WE GOING TO BE SLEEPING AT ALL THIS MORNING, MASTER BRUCE?
NOT TODAY, ALFRED...
...I'VE GOT TOO MUCH WORK TO DO.
SO IT WOULD APPEAR. I DO INSIST, HOWEVER, THAT YOU GE AT LEAST TEN MINUTES' REST AN MEDITATION BEFORE GOING BAC OUT TONIGHT IN THIS...

Took a blood sample from the reporter killed yesterday, and another from Claridge last night.

Hopefully I'll be able to analyze this poison.

Must be two variants, fast-acting and slow-acting, which may help me know what to look for.

If my hunch is right, and I'm sure it is, Claridge had already been exposed to the poison before Joker made his announcement.

Just as I get the chemical analysis running in the computer, Gotham's new nightmare makes a command performance...

GOOOOOD MOOOORNINNNGG GOTHAMCITAY!

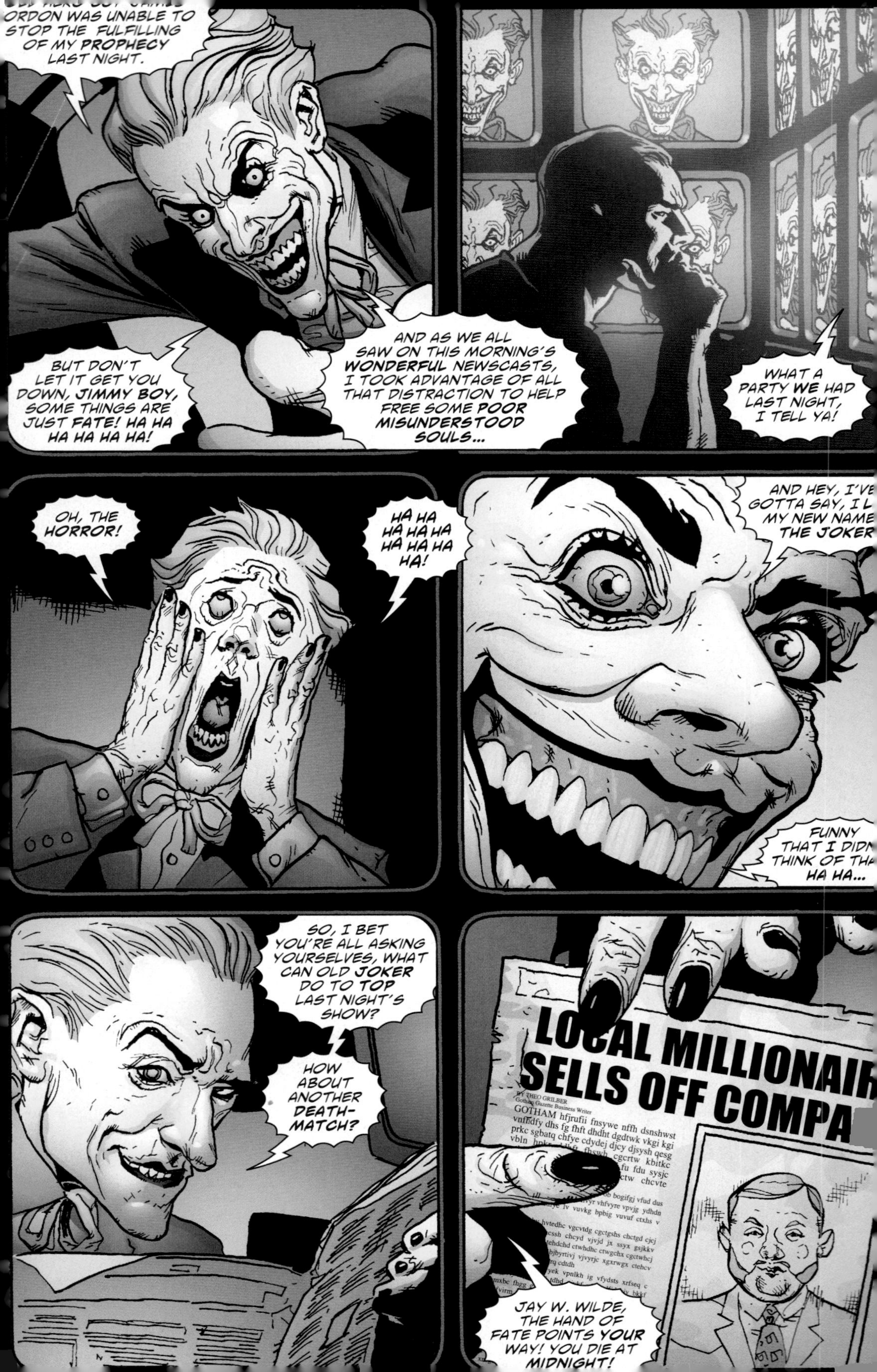
ORDON WAS UNABLE TO STOP THE FULFILLING OF MY PROPHECY LAST NIGHT.
BUT DON'T LET IT GET YOU DOWN, JIMMY BOY, SOME THINGS ARE JUST FATE! HA HA HA HA HA HA!
AND AS WE ALL SAW ON THIS MORNING'S WONDERFUL NEWSCASTS, I TOOK ADVANTAGE OF ALL THAT DISTRACTION TO HELP FREE SOME POOR MISUNDERSTOOD SOULS...
WHAT A PARTY WE HAD LAST NIGHT, I TELL YA!
OH, THE HORROR!
HA HA HA HA HA HA HA HA HA!
AND HEY, I'VE GOTTA SAY, I L MY NEW NAME THE JOKER
FUNNY THAT I DIDN THINK OF THA HA HA...
SO, I BET YOU'RE ALL ASKING YOURSELVES, WHAT CAN OLD JOKER DO TO TOP LAST NIGHT'S SHOW?
HOW ABOUT ANOTHER DEATH-MATCH?
LOCAL MILLIONAIR SELLS OFF COMPA
BY THEO GRILBER
Gotham Gazette Business Writer
JAY W. WILDE, THE HAND OF FATE POINTS YOUR WAY! YOU DIE AT MIDNIGHT!

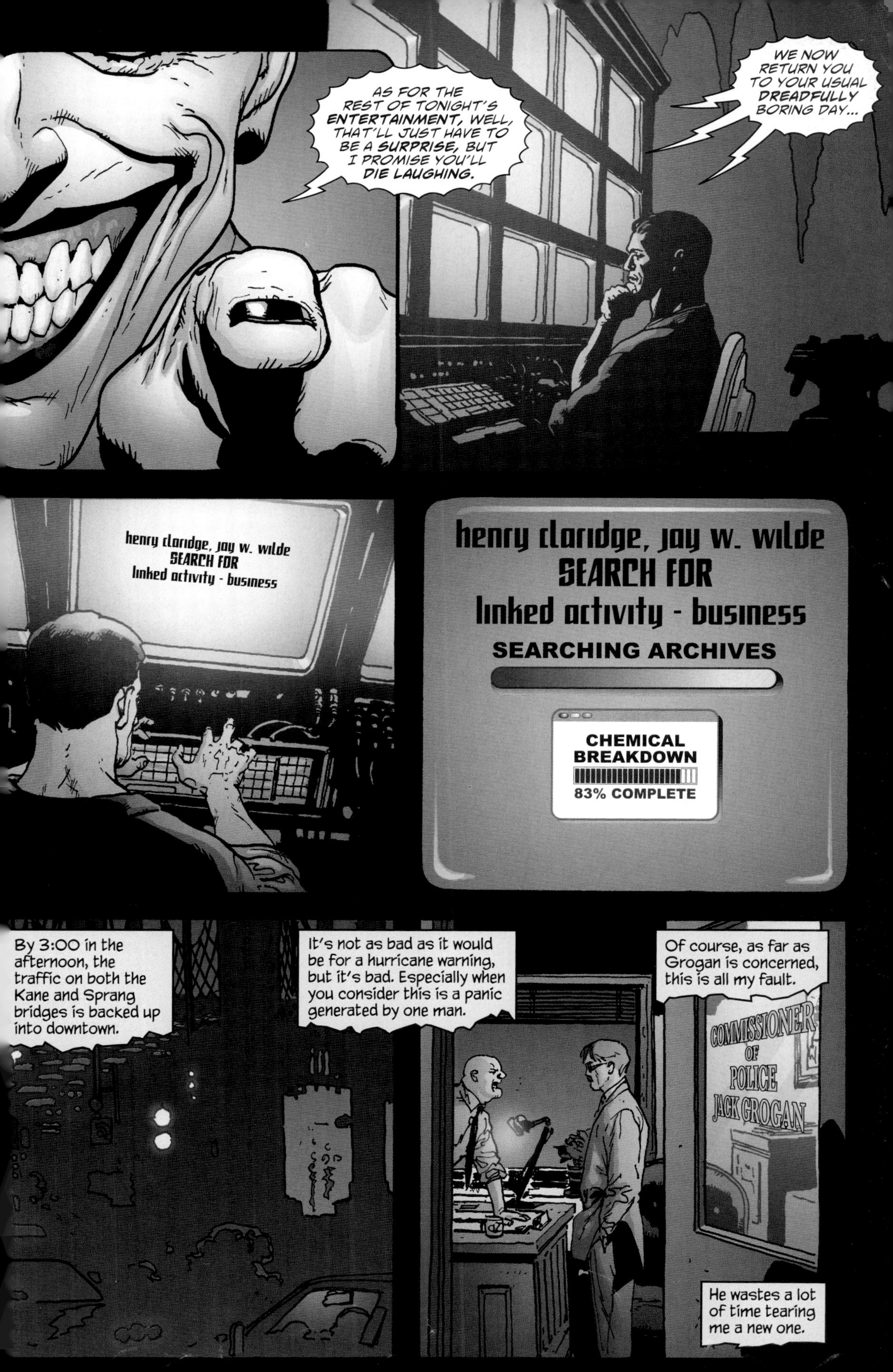

AS FOR THE REST OF TONIGHT'S ENTERTAINMENT, WELL, THAT'LL JUST HAVE TO BE A SURPRISE, BUT I PROMISE YOU'LL DIE LAUGHING.
WE NOW RETURN YOU TO YOUR USUAL DREADFULLY BORING DAY...
henry claridge, jay w. wilde
SEARCH FOR
linked activity - business
henry claridge, jay w. wilde
SEARCH FOR
linked activity - business
SEARCHING ARCHIVES
CHEMICAL BREAKDOWN
83% COMPLETE
By 3:00 in the afternoon, the traffic on both the Kane and Sprang bridges is backed up into downtown.
It's not as bad as it would be for a hurricane warning, but it's bad. Especially when you consider this is a panic generated by one man.
Of course, as far as Grogan is concerned, this is all my fault.
COMMISSIONER OF POLICE JACK GROGAN
He wastes a lot of time tearing me a new one.

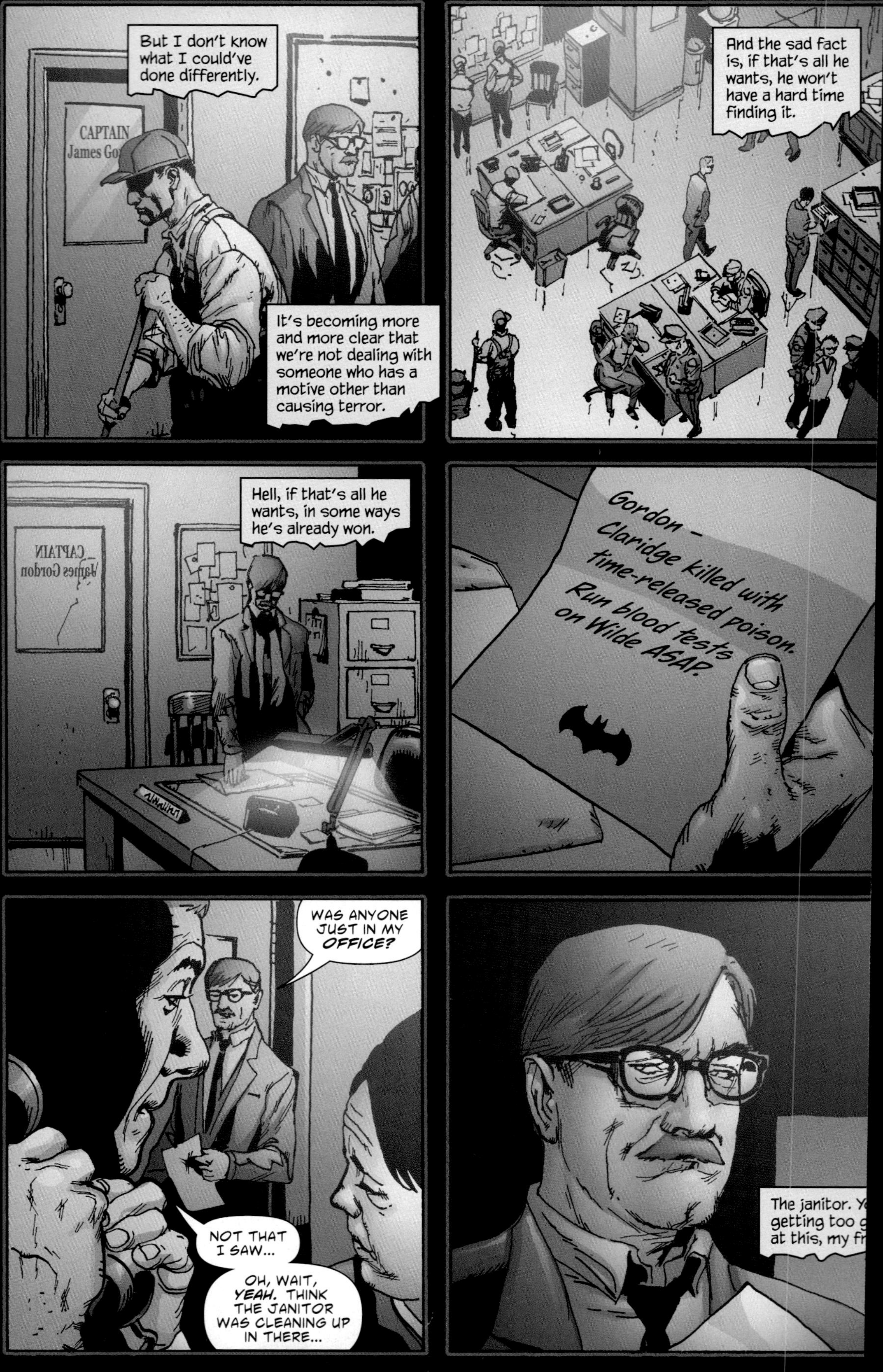
CAPTAIN
James Go
But I don't know what I could've done differently.
It's becoming more and more clear that we're not dealing with someone who has a motive other than causing terror.
And the sad fact is, if that's all he wants, he won't have a hard time finding it.
CAPTAIN
James Gordon
Hell, if that's all he wants, in some ways he's already won.
Gordon –
Claridge killed with time-released poison.
Run blood tests on Wilde ASAP.
WAS ANYONE JUST IN MY *OFFICE?*
NOT THAT I SAW...
OH, WAIT, *YEAH.* THINK THE JANITOR WAS CLEANING UP IN THERE...
The janitor. Y
getting too g
at this, my fr

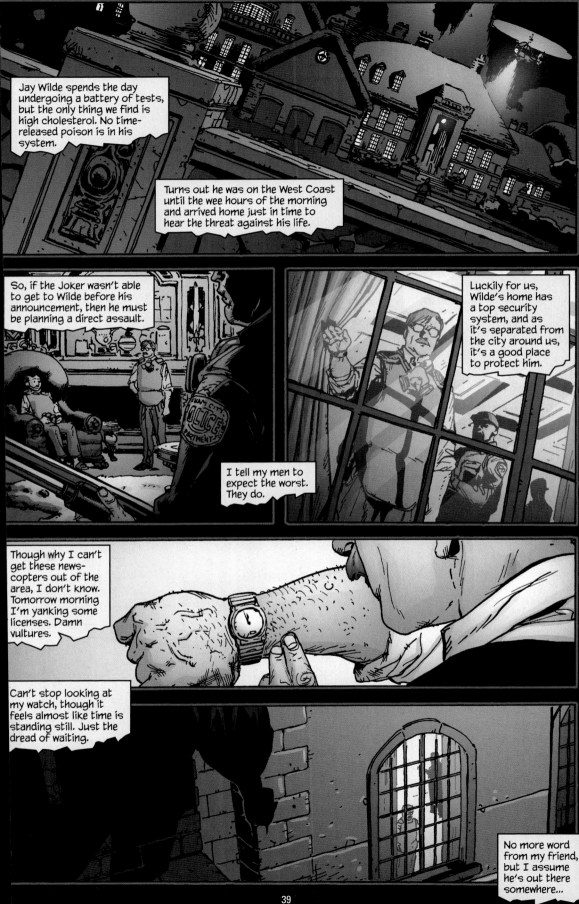

Jay Wilde spends the day undergoing a battery of tests, but the only thing we find is high cholesterol. No time-released poison is in his system.

Turns out he was on the West Coast until the wee hours of the morning and arrived home just in time to hear the threat against his life.

So, if the Joker wasn't able to get to Wilde before his announcement, then he must be planning a direct assault.

Luckily for us, Wilde's home has a top security system, and as it's separated from the city around us, it's a good place to protect him.

I tell my men to expect the worst. They do.

Though why I can't get these news-copters out of the area, I don't know. Tomorrow morning I'm yanking some licenses. Damn vultures.

Can't stop looking at my watch, though it feels almost like time is standing still. Just the dread of waiting.

No more word from my friend, but I assume he's out there somewhere...

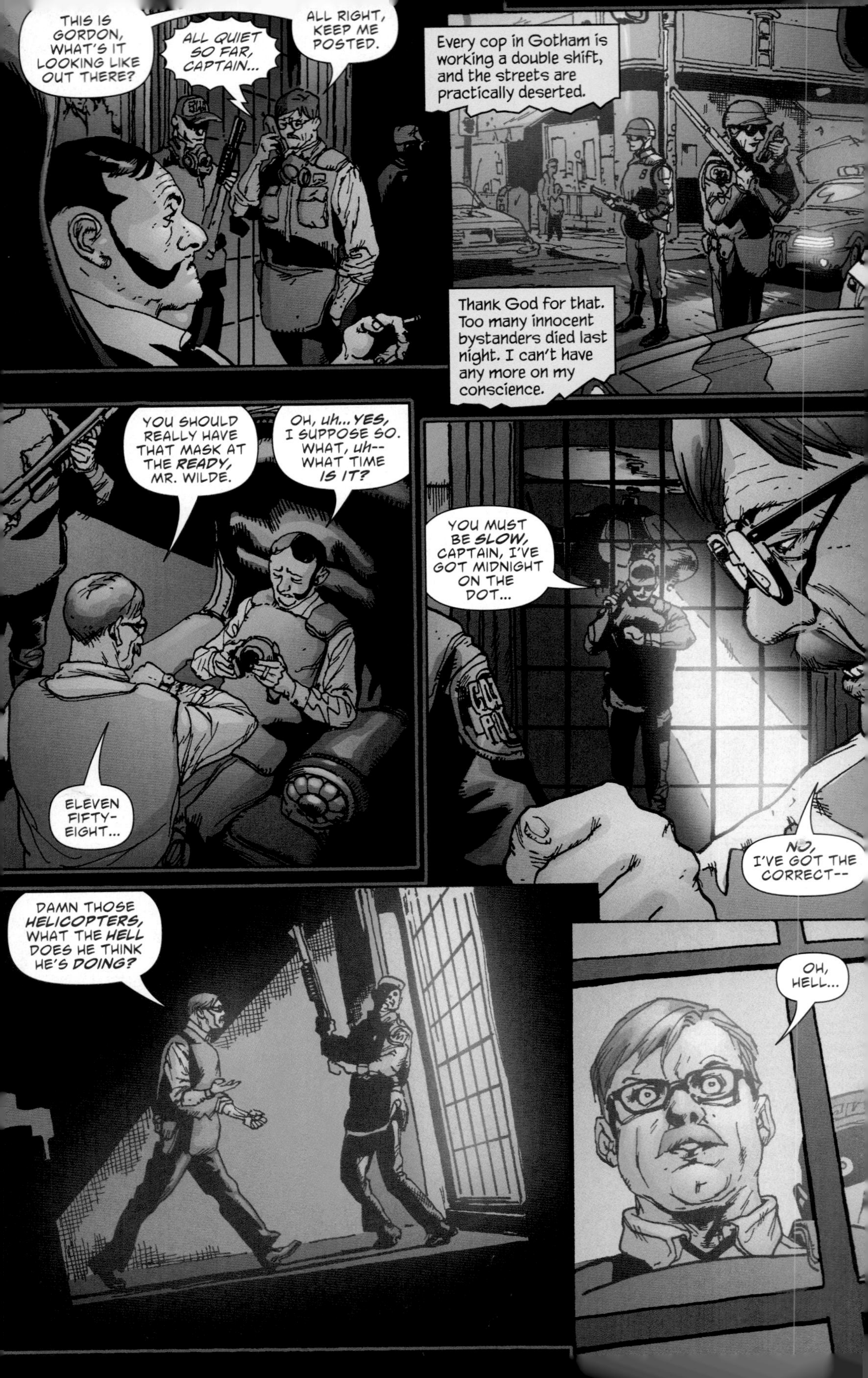
THIS IS GORDON, WHAT'S IT LOOKING LIKE OUT THERE?
ALL QUIET SO FAR, CAPTAIN...
ALL RIGHT, KEEP ME POSTED.
Every cop in Gotham is working a double shift, and the streets are practically deserted.
Thank God for that. Too many innocent bystanders died last night. I can't have any more on my conscience.
YOU SHOULD REALLY HAVE THAT MASK AT THE READY, MR. WILDE.
OH, uh... YES, I SUPPOSE SO. WHAT, uh-- WHAT TIME IS IT?
ELEVEN FIFTY-EIGHT...
YOU MUST BE SLOW, CAPTAIN, I'VE GOT MIDNIGHT ON THE DOT...
NO, I'VE GOT THE CORRECT--
DAMN THOSE HELICOPTERS, WHAT THE HELL DOES HE THINK HE'S DOING?
OH, HELL...

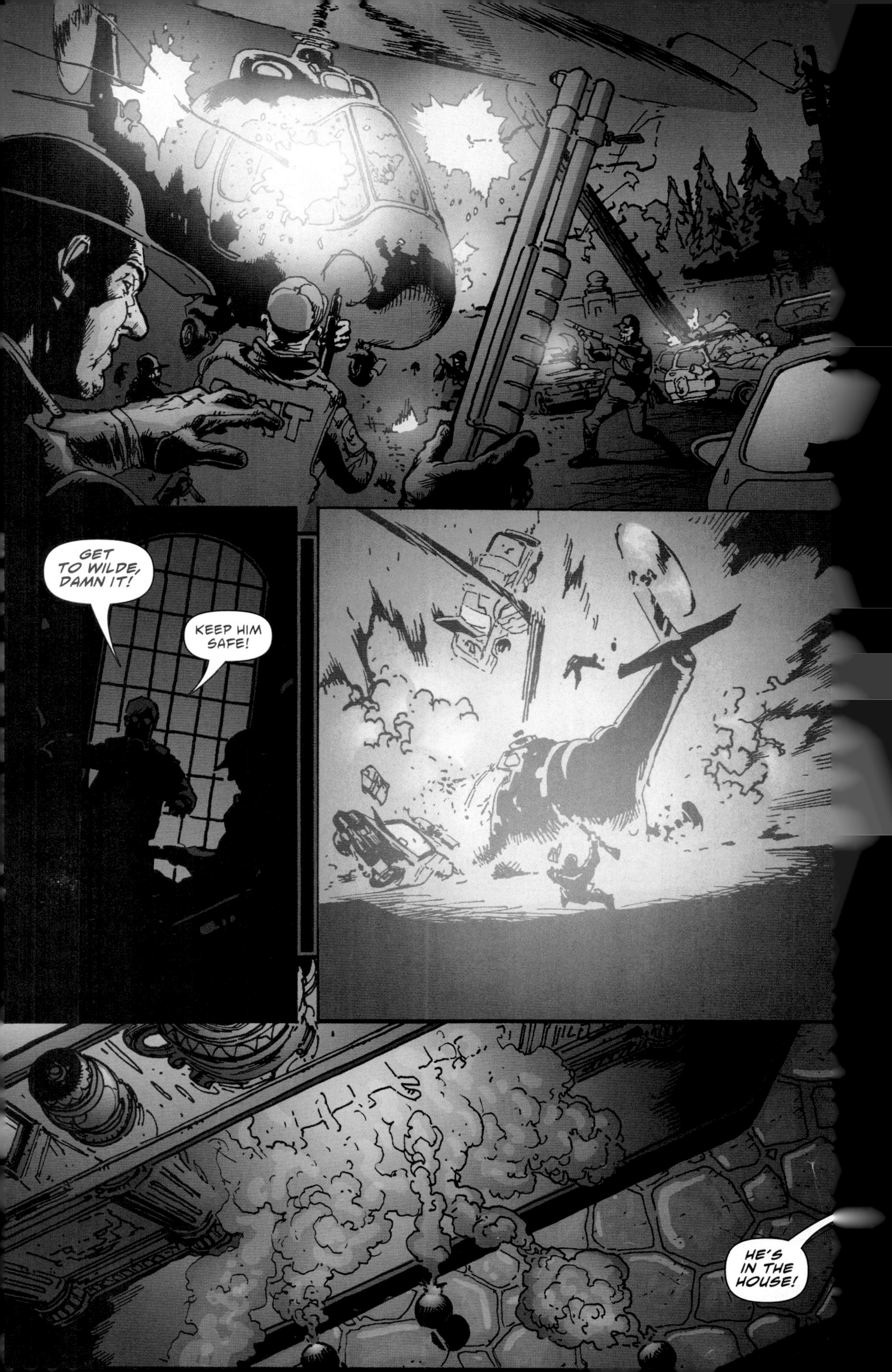
GET TO WILDE, DAMN IT!
KEEP HIM SAFE!
HE'S IN THE HOUSE!

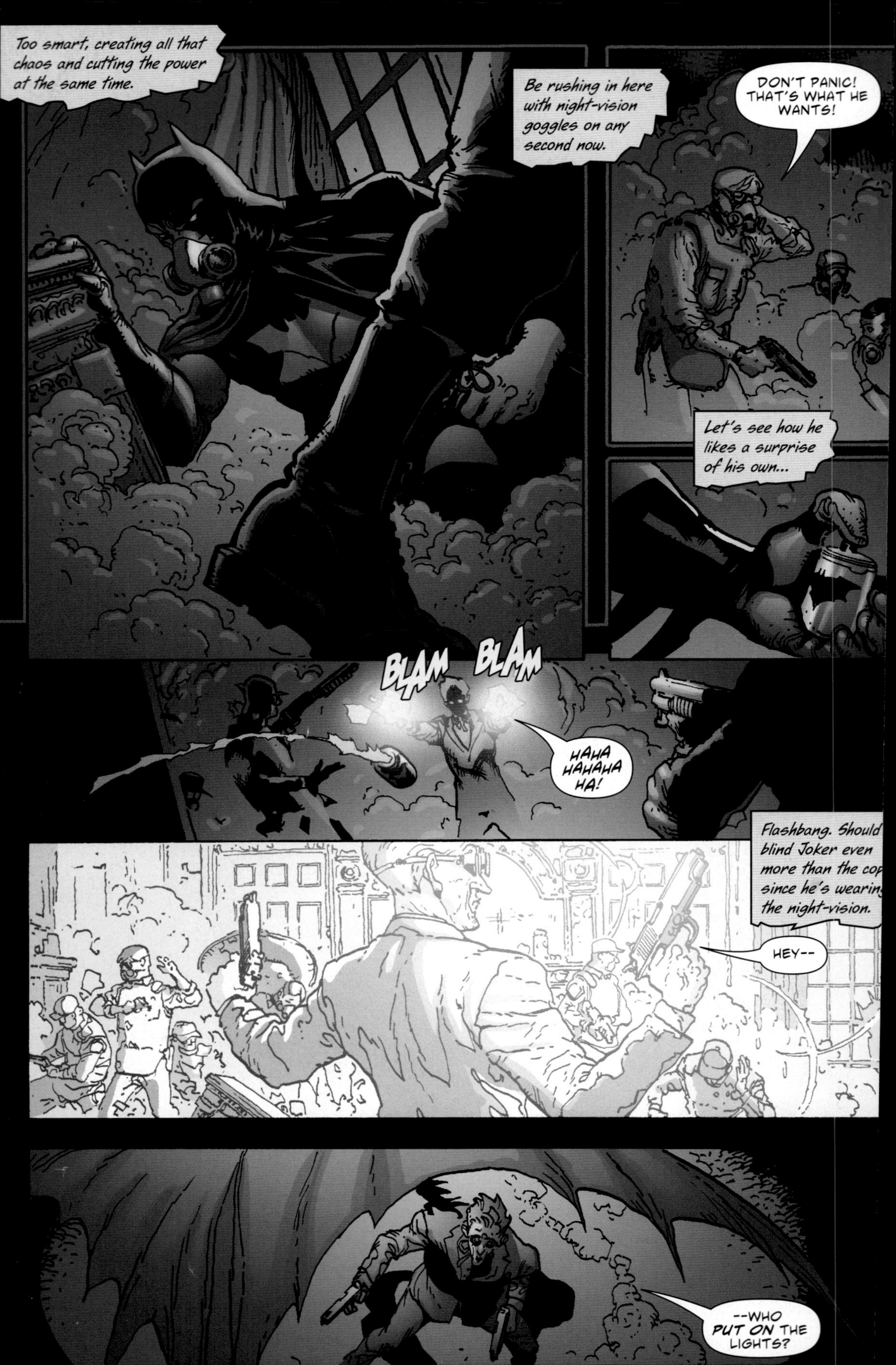
Too smart, creating all that chaos and cutting the power at the same time.
Be rushing in here with night-vision goggles on any second now.
DON'T PANIC! THAT'S WHAT HE WANTS!
Let's see how he likes a surprise of his own...
BLAM BLAM
HAHA HAHAHA HA!
Flashbang. Should blind Joker even more than the cops since he's wearing the night-vision.
HEY--
--WHO PUT ON THE LIGHTS?

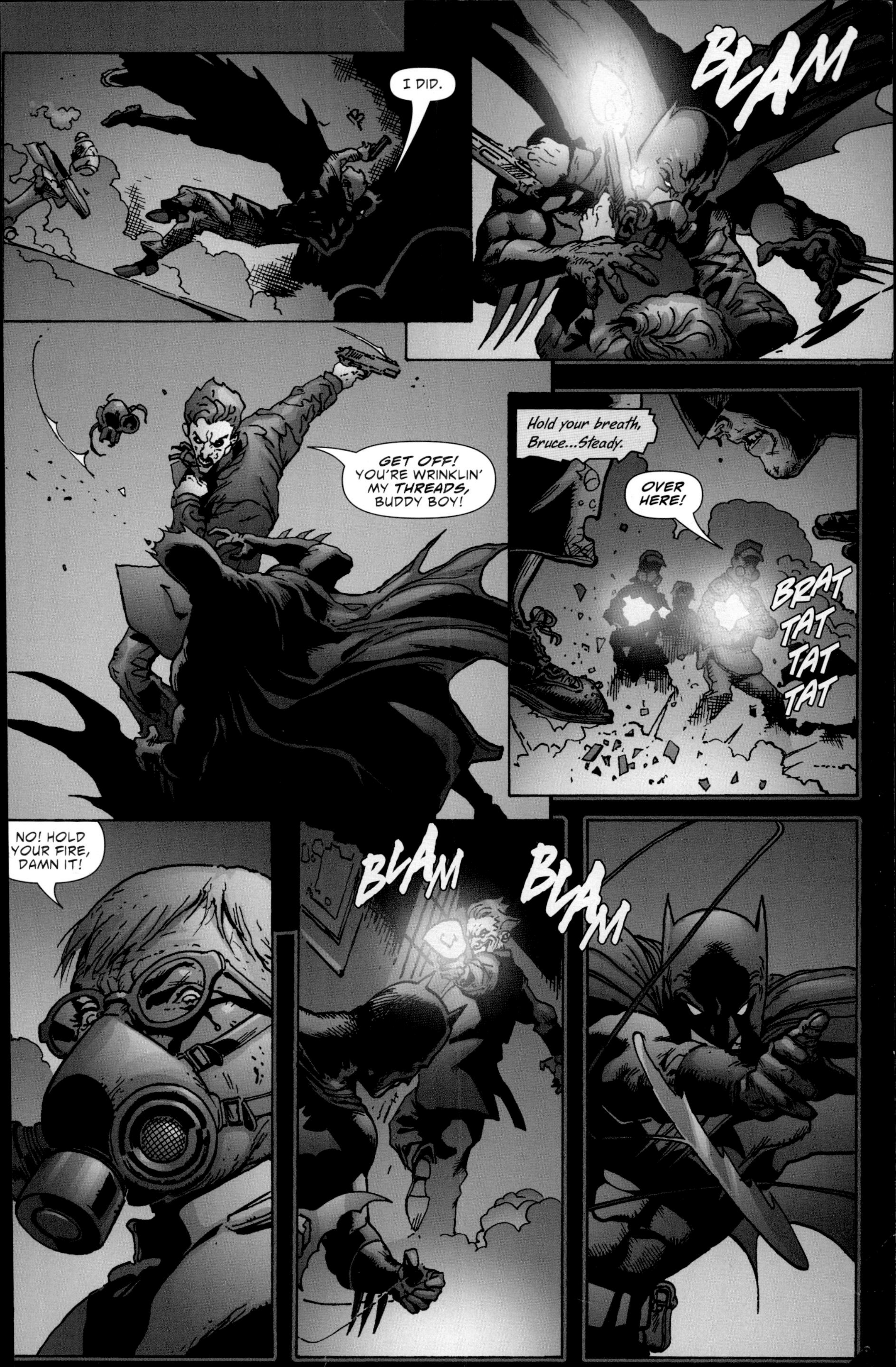
I DID.
BLAM
GET OFF! YOU'RE WRINKLIN' MY THREADS, BUDDY BOY!
Hold your breath, Bruce...Steady.
OVER HERE!
BRAT TAT TAT TAT
NO! HOLD YOUR FIRE, DAMN IT!
BLAM
BLAM

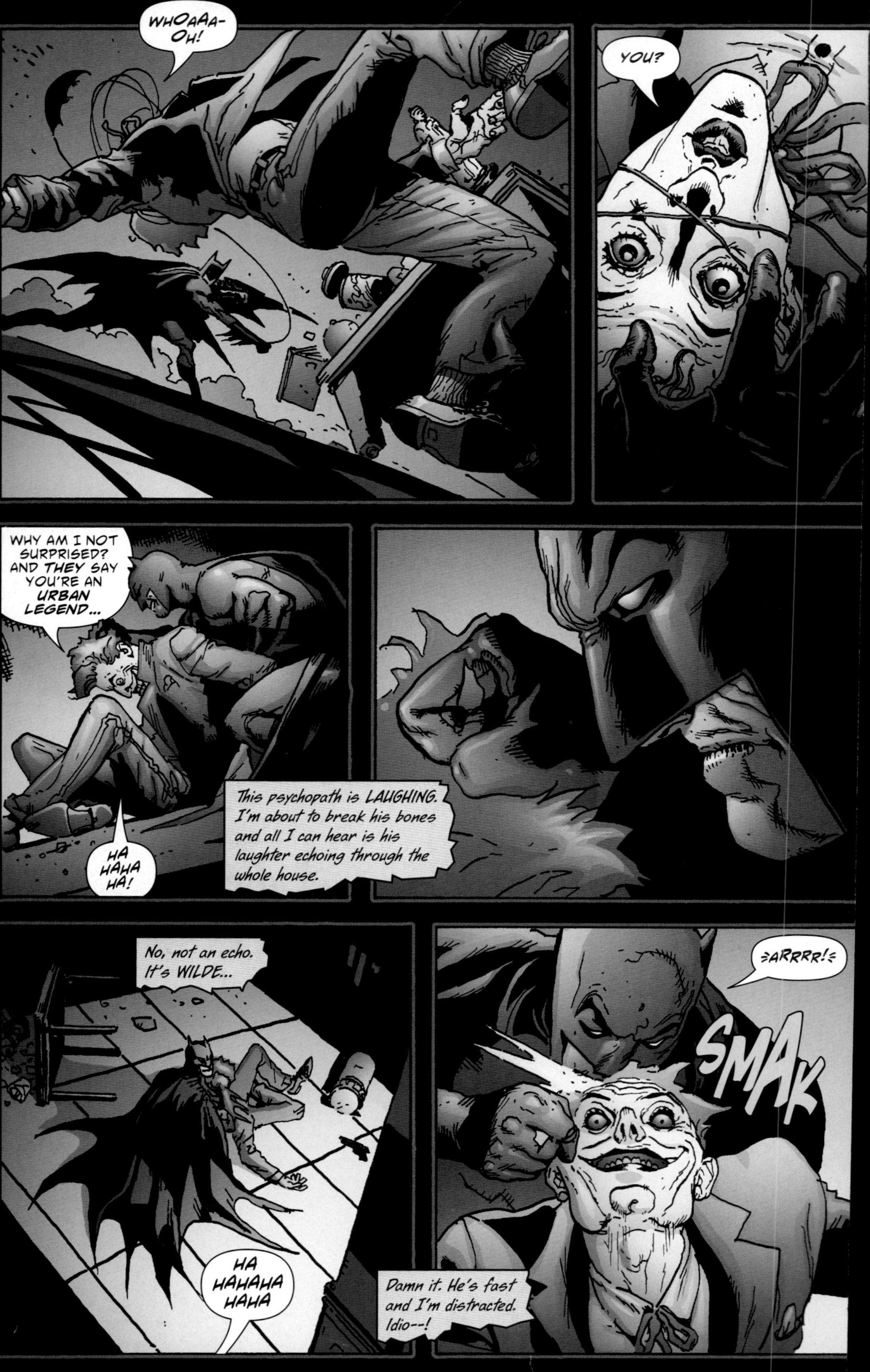
WHOAAA-OH!
YOU?
WHY AM I NOT SURPRISED? AND THEY SAY YOU'RE AN URBAN LEGEND...
HA HAHA HA!
This psychopath is LAUGHING. I'm about to break his bones and all I can hear is his laughter echoing through the whole house.
No, not an echo. It's WILDE...
HA HAHAHA HAHA
ARRRR!
SMAK
Damn it. He's fast and I'm distracted. Idio--!

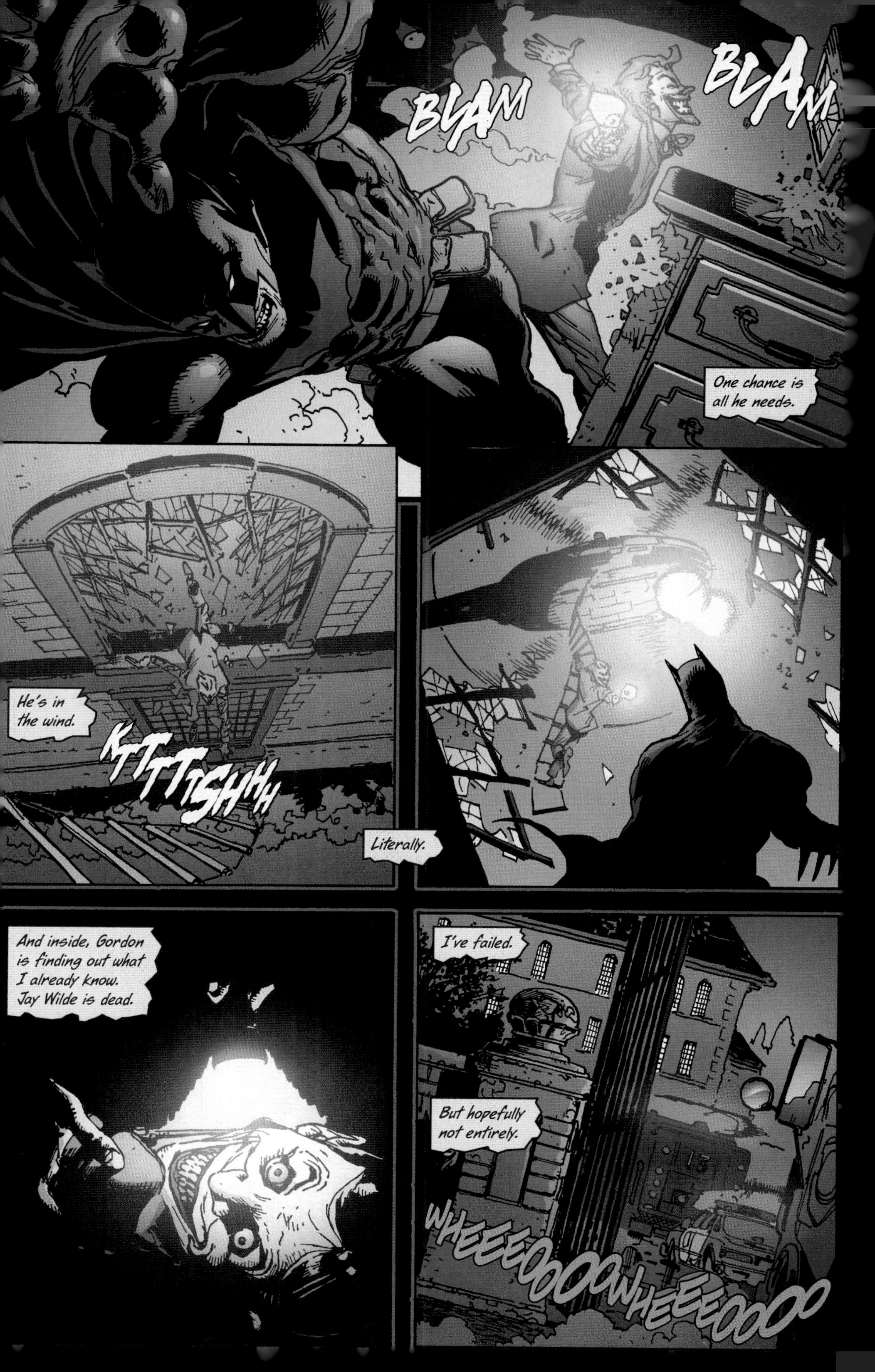
BLAM
BLAM
One chance is all he needs.
He's in the wind.
KTTTTSHHHH
Literally.
And inside, Gordon is finding out what I already know. Jay Wilde is dead.
I've failed.
But hopefully not entirely.
WHEEEOOOOWHEEEOOOOO

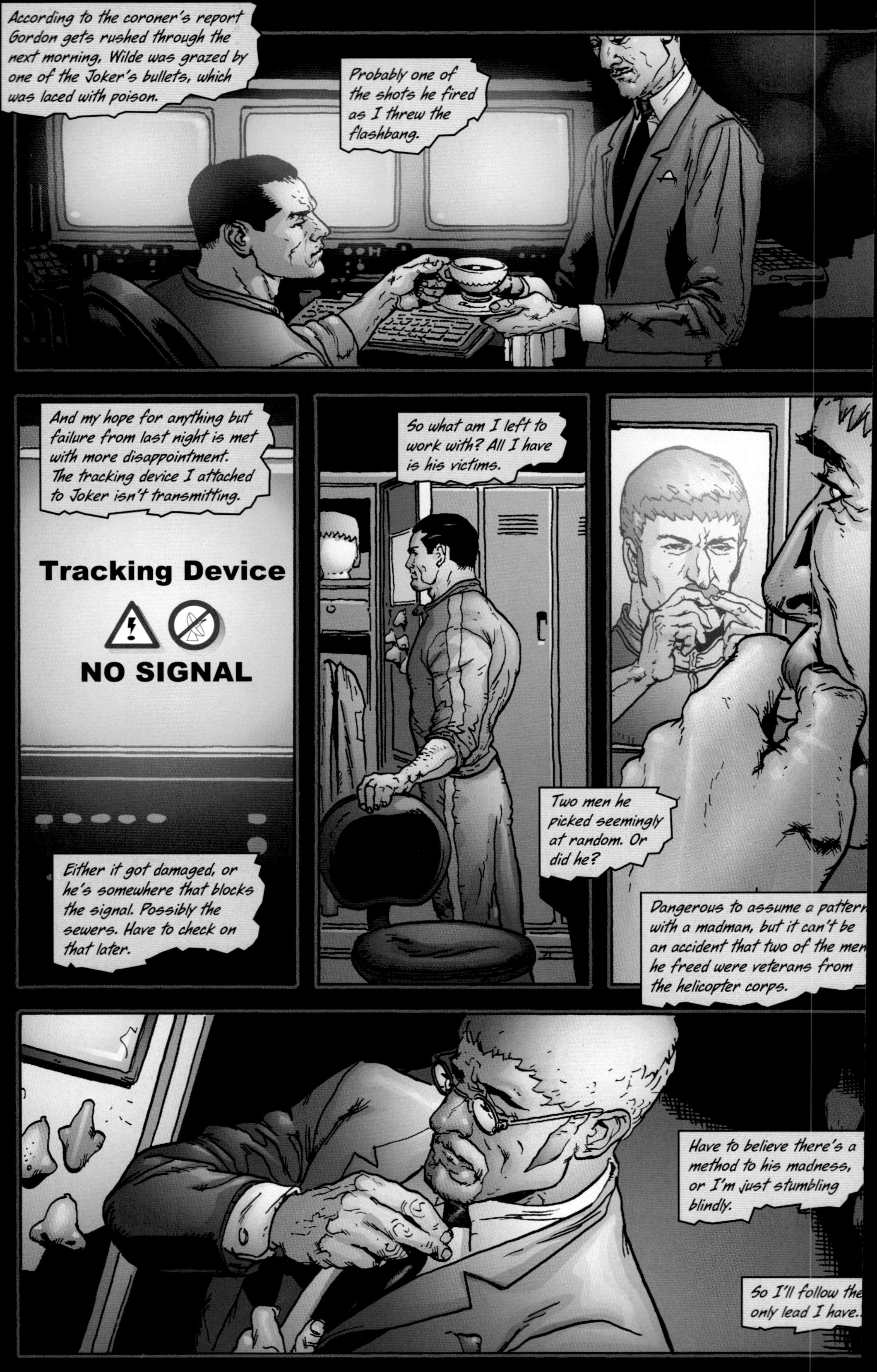
According to the coroner's report Gordon gets rushed through the next morning, Wilde was grazed by one of the Joker's bullets, which was laced with poison.
Probably one of the shots he fired as I threw the flashbang.
And my hope for anything but failure from last night is met with more disappointment. The tracking device I attached to Joker isn't transmitting.
Tracking Device
NO SIGNAL
Either it got damaged, or he's somewhere that blocks the signal. Possibly the sewers. Have to check on that later.
So what am I left to work with? All I have is his victims.
Two men he picked seemingly at random. Or did he?
Dangerous to assume a pattern with a madman, but it can't be an accident that two of the men he freed were veterans from the helicopter corps.
Have to believe there's a method to his madness, or I'm just stumbling blindly.
So I'll follow the only lead I have...

There were numerous links between Wilde and Claridge; both were investors and on the boards of many different corporate entities.

But the only one that sticks out is Ace Chemical Processing. Wilde and Claridge were the main investors in the plant when it opened 20 years ago.

CLOSED BY ORDER OF E.P.A.

And this is the place where, three months ago, Batman fought the Red Hood. Too much of a coincidence not to look into...

WHO DID YOU SAY YOU WERE *WITH* AGAIN?

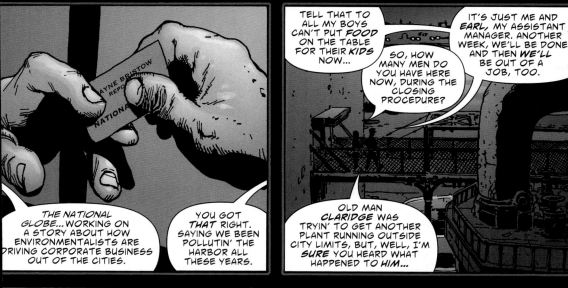

WAYNE BRISTOW REPO...

NATIONA...

THE *NATIONAL GLOBE*...WORKING ON A STORY ABOUT HOW ENVIRONMENTALISTS ARE DRIVING CORPORATE BUSINESS OUT OF THE CITIES.

YOU GOT *THAT* RIGHT. SAYING WE BEEN POLLUTIN' THE HARBOR ALL THESE YEARS.

TELL THAT TO ALL MY BOYS CAN'T PUT *FOOD* ON THE TABLE FOR THEIR *KIDS* NOW...

SO, HOW MANY MEN DO YOU HAVE HERE NOW, DURING THE CLOSING PROCEDURE?

IT'S JUST ME AND *EARL*, MY ASSISTANT MANAGER. ANOTHER WEEK, WE'LL BE DONE AND THEN *WE'LL* BE OUT OF A JOB, TOO.

OLD MAN *CLARIDGE* WAS TRYIN' TO GET ANOTHER PLANT RUNNING OUTSIDE CITY LIMITS, BUT, WELL, I'M *SURE* YOU HEARD WHAT HAPPENED TO *HIM*...

NOW, WORD IS YOU HAD A *WHISTLE-BLOWER* HERE.

WHAT? THAT'S THE FIRST I HEARD'A THAT...

OH YEAH, I'M *CERTAIN* THERE WAS A NAME LISTED ON THE REPORT I SAW...

I DON'T HAVE IT WRITTEN DOWN HERE, BUT IF I COULD GET A LOOK AT YOUR *PERSONNEL RECORDS*, THEY MIGHT JOG MY MEMORY.

YOU'RE *OUT OF LUCK* THERE...HAD A *FIRE* IN THE RECORDS ROOM JUST AFTER THE PLANT SHUT. LOST *EVERYTHING*...

YOU SURE WE HAD AN INSIDER LEAKING STUFF TO THOSE BASTARDS?

ABSOLUTELY.

HEY, *EARL*, LISTEN TO *THIS*... WE'RE ALL OUT OF WORK BECAUSE ONE OF OUR OWN GUYS WAS TALKIN' TO THE FEDS.

REALLY? WELL, I'D SURE LIKE TO GET MY HANDS ON THAT S.O.B. ....

I'M SORRY TO ASK, EARL, BUT HOW DID YOU GET THAT *WHITE STAIN* THERE?

OH...*THIS*. GOT TOO CLOSE TO THE DISPOSAL TANKS ONE DAY, HIT WITH SOME SPLASH-BACK. NO *BIGGIE*. I HARDLY EVEN *NOTICE IT* ANYMORE...

SHOULD'A SEEN SOME OF THE *OTHER GUYS.*

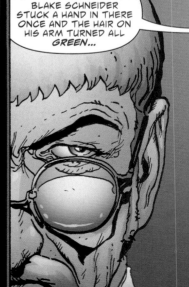

BLAKE SCHNEIDER STUCK A HAND IN THERE ONCE AND THE HAIR ON HIS ARM TURNED ALL *GREEN*...

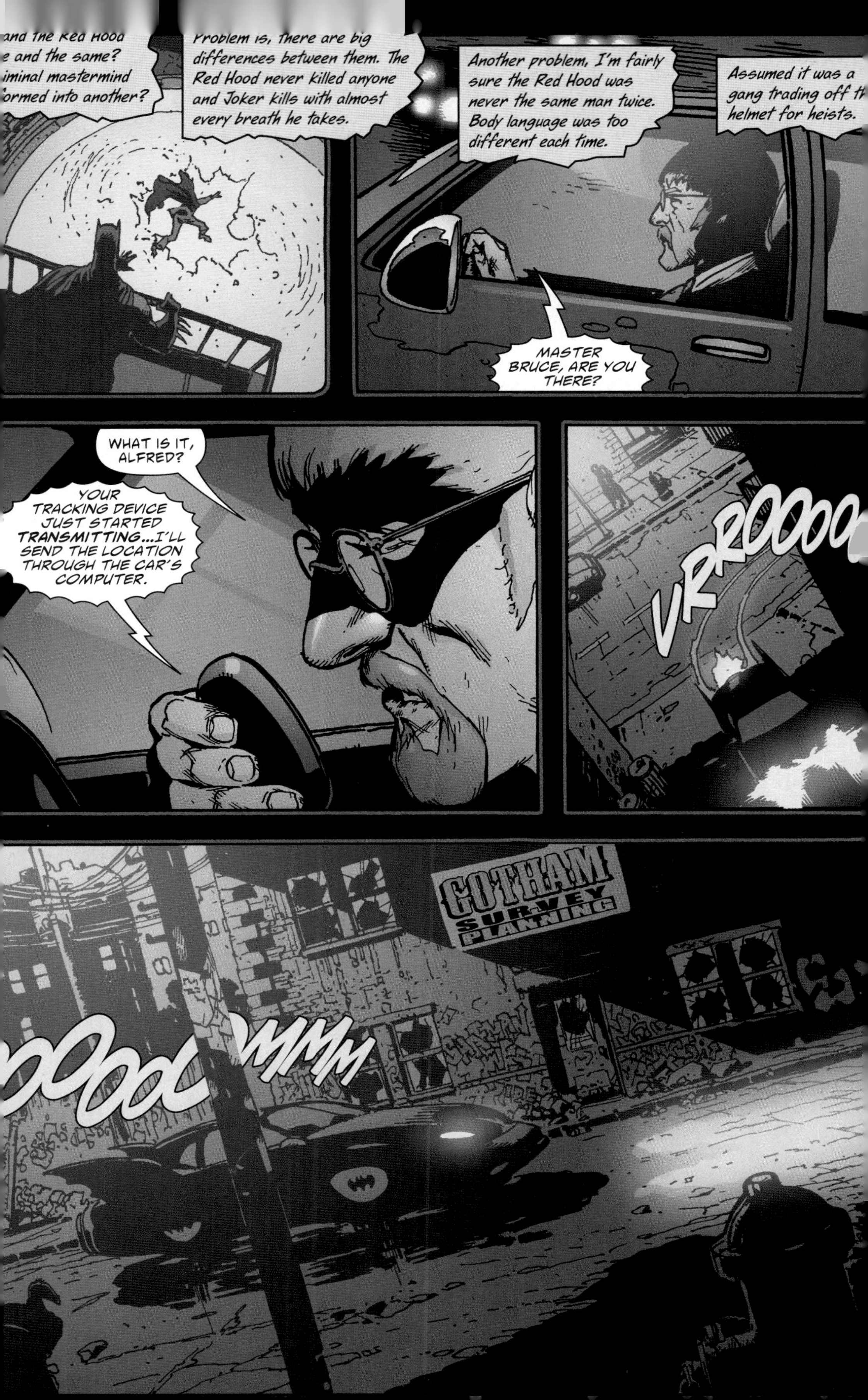
and the Red Hood
e and the same?
iminal mastermind
formed into another?
Problem is, there are big differences between them. The Red Hood never killed anyone and Joker kills with almost every breath he takes.
Another problem, I'm fairly sure the Red Hood was never the same man twice. Body language was too different each time.
Assumed it was a gang trading off th helmet for heists.
MASTER BRUCE, ARE YOU THERE?
WHAT IS IT, ALFRED?
YOUR TRACKING DEVICE JUST STARTED TRANSMITTING...I'LL SEND THE LOCATION THROUGH THE CAR'S COMPUTER.
VRROOOOO
OOOOOMMMM
GOTHAM SURVEY PLANNING

The signal emanates from an abandoned Survey and Planning office in Old Gotham. Like a lot of this area, the office has been unused since the early '50s.

I find the tracking device on the floor near a recently shattered window. Must have gotten pried loose as he wriggled through the broken glass.

So, what did the Joker WANT here?

Most of this information is completely out of date. It'd be useless.

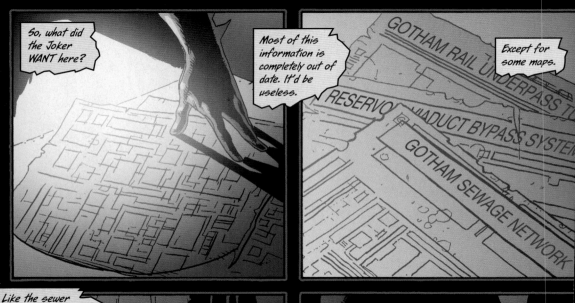

GOTHAM RAIL UNDERPASS T
RESERVO
DUCT BYPASS SYSTEM
GOTHAM SEWAGE NETWORK

Except for some maps.

Like the sewer system. The current network is built in conjunction with the original structure the city was built around.

So, if someone knew what they were doing, they could get all the way from one side of Gotham to the other without ever leaving those tunnels.

I was planning to check the sewers tonight anyway.

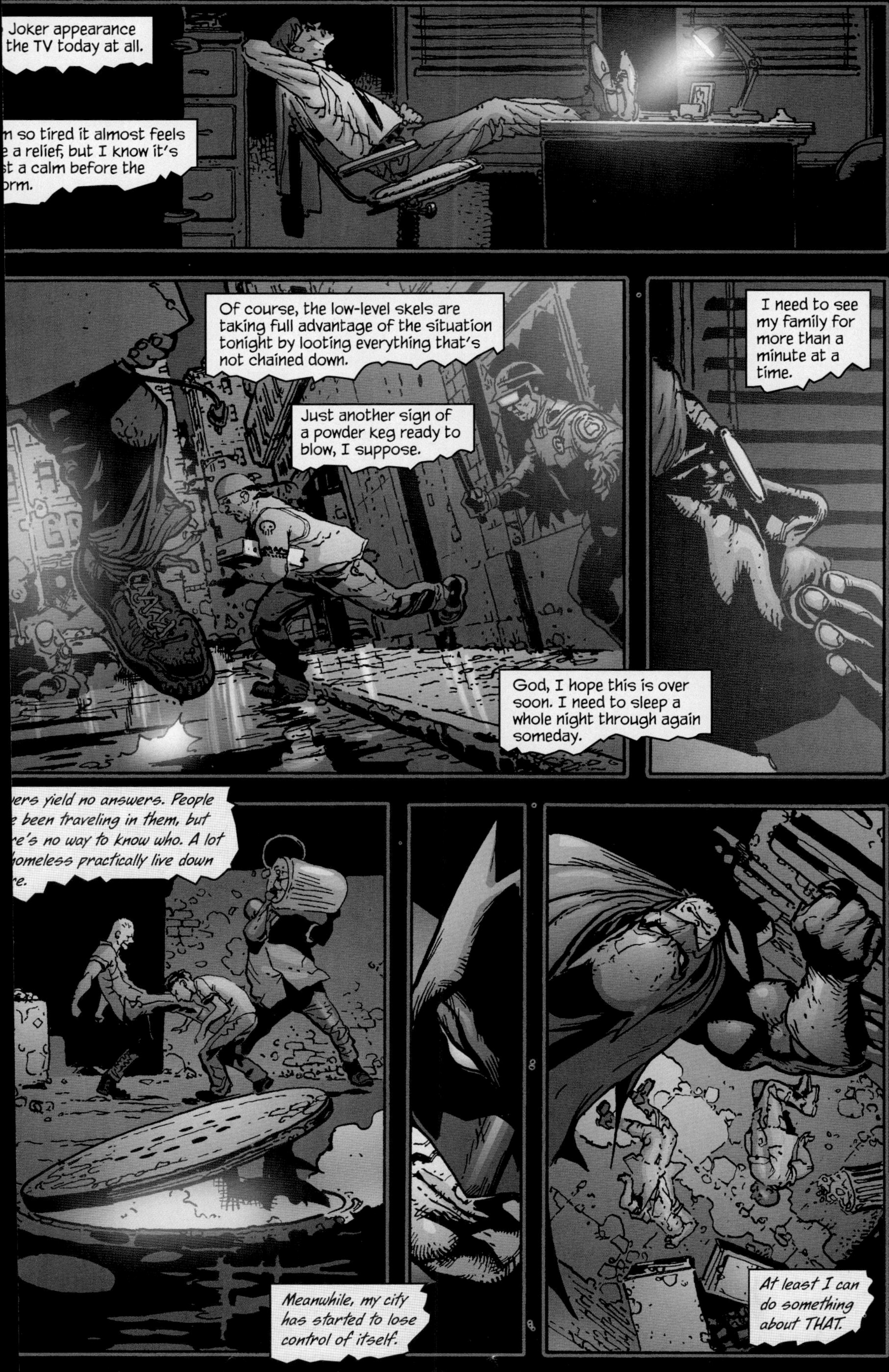
Joker appearance
the TV today at all.
m so tired it almost feels
a relief, but I know it's
st a calm before the
orm.
Of course, the low-level skels are taking full advantage of the situation tonight by looting everything that's not chained down.
Just another sign of a powder keg ready to blow, I suppose.
I need to see my family for more than a minute at a time.
God, I hope this is over soon. I need to sleep a whole night through again someday.
wers yield no answers. People
been traveling in them, but
re's no way to know who. A lot
homeless practically live down
re.
Meanwhile, my city has started to lose control of itself.
At least I can do something about THAT.

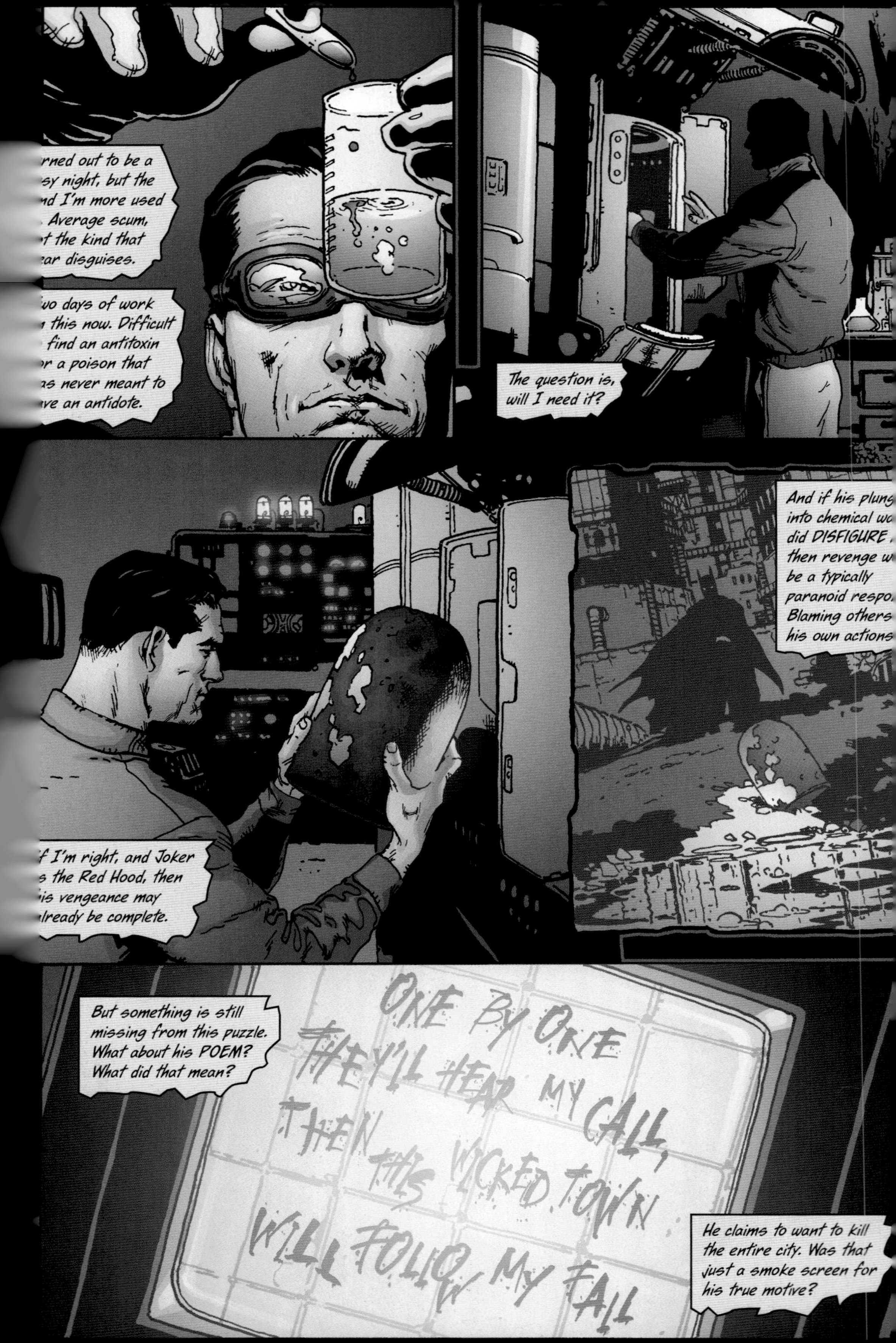

rned out to be a sy night, but the nd I'm more used Average scum, t the kind that ear disguises.
wo days of work this now. Difficult find an antitoxin r a poison that as never meant to ve an antidote.
The question is, will I need it?
f I'm right, and Joker s the Red Hood, then is vengeance may lready be complete.
And if his plung into chemical wa did DISFIGURE then revenge w be a typically paranoid respo Blaming others his own actions
But something is still missing from this puzzle. What about his POEM? What did that mean?
ONE BY ONE THEY'LL HEAR MY CALL, THEN THIS WICKED TOWN WILL FOLLOW MY FALL
He claims to want to kill the entire city. Was that just a smoke screen for his true motive?

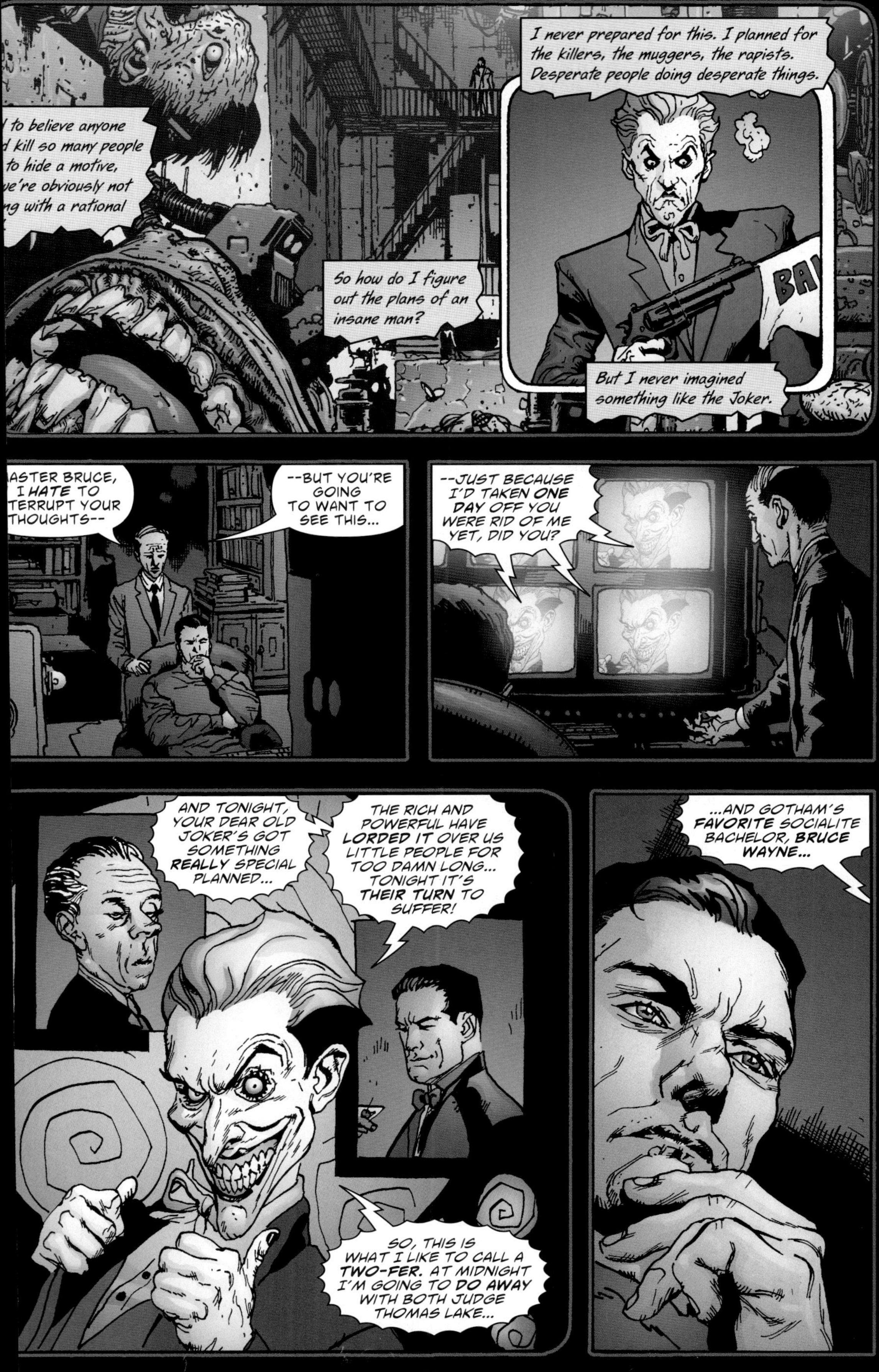
to believe anyone
d kill so many people
to hide a motive,
ve're obviously not
ng with a rational
So how do I figure out the plans of an insane man?
I never prepared for this. I planned for the killers, the muggers, the rapists. Desperate people doing desperate things.
But I never imagined something like the Joker.
ASTER BRUCE, I HATE TO TERRUPT YOUR THOUGHTS--
--BUT YOU'RE GOING TO WANT TO SEE THIS...
--JUST BECAUSE I'D TAKEN ONE DAY OFF YOU WERE RID OF ME YET, DID YOU?
AND TONIGHT, YOUR DEAR OLD JOKER'S GOT SOMETHING REALLY SPECIAL PLANNED...
THE RICH AND POWERFUL HAVE LORDED IT OVER US LITTLE PEOPLE FOR TOO DAMN LONG... TONIGHT IT'S THEIR TURN TO SUFFER!
SO, THIS IS WHAT I LIKE TO CALL A TWO-FER. AT MIDNIGHT I'M GOING TO DO AWAY WITH BOTH JUDGE THOMAS LAKE...
...AND GOTHAM'S FAVORITE SOCIALITE BACHELOR, BRUCE WAYNE...

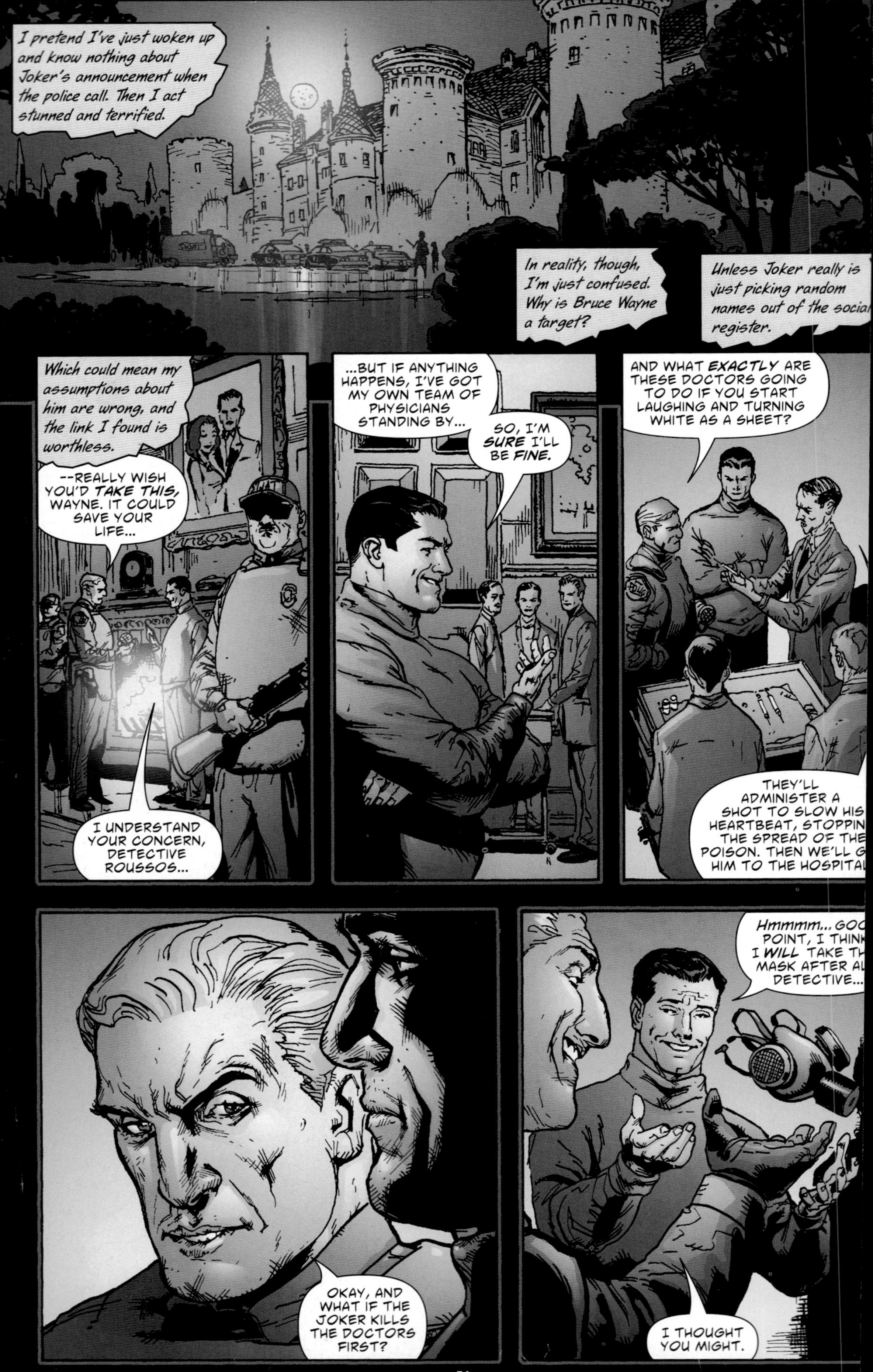
I pretend I've just woken up and know nothing about Joker's announcement when the police call. Then I act stunned and terrified.
In reality, though, I'm just confused. Why is Bruce Wayne a target?
Unless Joker really is just picking random names out of the social register.
Which could mean my assumptions about him are wrong, and the link I found is worthless.
--REALLY WISH YOU'D TAKE THIS, WAYNE. IT COULD SAVE YOUR LIFE...
I UNDERSTAND YOUR CONCERN, DETECTIVE ROUSSOS...
...BUT IF ANYTHING HAPPENS, I'VE GOT MY OWN TEAM OF PHYSICIANS STANDING BY...
SO, I'M SURE I'LL BE FINE.
AND WHAT EXACTLY ARE THESE DOCTORS GOING TO DO IF YOU START LAUGHING AND TURNING WHITE AS A SHEET?
THEY'LL ADMINISTER A SHOT TO SLOW HIS HEARTBEAT, STOPPIN THE SPREAD OF THE POISON. THEN WE'LL G HIM TO THE HOSPITAL
OKAY, AND WHAT IF THE JOKER KILLS THE DOCTORS FIRST?
Hmmmm... GOO POINT, I THINK I WILL TAKE TH MASK AFTER AL DETECTIVE...
I THOUGHT YOU MIGHT.

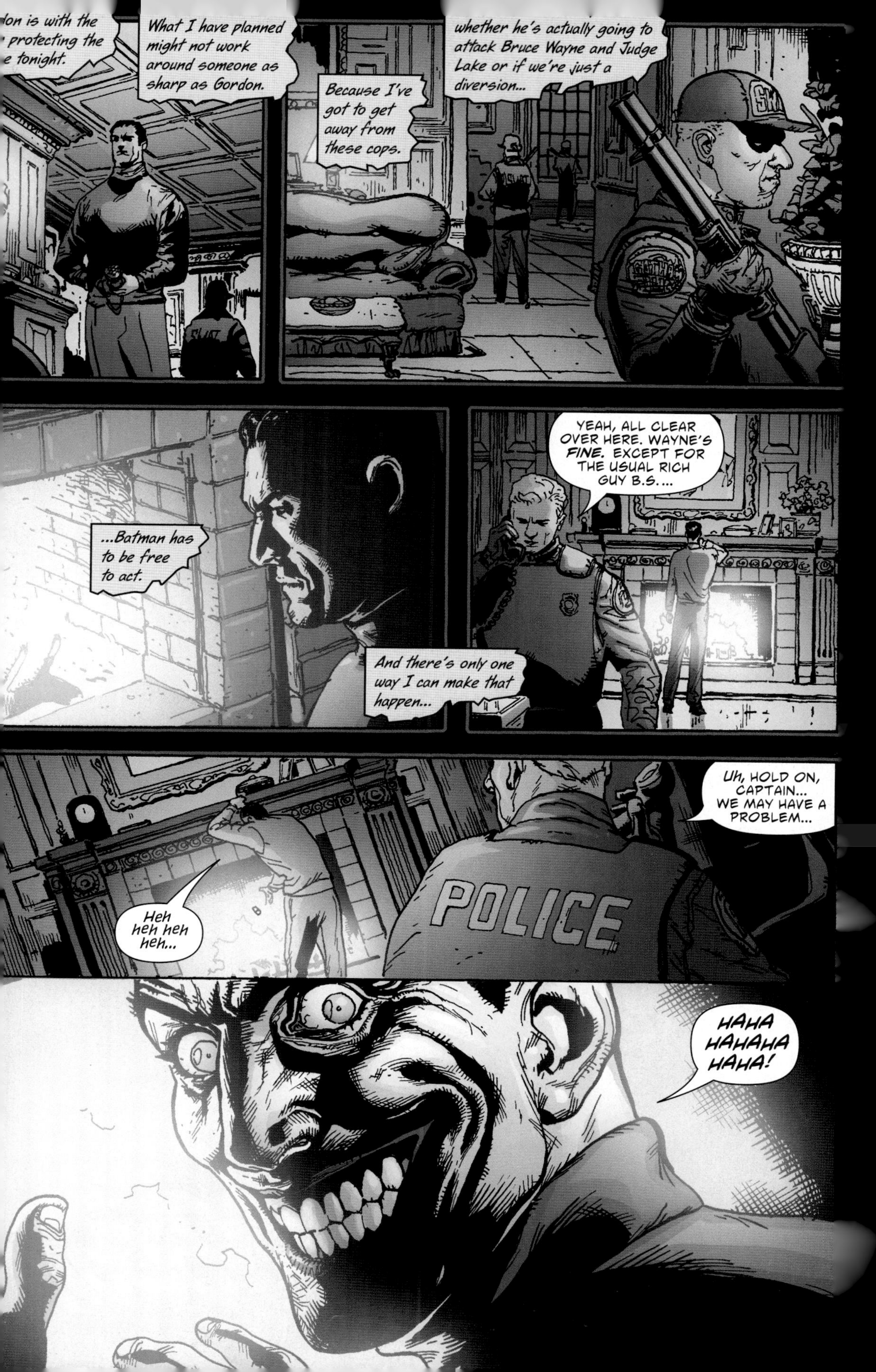
don is with the
protecting the
e tonight.
What I have planned might not work around someone as sharp as Gordon.
Because I've got to get away from these cops.
whether he's actually going to attack Bruce Wayne and Judge Lake or if we're just a diversion...
...Batman has to be free to act.
And there's only one way I can make that happen...
YEAH, ALL CLEAR OVER HERE. WAYNE'S FINE. EXCEPT FOR THE USUAL RICH GUY B.S....
Heh heh heh heh...
POLICE
UH, HOLD ON, CAPTAIN... WE MAY HAVE A PROBLEM...
HAHA HAHAHA HAHA!

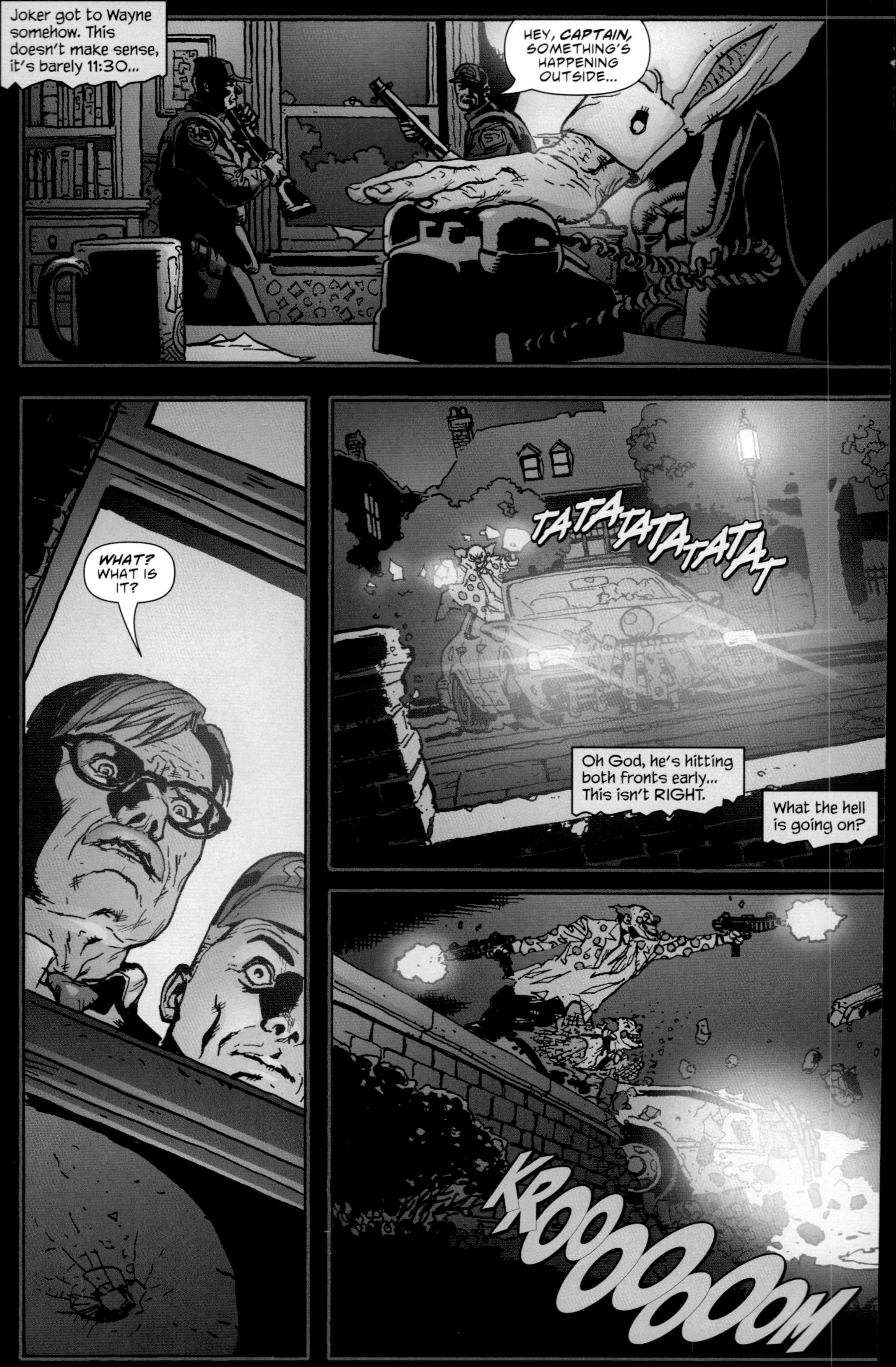
Joker got to Wayne somehow. This doesn't make sense, it's barely 11:30...
HEY, CAPTAIN, SOMETHING'S HAPPENING OUTSIDE...
WHAT? WHAT IS IT?
TATATATATATATAT
Oh God, he's hitting both fronts early... This isn't RIGHT.
What the hell is going on?
KROOOOOOOM

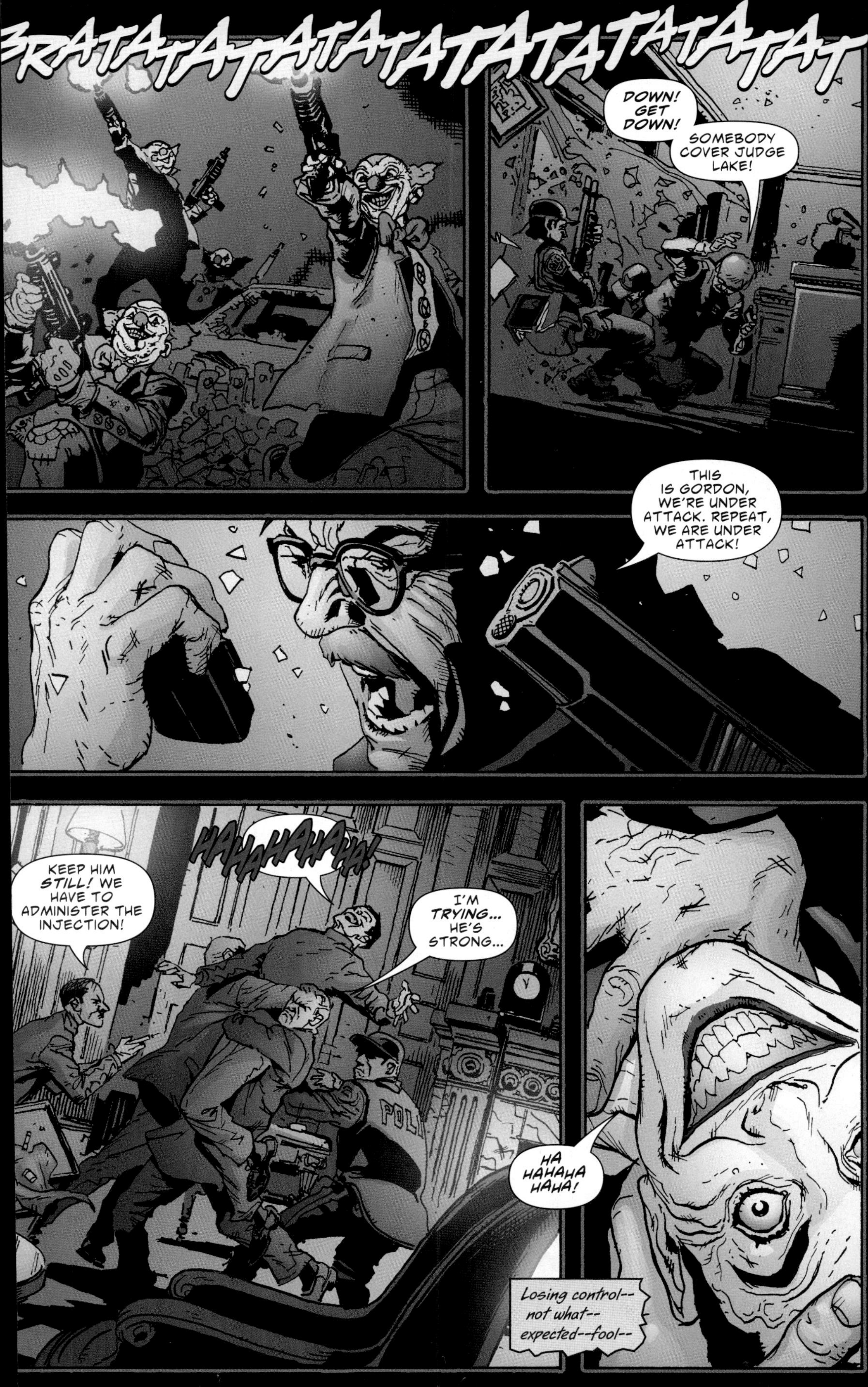
BRATATATATATATATATATATATATAT
DOWN! GET DOWN!
SOMEBODY COVER JUDGE LAKE!
THIS IS GORDON, WE'RE UNDER ATTACK. REPEAT, WE ARE UNDER ATTACK!
KEEP HIM STILL! WE HAVE TO ADMINISTER THE INJECTION!
HAHAHAHAHA!
I'M TRYING... HE'S STRONG...
HA HAHAHA HAHA!
Losing control-- not what-- expected--fool--

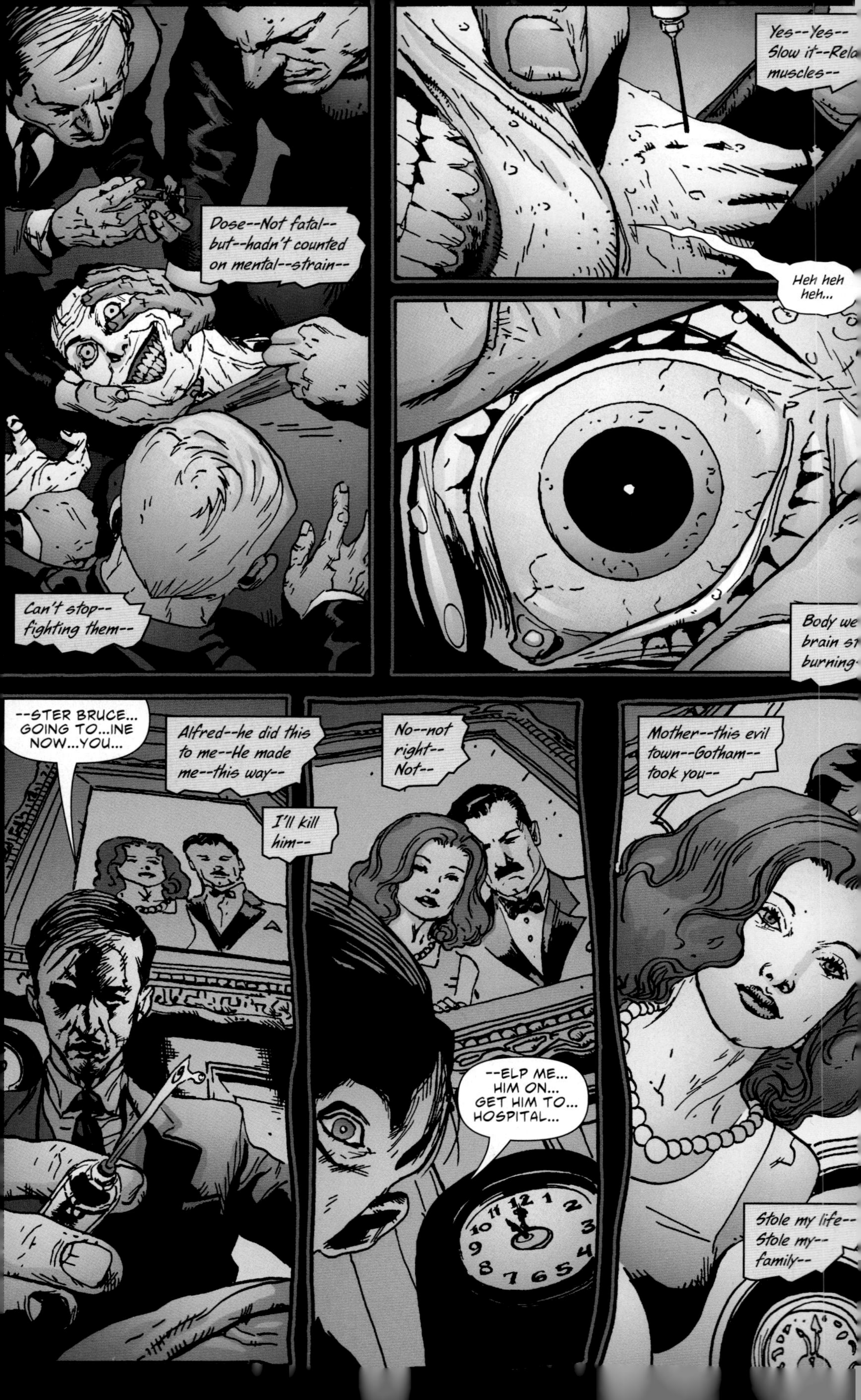
Dose--Not fatal--
but--hadn't counted
on mental--strain--
Can't stop--
fighting them--
Yes--Yes--
Slow it--Rela
muscles--
Heh heh
heh...
Body we
brain st
burning
--STER BRUCE...
GOING TO...INE
NOW...YOU...
Alfred--he did this
to me--He made
me--this way--
I'll kill
him--
No--not
right--
Not--
--ELP ME...
HIM ON...
GET HIM TO...
HOSPITAL...
Mother--this evil
town--Gotham--
took you--
Stole my life--
Stole my--
family--

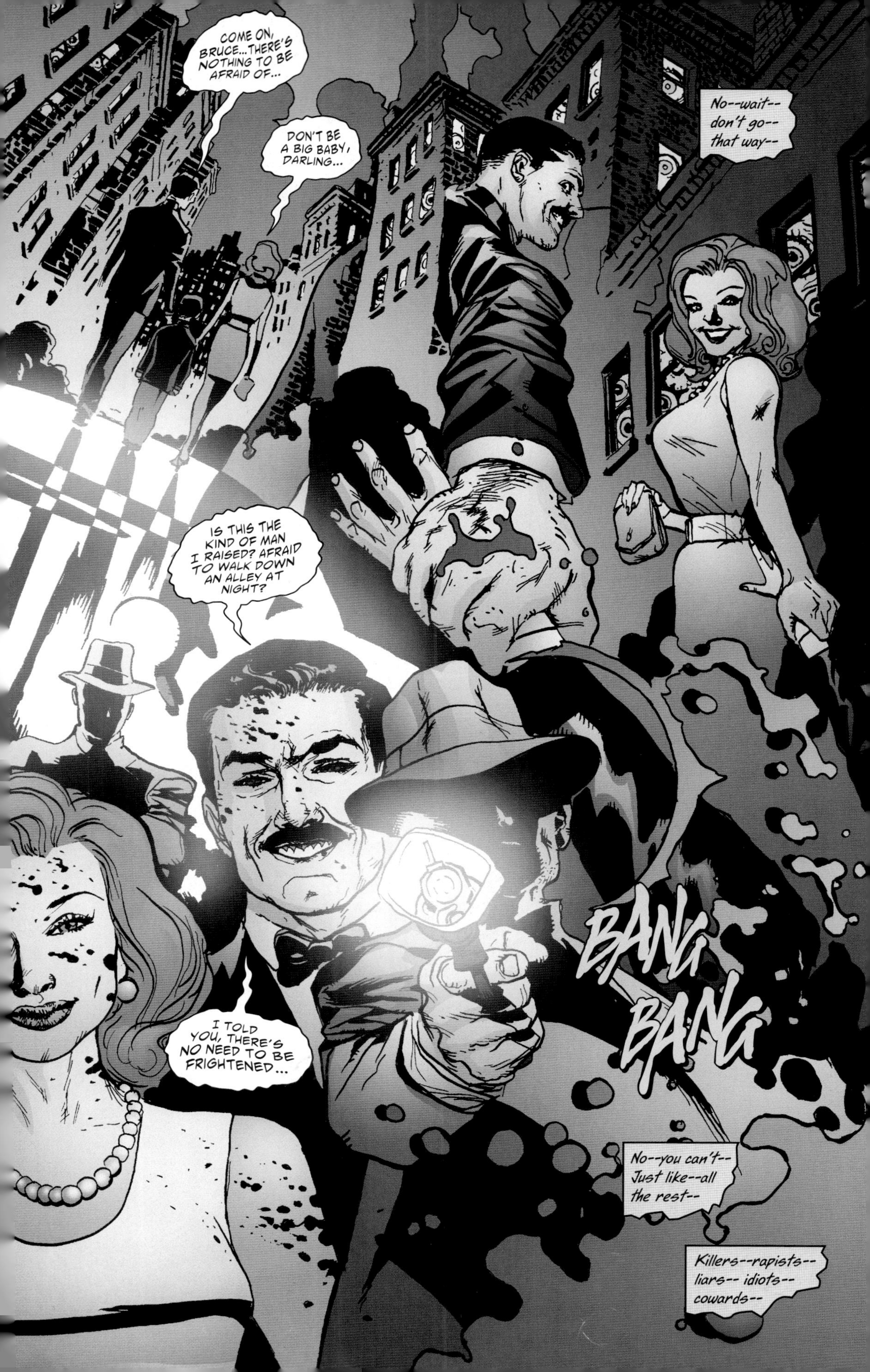
COME ON, BRUCE...THERE'S NOTHING TO BE AFRAID OF...
DON'T BE A BIG BABY, DARLING...
No--wait-- don't go-- that way--
IS THIS THE KIND OF MAN I RAISED? AFRAID TO WALK DOWN AN ALLEY AT NIGHT?
I TOLD YOU, THERE'S NO NEED TO BE FRIGHTENED...
BANG
BANG
No--you can't-- Just like--all the rest--
Killers--rapists-- liars-- idiots-- cowards--

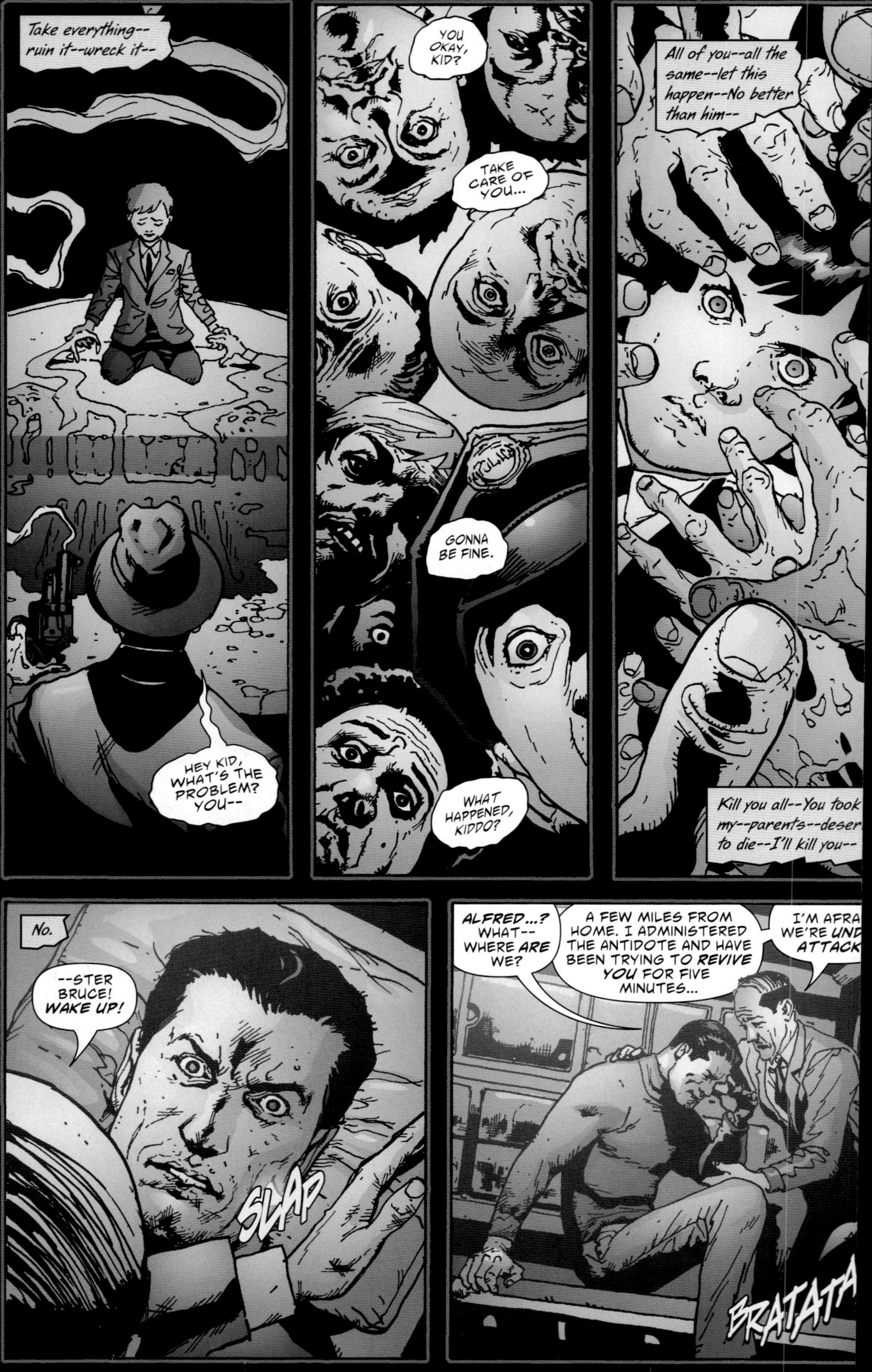
Take everything--ruin it--wreck it--
HEY KID, WHAT'S THE PROBLEM? YOU--
YOU OKAY, KID?
TAKE CARE OF YOU...
GONNA BE FINE.
WHAT HAPPENED, KIDDO?
All of you--all the same--let this happen--No better than him--
Kill you all--You took my--parents--deser to die--I'll kill you--
No.
--STER BRUCE! WAKE UP!
SLAP
ALFRED...? WHAT-- WHERE ARE WE?
A FEW MILES FROM HOME. I ADMINISTERED THE ANTIDOTE AND HAVE BEEN TRYING TO REVIVE YOU FOR FIVE MINUTES...
I'M AFRA WE'RE UND ATTACK
BRATATA

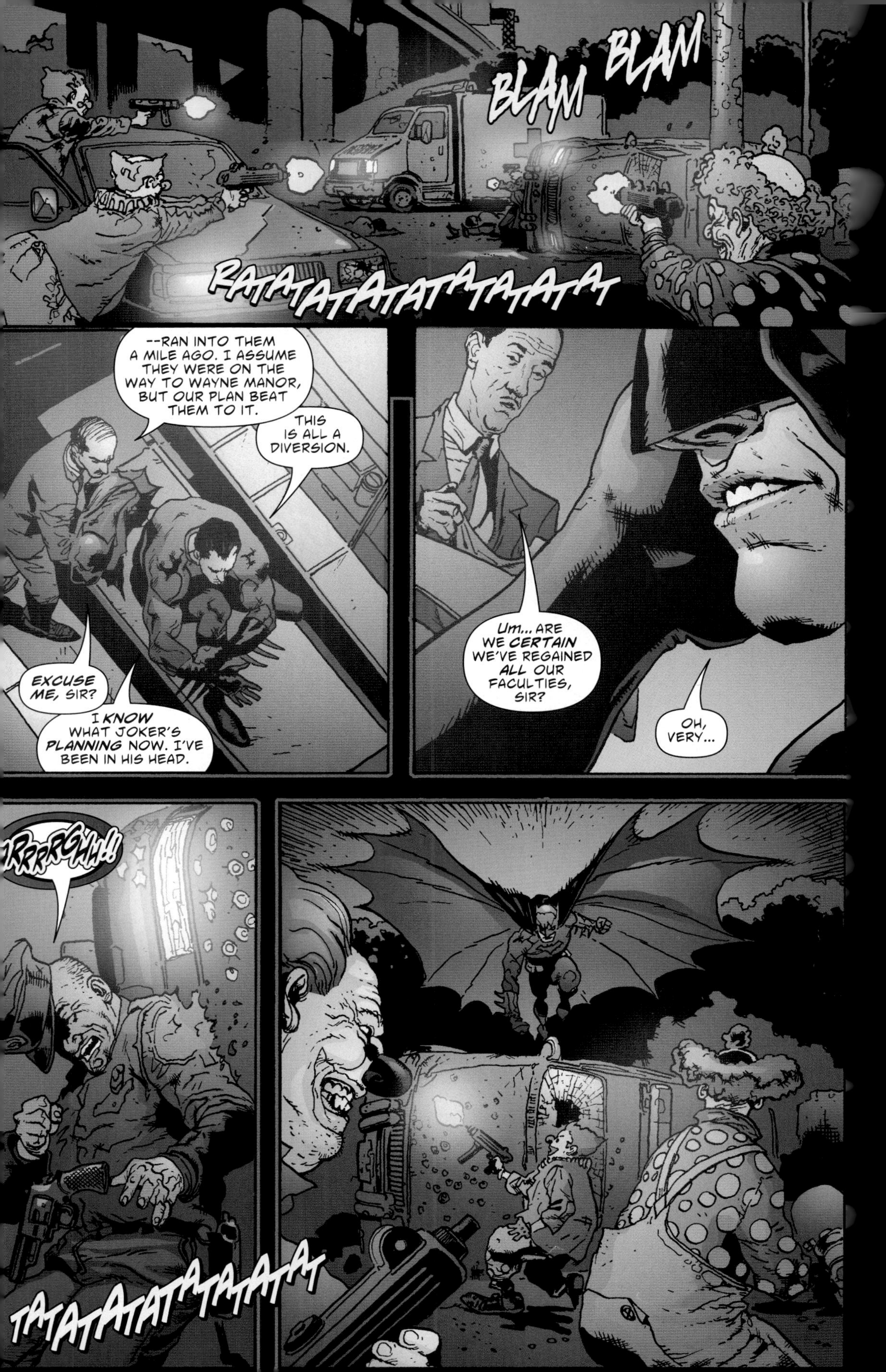
BLAM BLAM
RATATATATATATATATATAT
--RAN INTO THEM A MILE AGO. I ASSUME THEY WERE ON THE WAY TO WAYNE MANOR, BUT OUR PLAN BEAT THEM TO IT.
THIS IS ALL A DIVERSION.
EXCUSE ME, SIR?
I KNOW WHAT JOKER'S PLANNING NOW. I'VE BEEN IN HIS HEAD.
Um... ARE WE CERTAIN WE'VE REGAINED ALL OUR FACULTIES, SIR?
OH, VERY...
RRRRGHH!!
TATATATATATATATAT

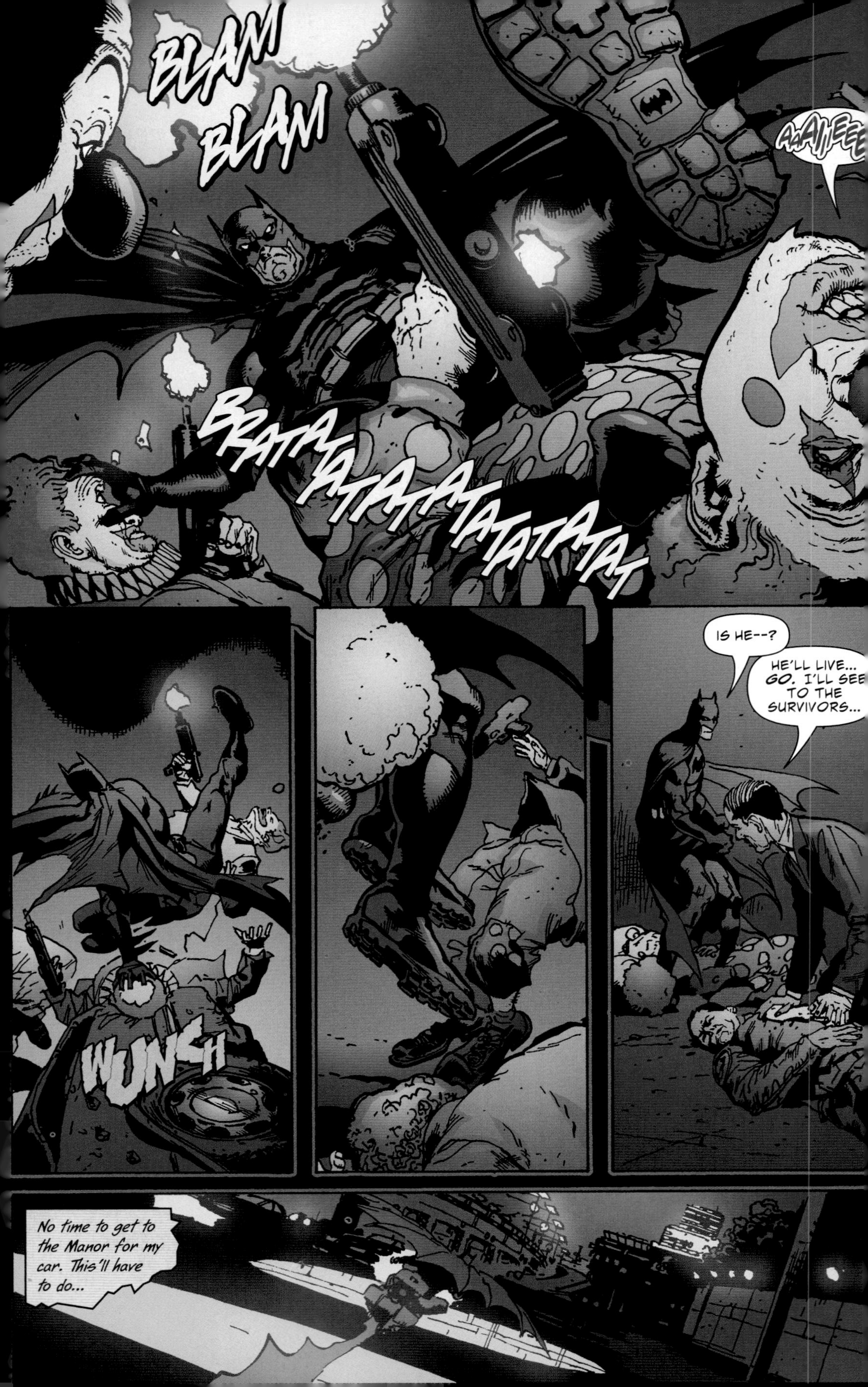
BLAM
BLAM
AaAIIIEEE
BRATATATATATATATATATAT
WUNCH
IS HE--?
HE'LL LIVE... GO. I'LL SEE TO THE SURVIVORS...
No time to get to the Manor for my car. This'll have to do...

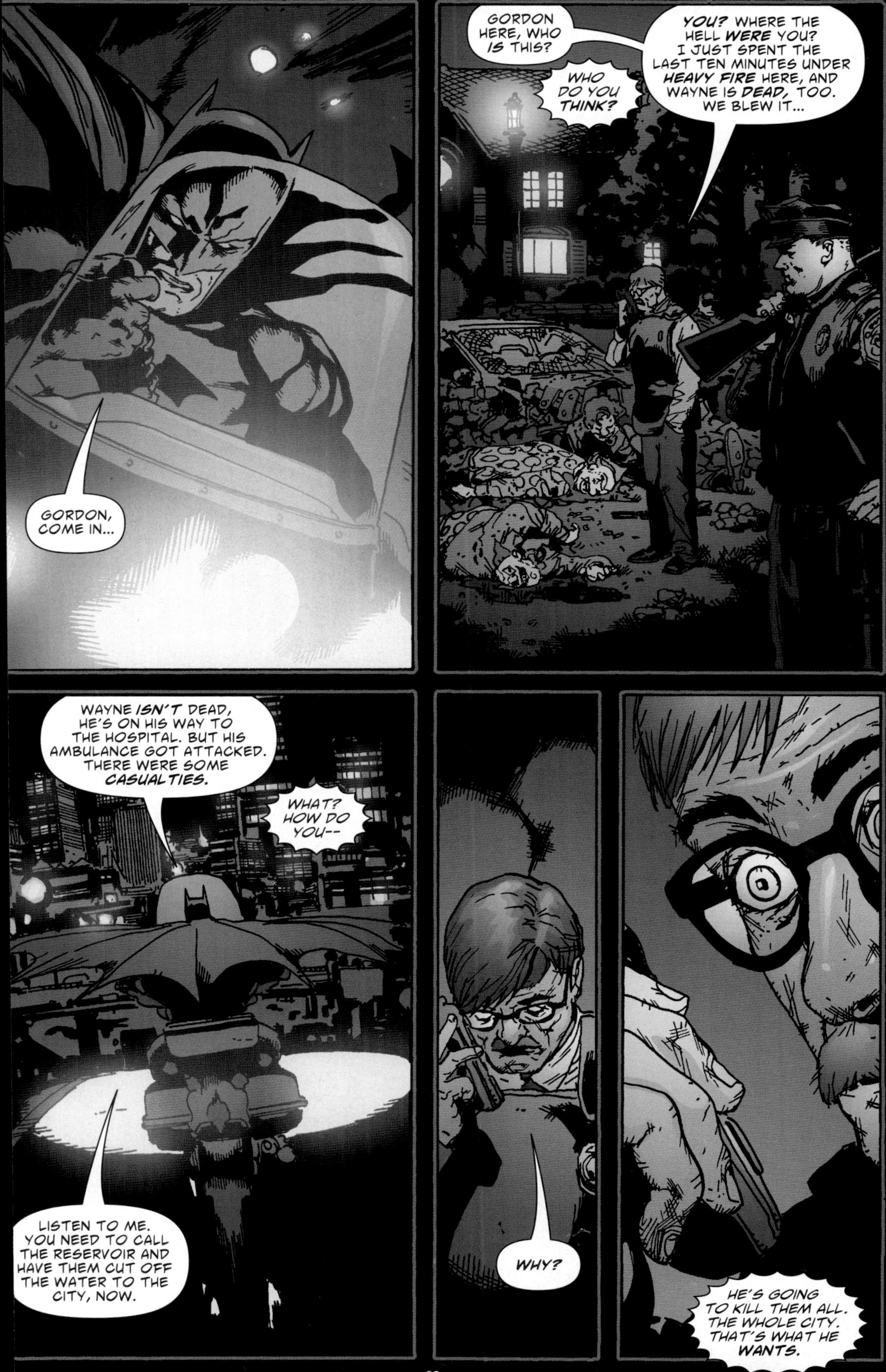

GORDON, COME IN...
GORDON HERE, WHO IS THIS?
WHO DO YOU THINK?
YOU? WHERE THE HELL WERE YOU? I JUST SPENT THE LAST TEN MINUTES UNDER HEAVY FIRE HERE, AND WAYNE IS DEAD, TOO. WE BLEW IT...
WAYNE ISN'T DEAD, HE'S ON HIS WAY TO THE HOSPITAL. BUT HIS AMBULANCE GOT ATTACKED. THERE WERE SOME CASUALTIES.
WHAT? HOW DO YOU--
LISTEN TO ME. YOU NEED TO CALL THE RESERVOIR AND HAVE THEM CUT OFF THE WATER TO THE CITY, NOW.
WHY?
HE'S GOING TO KILL THEM ALL. THE WHOLE CITY. THAT'S WHAT HE WANTS.

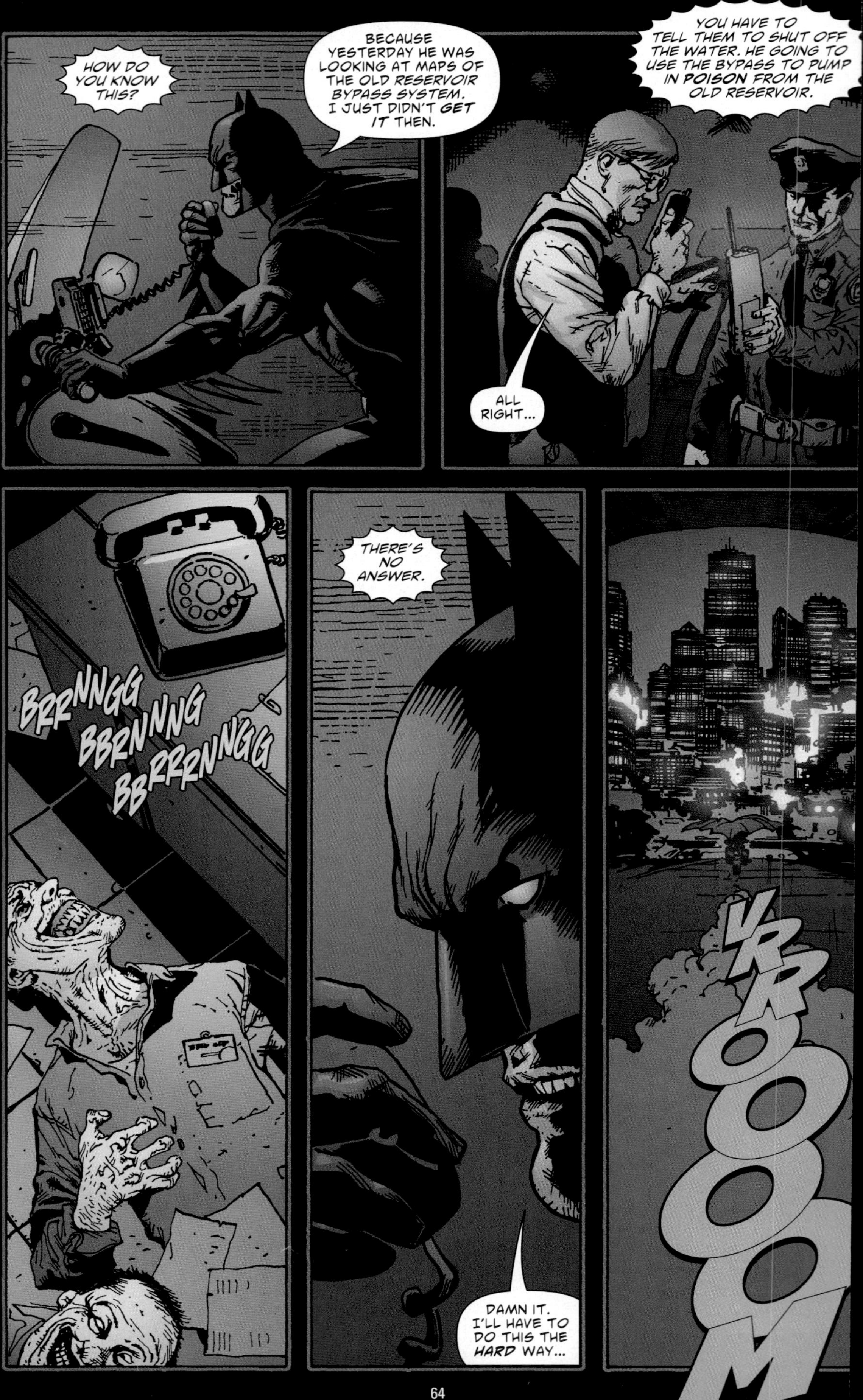

HOW DO YOU KNOW THIS?
BECAUSE YESTERDAY HE WAS LOOKING AT MAPS OF THE OLD RESERVOIR BYPASS SYSTEM. I JUST DIDN'T GET IT THEN.
YOU HAVE TO TELL THEM TO SHUT OFF THE WATER. HE GOING TO USE THE BYPASS TO PUMP IN POISON FROM THE OLD RESERVOIR.
ALL RIGHT...
BRRNNGG BBRNNNG BBRRRNNGG
THERE'S NO ANSWER.
DAMN IT. I'LL HAVE TO DO THIS THE HARD WAY...
VRROOOOOM

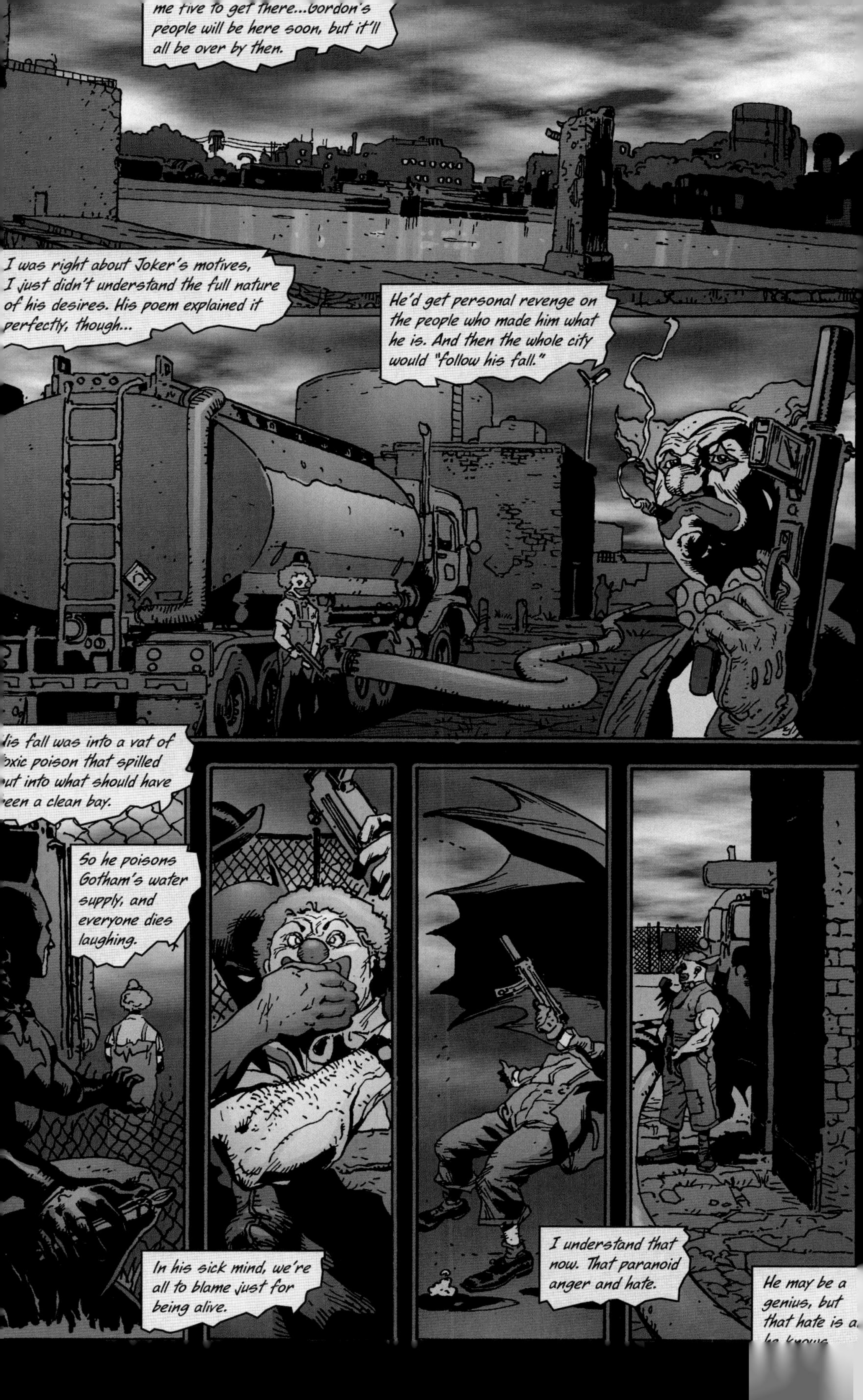
me five to get there...Gordon's people will be here soon, but it'll all be over by then.
I was right about Joker's motives, I just didn't understand the full nature of his desires. His poem explained it perfectly, though...
He'd get personal revenge on the people who made him what he is. And then the whole city would "follow his fall."
lis fall was into a vat of oxic poison that spilled ut into what should have een a clean bay.
So he poisons Gotham's water supply, and everyone dies laughing.
In his sick mind, we're all to blame just for being alive.
I understand that now. That paranoid anger and hate.
He may be a genius, but that hate is a

IT'S OVER, JOKER. GIVE IT UP.

YOU AGAIN? YOU'RE LIKE MY OWN PERSONAL BAD PENNY, AREN'T YOU? ALWAYS TURNING UP...

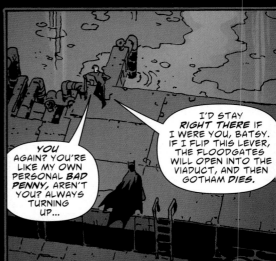

I'D STAY RIGHT THERE IF I WERE YOU, BATSY. IF I FLIP THIS LEVER, THE FLOODGATES WILL OPEN INTO THE VIADUCT, AND THEN GOTHAM DIES.

I CAN'T LET YOU DO THAT.

REALLY? AND HOW THE HELL DO YOU THINK YOU'RE GOING TO STOP ME?

LIKE THIS.

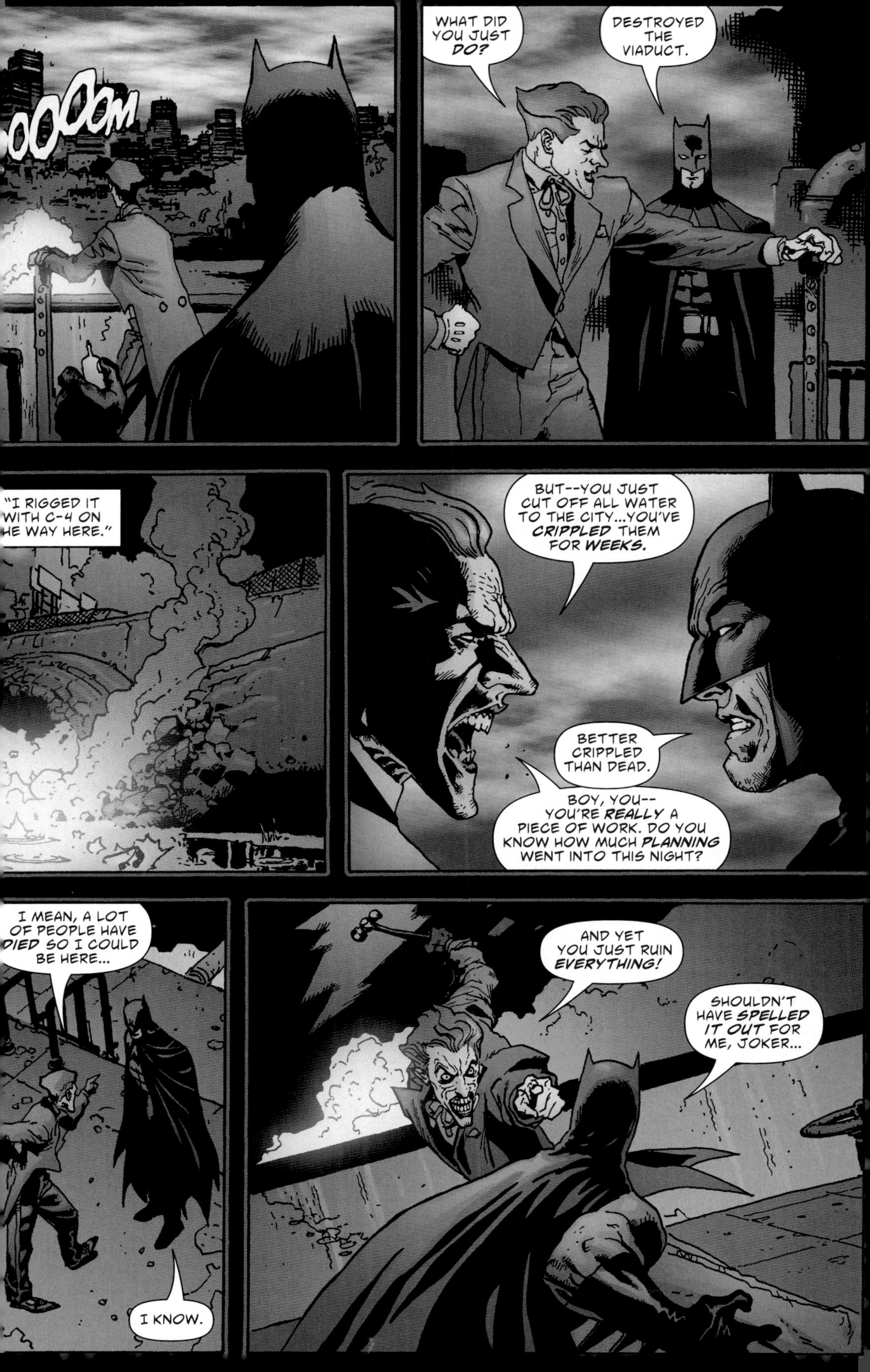
OOOOOM
WHAT DID YOU JUST *DO?*
DESTROYED THE VIADUCT.
"I RIGGED IT WITH C-4 ON HE WAY HERE."
BUT--YOU JUST CUT OFF ALL WATER TO THE CITY...YOU'VE *CRIPPLED* THEM FOR *WEEKS.*
BETTER CRIPPLED THAN DEAD.
BOY, YOU-- YOU'RE *REALLY* A PIECE OF WORK. DO YOU KNOW HOW MUCH *PLANNING* WENT INTO THIS NIGHT?
I MEAN, A LOT OF PEOPLE HAVE *DIED* SO I COULD BE HERE...
I KNOW.
AND YET YOU JUST RUIN *EVERYTHING!*
SHOULDN'T HAVE *SPELLED IT OUT* FOR ME, JOKER...

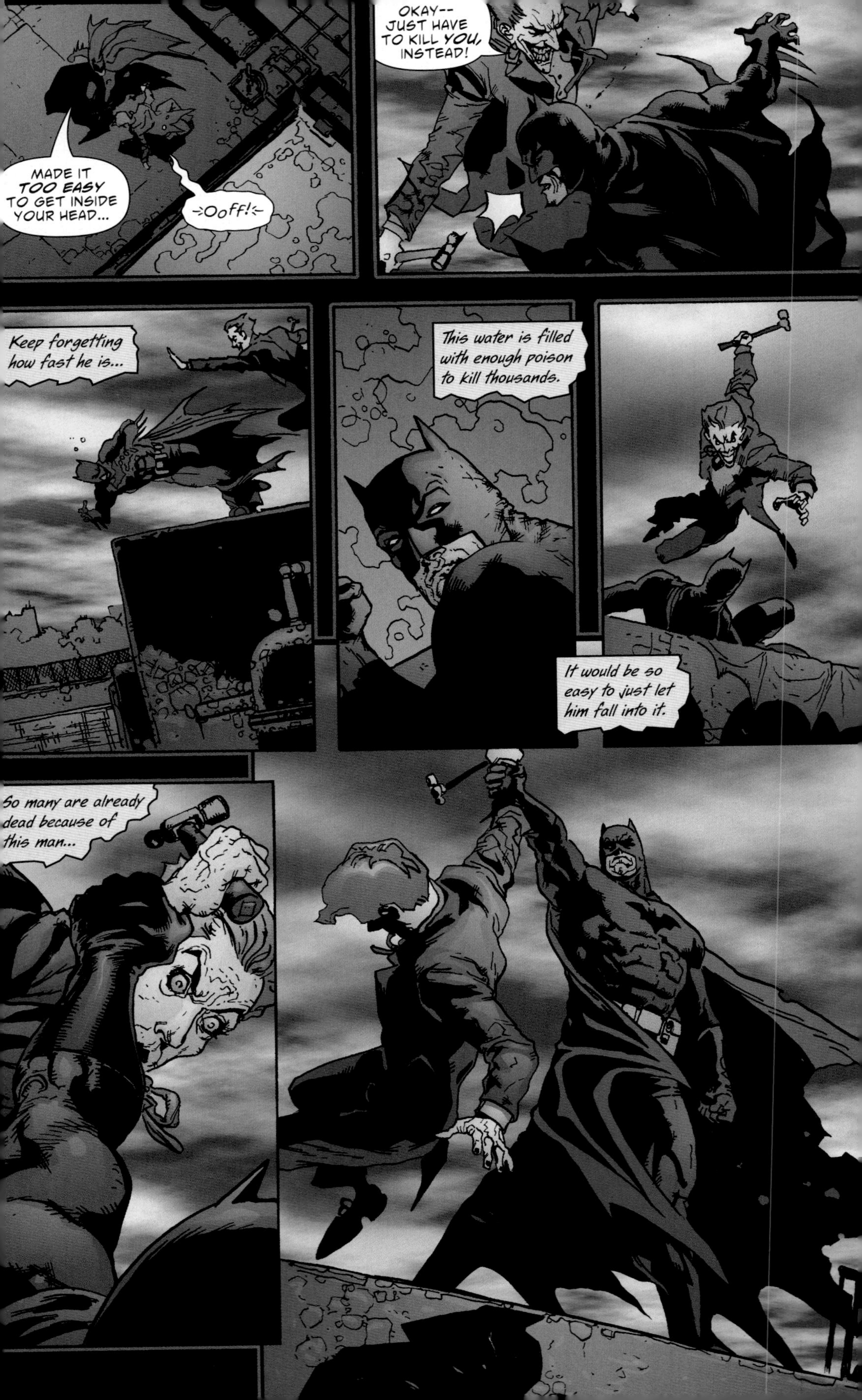
MADE IT TOO EASY TO GET INSIDE YOUR HEAD...
-Ooff!-
OKAY-- JUST HAVE TO KILL YOU, INSTEAD!
Keep forgetting how fast he is...
This water is filled with enough poison to kill thousands.
It would be so easy to just let him fall into it.
So many are already dead because of this man...

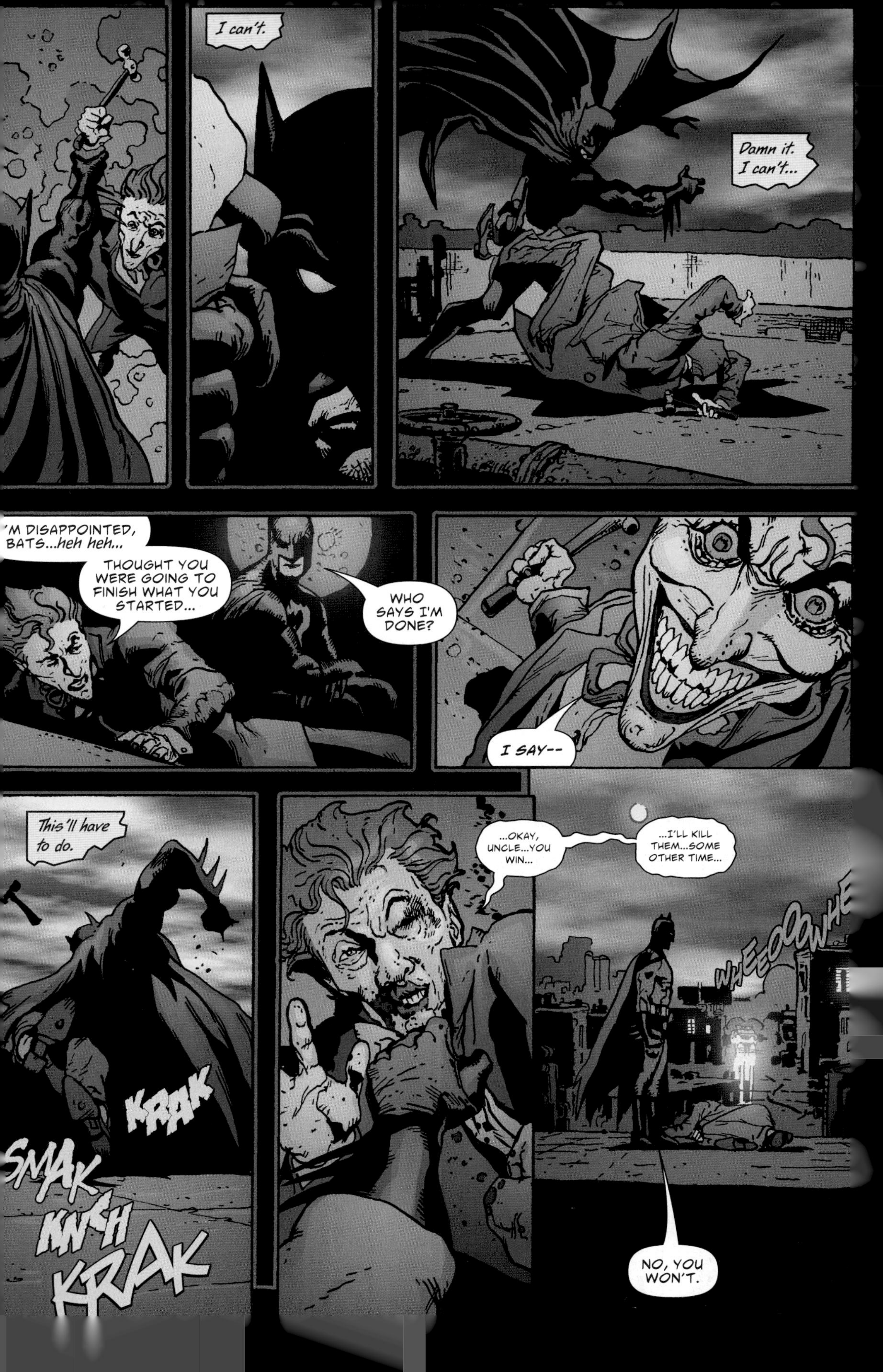
I can't.
Damn it. I can't...
'M DISAPPOINTED, BATS...heh heh...
THOUGHT YOU WERE GOING TO FINISH WHAT YOU STARTED...
WHO SAYS I'M DONE?
I SAY--
This'll have to do.
KRAK
SMAK
KNCH
KRAK
...OKAY, UNCLE...YOU WIN...
...I'LL KILL THEM...SOME OTHER TIME...
WHEEOOOWHE
NO, YOU WON'T.

...ack's to calm back down even after Joker locked safely away Arkham. I can hardly blame them.

His prints aren't in any database, so we'll probably never know who he really is. He's certainly not saying, if he even knows.

Wayne was so glad to survive his part in all this that his company rebuilt the Gotham viaduct at no charge.

People were sweaty and miserable for a week, and by the end of it water was going for ten bucks a bottle, but we survived.

SO...HOW ARE **YOU** DOING?

I'VE BEEN BETTER.

STILL BLAMING YOURSELF FOR ALL THOSE DEAD PEOPLE?

MAYBE. IF JOKER WAS THE RED HOOD, THEN I **DID** PLAY A HAND IN HIS CREATION...

DID YOU PUT THE **HOOD** ON HIS HEAD AND THE **GUN** IN HIS HAND? NO, YOU **DIDN'T.**

YOU SAVED THE ENTIRE **CITY** FROM THAT DERANGED MADMAN. GIVE YOURSELF A PAT ON THE BACK, I SAY.

I'LL TAKE IT UNDER ADVISEMENT.

YOU DO THAT.

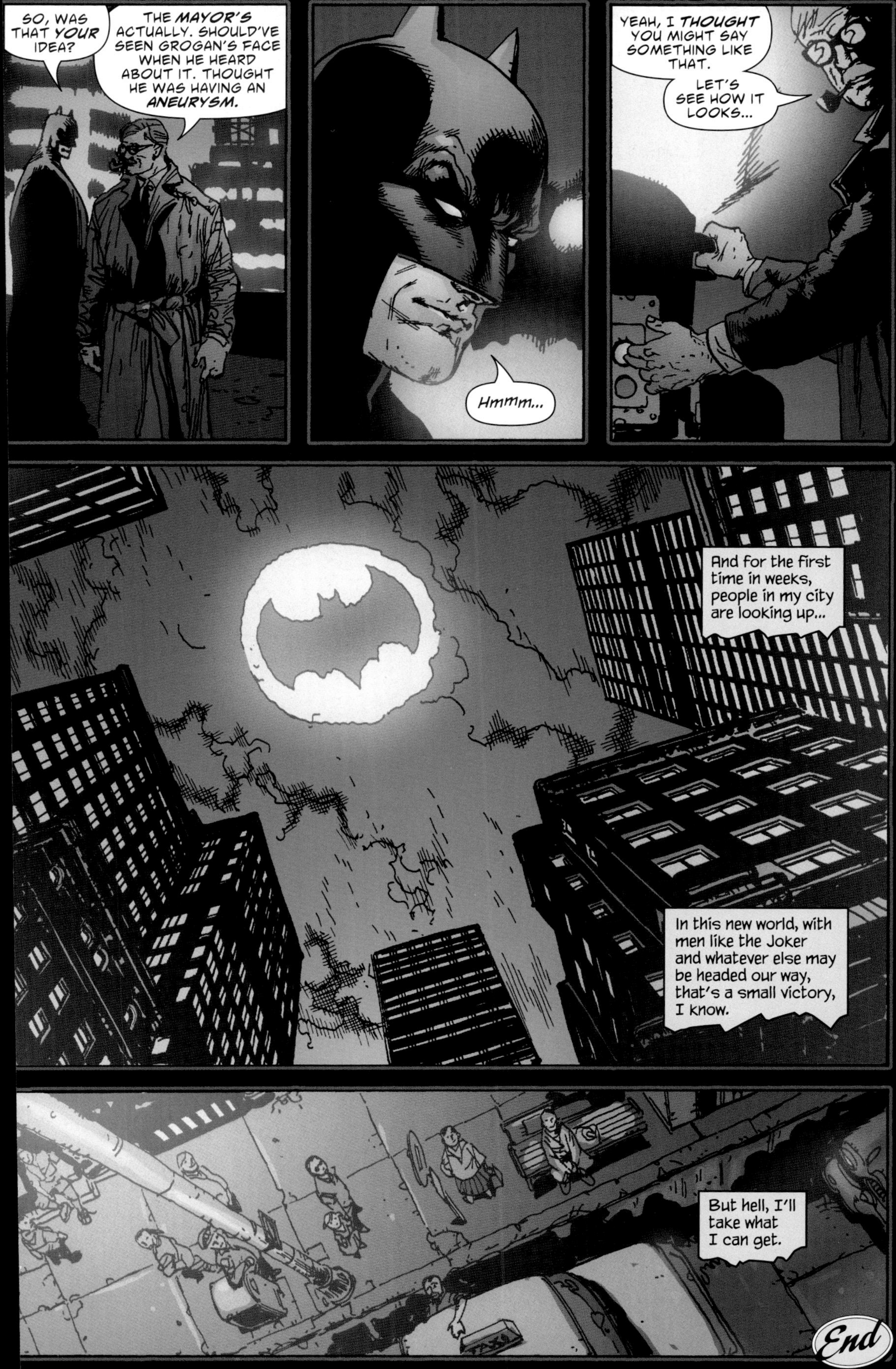
SO, WAS THAT YOUR IDEA?
THE MAYOR'S ACTUALLY. SHOULD'VE SEEN GROGAN'S FACE WHEN HE HEARD ABOUT IT. THOUGHT HE WAS HAVING AN ANEURYSM.
Hmmm...
YEAH, I THOUGHT YOU MIGHT SAY SOMETHING LIKE THAT.
LET'S SEE HOW IT LOOKS...
And for the first time in weeks, people in my city are looking up...
In this new world, with men like the Joker and whatever else may be headed our way, that's a small victory, I know.
But hell, I'll take what I can get.
TAXI
End

MADE OF WOOD

Pencils by Patrick Zircher
Inks by Aaron Sowd (Parts 1-3) and Steve Bird (Part 3)
Color by Jason Wright
Lettering by Todd Klein

Cover art by Tim Sale

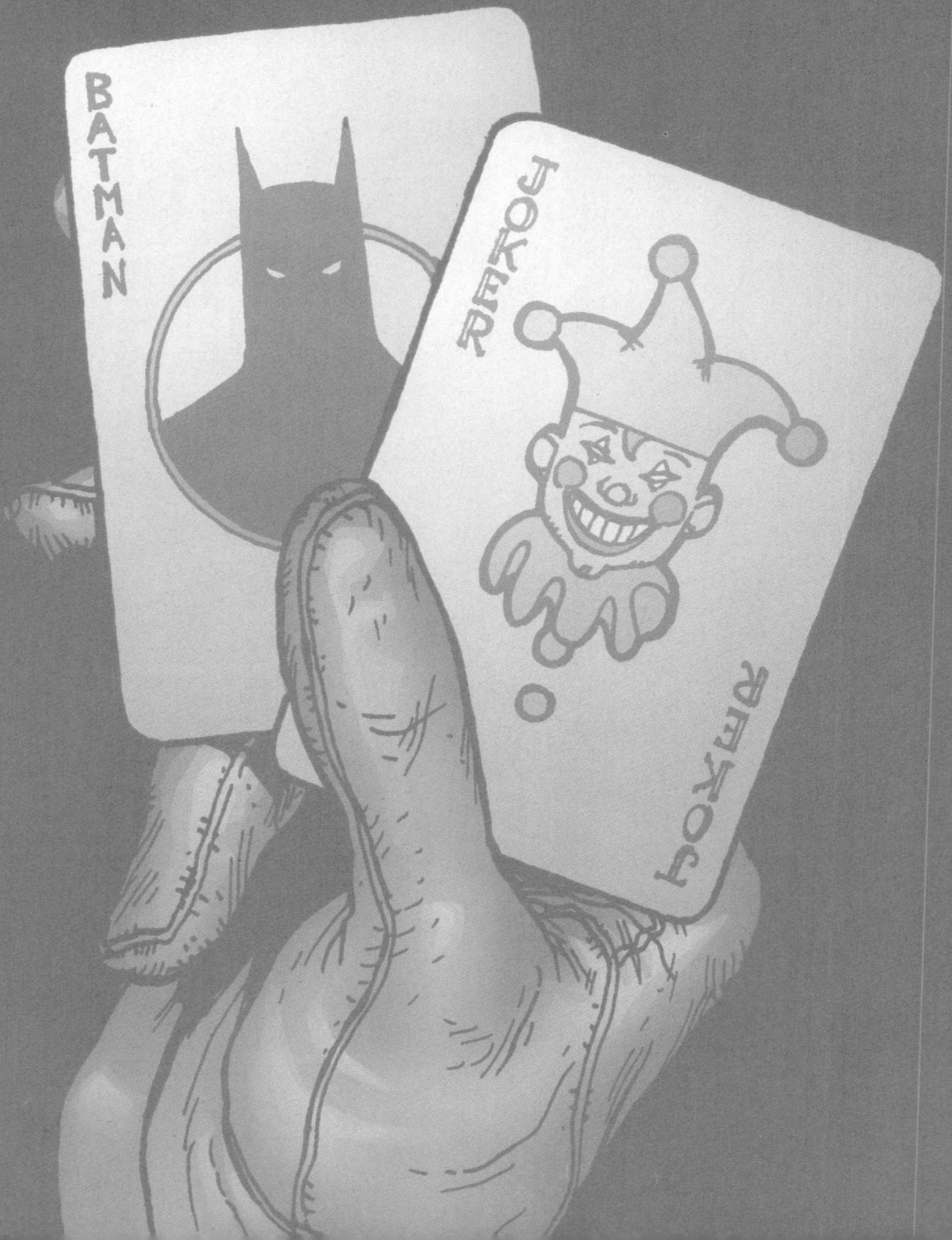
BATMAN
JOKER
JOKER

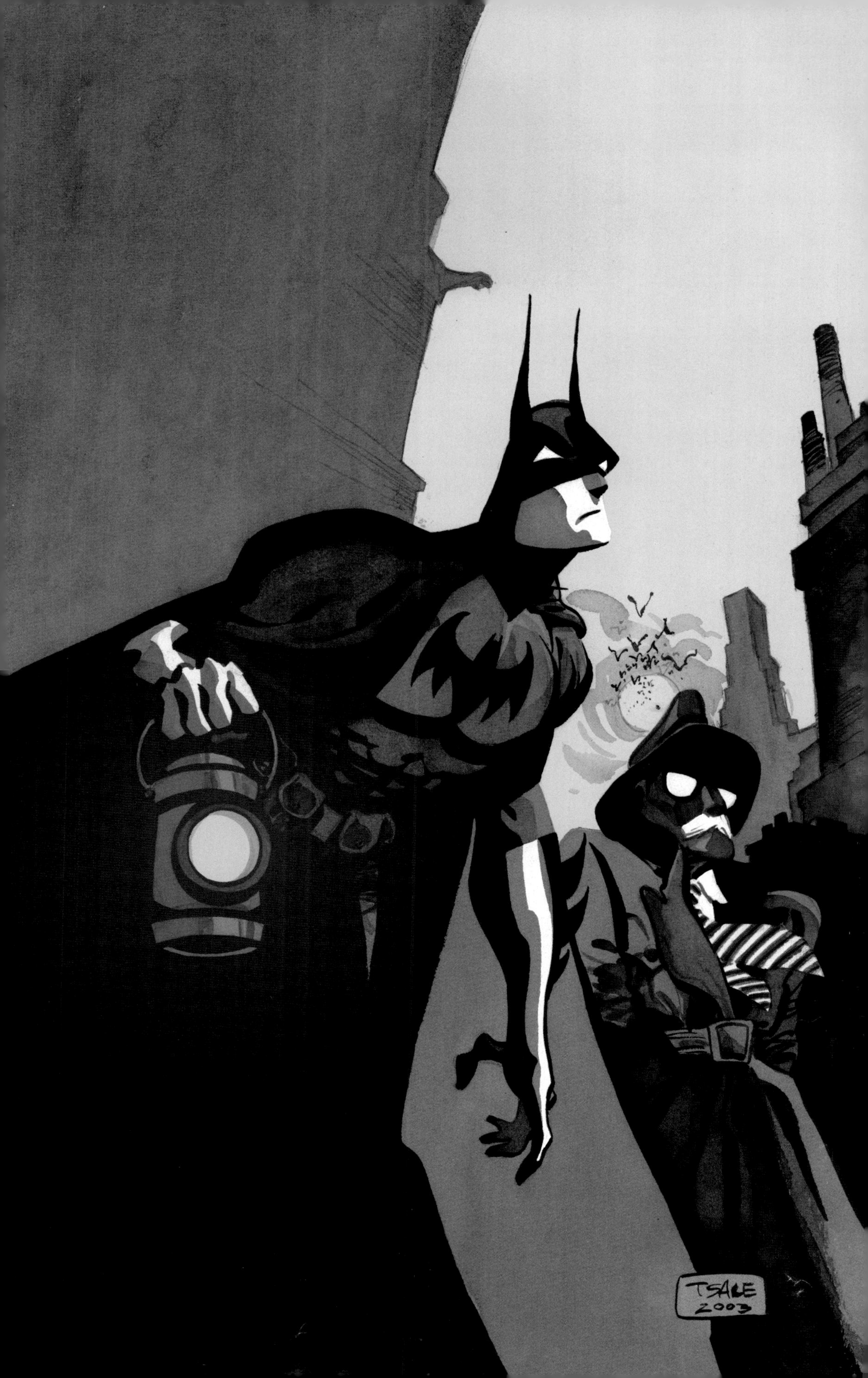
T SALE
2003

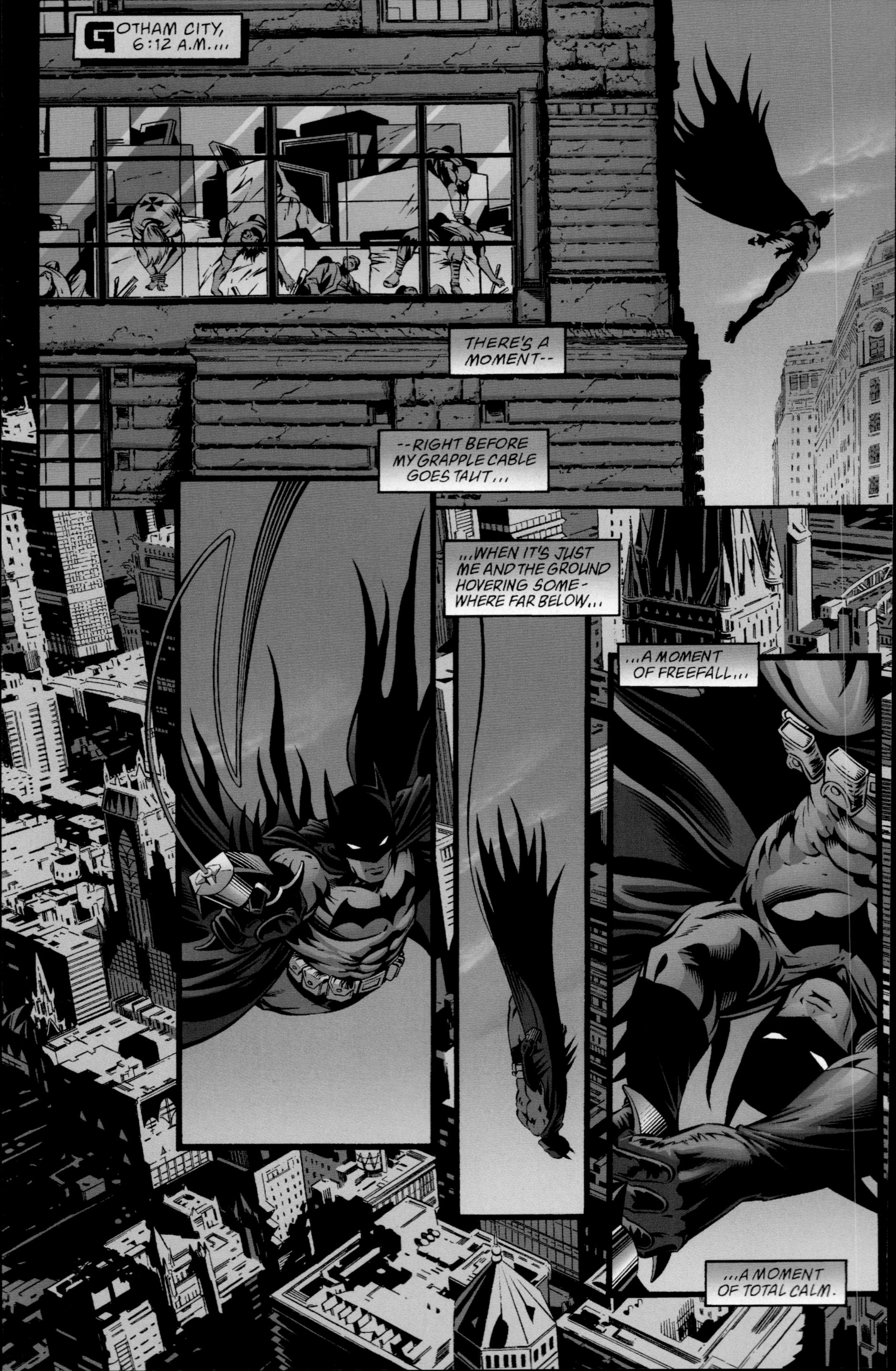
GOTHAM CITY, 6:12 A.M....
THERE'S A MOMENT--
--RIGHT BEFORE MY GRAPPLE CABLE GOES TAUT...
...WHEN IT'S JUST ME AND THE GROUND HOVERING SOME-WHERE FAR BELOW...
...A MOMENT OF FREEFALL...
...A MOMENT OF TOTAL CALM.

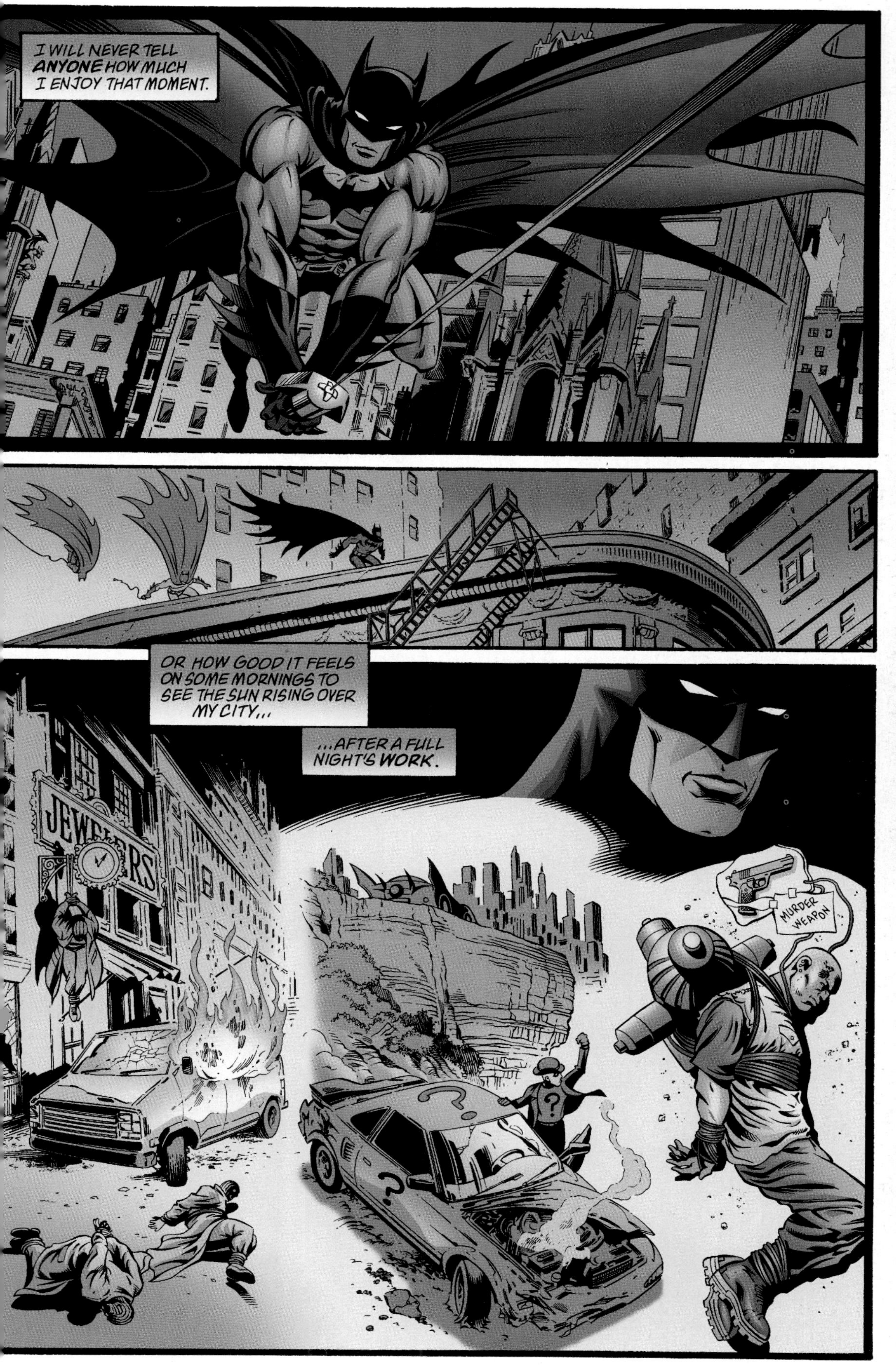
I WILL NEVER TELL ANYONE HOW MUCH I ENJOY THAT MOMENT.
OR HOW GOOD IT FEELS ON SOME MORNINGS TO SEE THE SUN RISING OVER MY CITY...
...AFTER A FULL NIGHT'S WORK.
JEWELERS
MURDER WEAPON

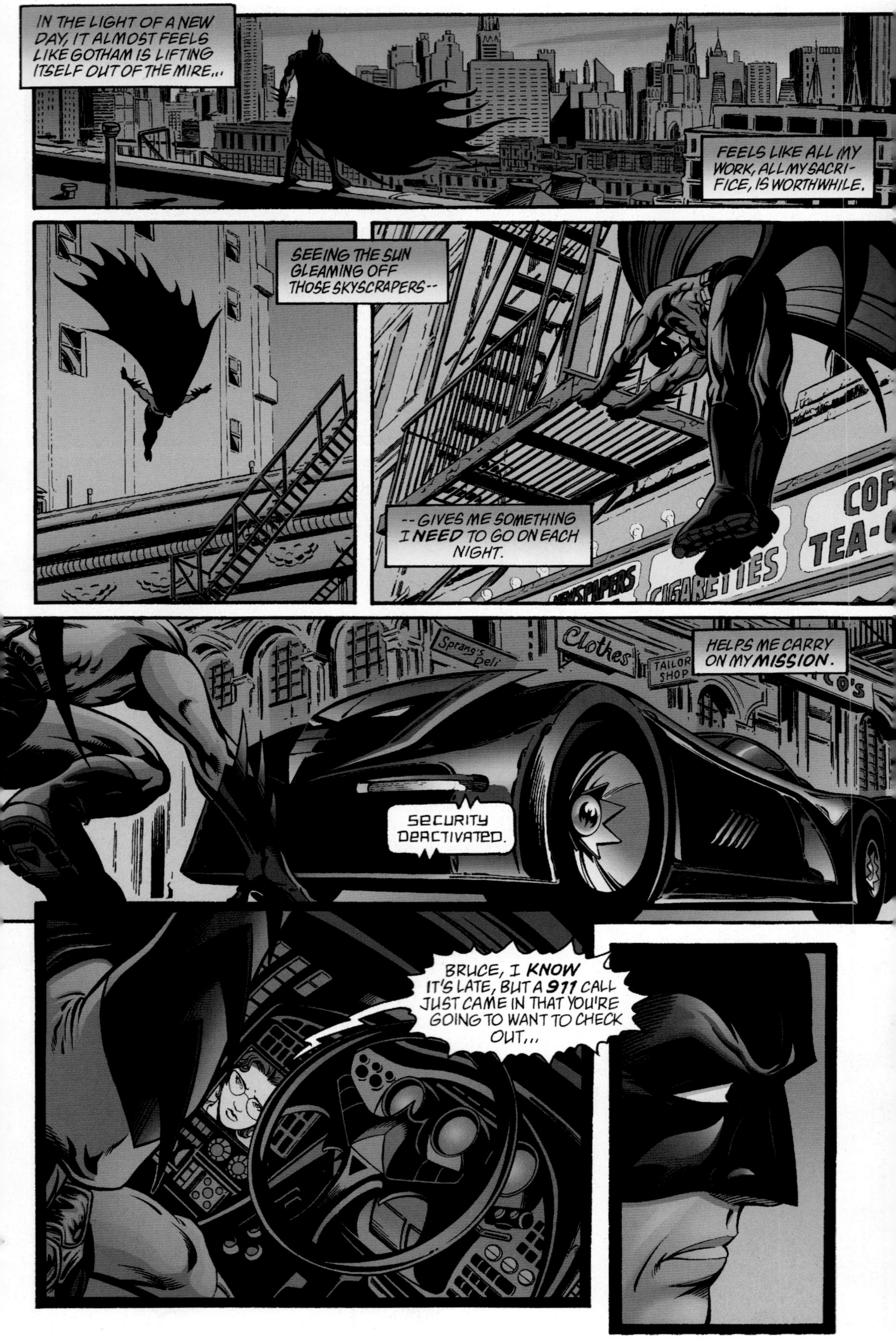
IN THE LIGHT OF A NEW DAY, IT ALMOST FEELS LIKE GOTHAM IS LIFTING ITSELF OUT OF THE MIRE...
FEELS LIKE ALL MY WORK, ALL MY SACRI-FICE, IS WORTHWHILE.
SEEING THE SUN GLEAMING OFF THOSE SKYSCRAPERS--
--GIVES ME SOMETHING I NEED TO GO ON EACH NIGHT.
CIGARETTES
NEWSPAPERS
Sprang's Deli
Clothes
TAILOR SHOP
HELPS ME CARRY ON MY MISSION.
SECURITY DEACTIVATED.
BRUCE, I KNOW IT'S LATE, BUT A 911 CALL JUST CAME IN THAT YOU'RE GOING TO WANT TO CHECK OUT...

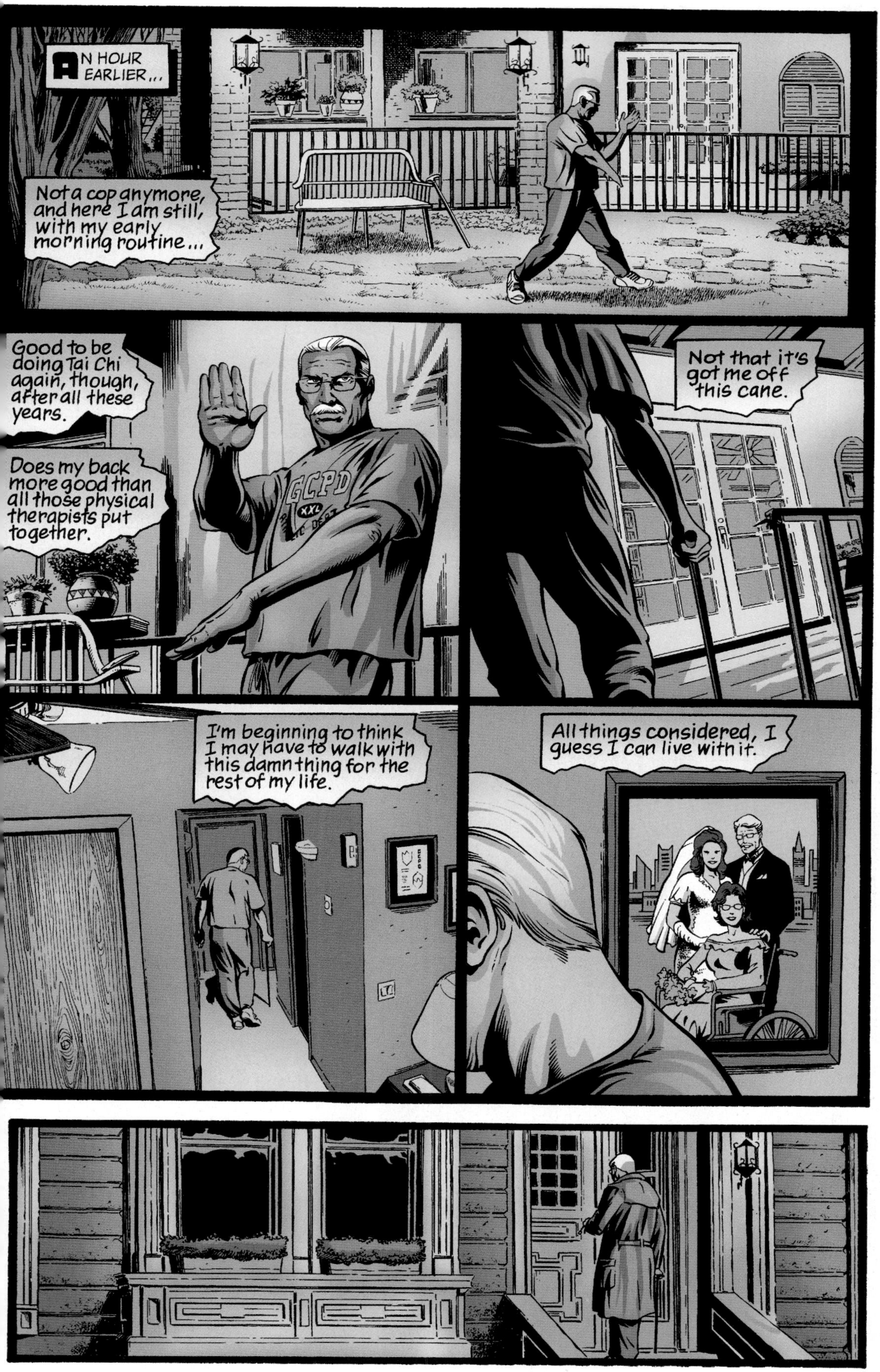
AN HOUR EARLIER...
Not a cop anymore, and here I am still, with my early morning routine...
Good to be doing Tai Chi again, though, after all these years.
Does my back more good than all those physical therapists put together.
GCPD
XXL
Not that it's got me off this cane.
I'm beginning to think I may have to walk with this damn thing for the rest of my life.
All things considered, I guess I can live with it.

Sarah never understood why I had to take this walk so early every day.

I always told her it was a habit left over from my time in the service...

...but the truth is, I just liked to see the city at this time of the day.

While it was wrapped in a blanket of fog. Before all the people and the noise took it over.

Until then, these were my streets.

TAKE 'ER EASY, COMMISH...

ALWAYS *TRY* TO, MICK...

Gotham Gazette

Of course, I'll never get Mickey to stop calling me that.

Hell, it's a full-time job just trying not to think of myself as a cop, I can hardly expect more from anyone else.

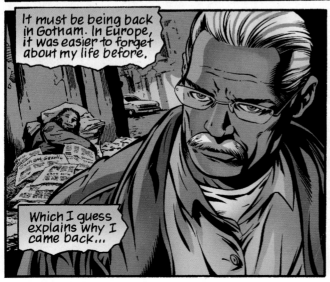

It must be being back in Gotham. In Europe, it was easier to forget about my life before.

Which I guess explains why I came back...

...because I don't want to forget, or run away. This is where my life has been...

...this is my city.

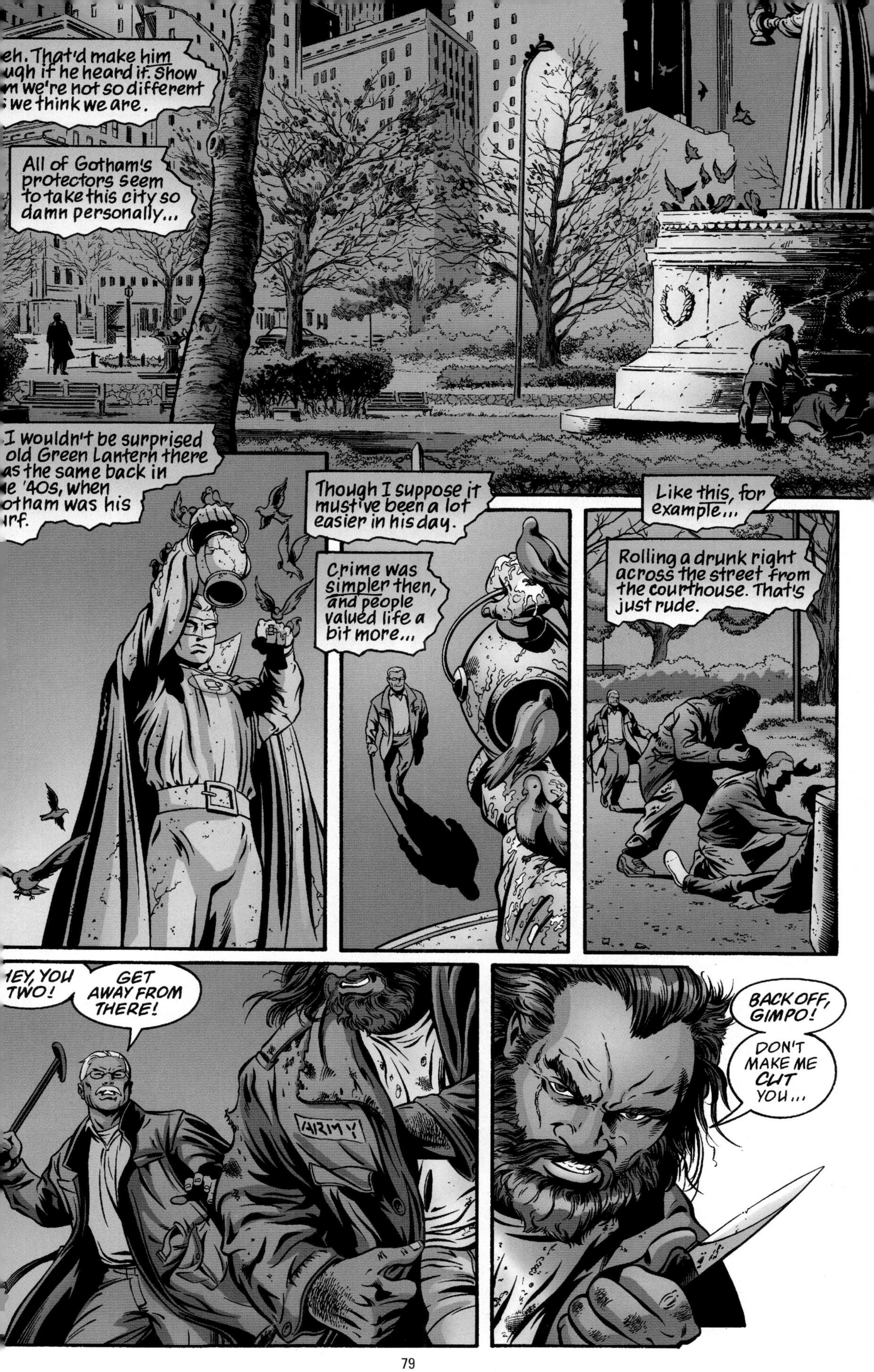
eh. That'd make him
ugh if he heard it. Show
m we're not so different
we think we are.
All of Gotham's protectors seem to take this city so damn personally...
I wouldn't be surprised old Green Lantern there as the same back in e '40s, when otham was his urf.
Though I suppose it must've been a lot easier in his day.
Crime was simpler then, and people valued life a bit more...
Like this, for example...
Rolling a drunk right across the street from the courthouse. That's just rude.
ARMY
EY, YOU TWO!
GET AWAY FROM THERE!
BACK OFF, GIMPO!
DON'T MAKE ME CUT YOU...

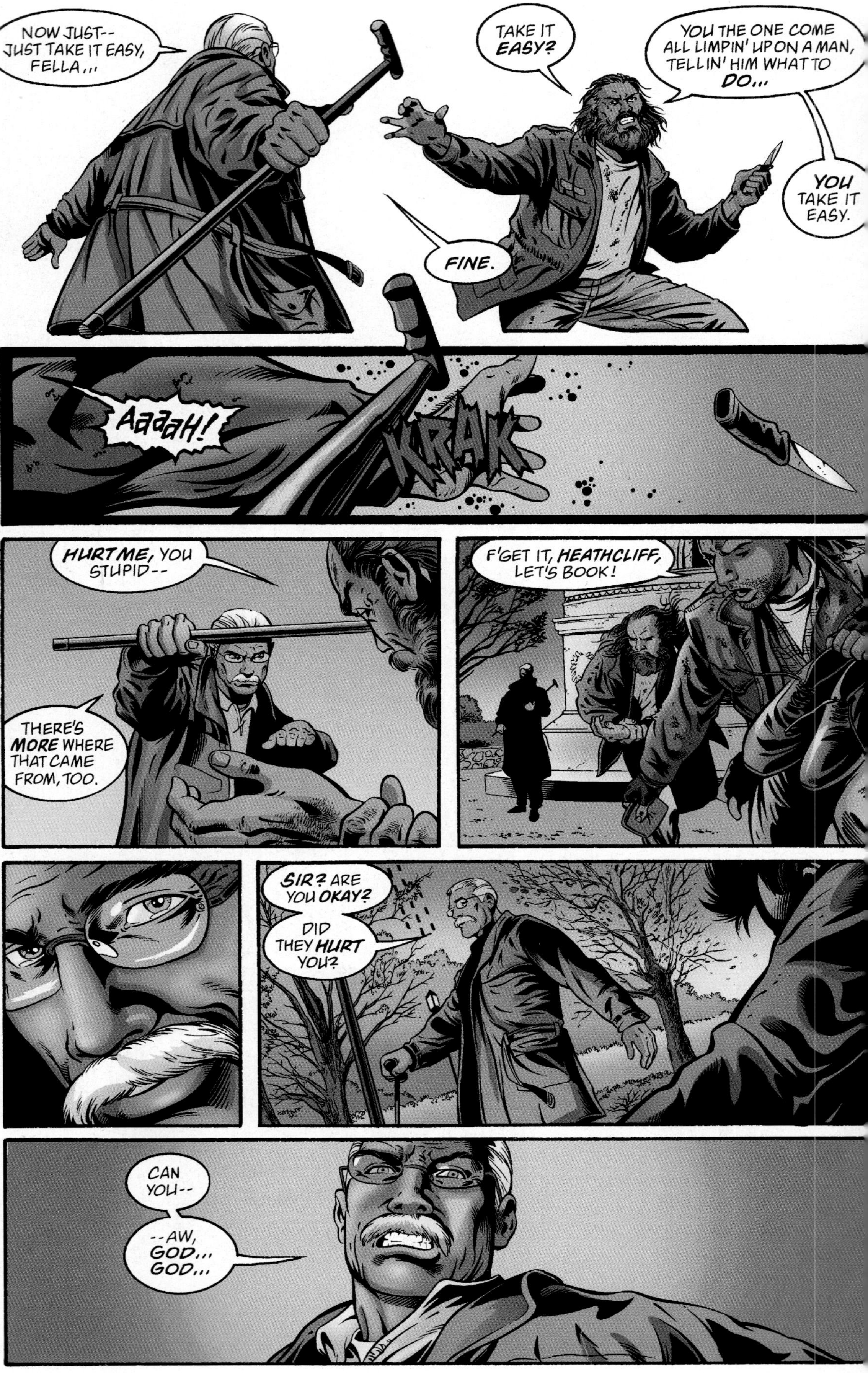
NOW JUST--
JUST TAKE IT EASY, FELLA...
TAKE IT EASY?
YOU THE ONE COME ALL LIMPIN' UP ON A MAN, TELLIN' HIM WHAT TO DO...
YOU TAKE IT EASY.
FINE.
AaaaH!
KRAK
HURT ME, YOU STUPID--
THERE'S MORE WHERE THAT CAME FROM, TOO.
F'GET IT, HEATHCLIFF, LET'S BOOK!
SIR? ARE YOU OKAY?
DID THEY HURT YOU?
CAN YOU--
--AW, GOD... GOD...

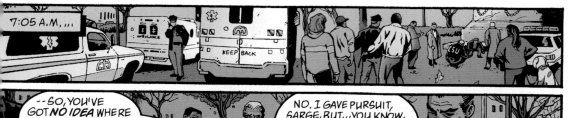

7:05 A.M. ...
AMBULANCE
KEEP BACK
CSU
--SO, YOU'VE GOT NO IDEA WHERE THESE SKELS TOOK OFF TO?
NO. I GAVE PURSUIT, SARGE, BUT... YOU KNOW, WITH THIS CANE AND ALL, I'M JUST NOT MUCH GOOD FOR RUNNING.
EL LIKE SUCH A FOOL. E SEEN ENOUGH DEAD DIES IN MY LIFE, I OULD'VE KNOWN RIGHT AWAY.
UST THOUGHT AT SMELL WAS OSE MEN, NOT A CORPSE.
NOT YOUR FAULT, COMMISSIONER... I MEAN, JIM.
TURNING INTO A BAD HABIT WITH YOU NOW, ISN'T IT? STUMBLING ONTO CRIMES.
AH, I WAS ALWAYS A TROUBLE MAGNET, SARGE...
YOU HAVE ANY IDEAS ON WHAT THAT'S SUPPOSED TO MEAN?
MADE OF WOOD
NO, DETECTIVE CROWE, I DON'T.

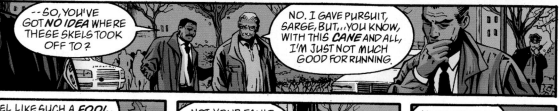

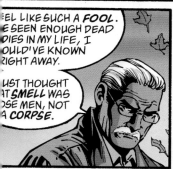

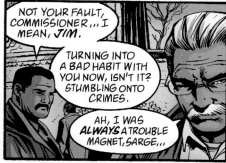

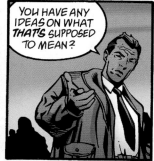

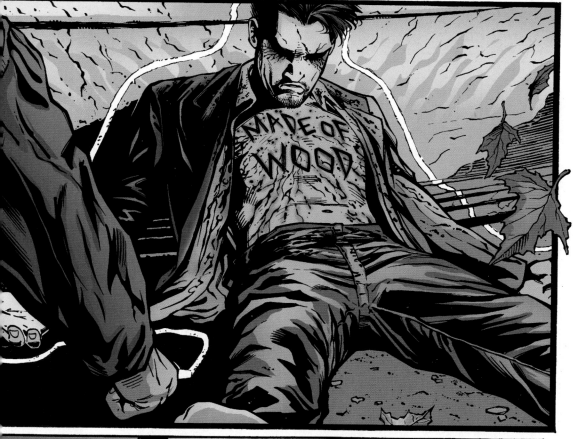

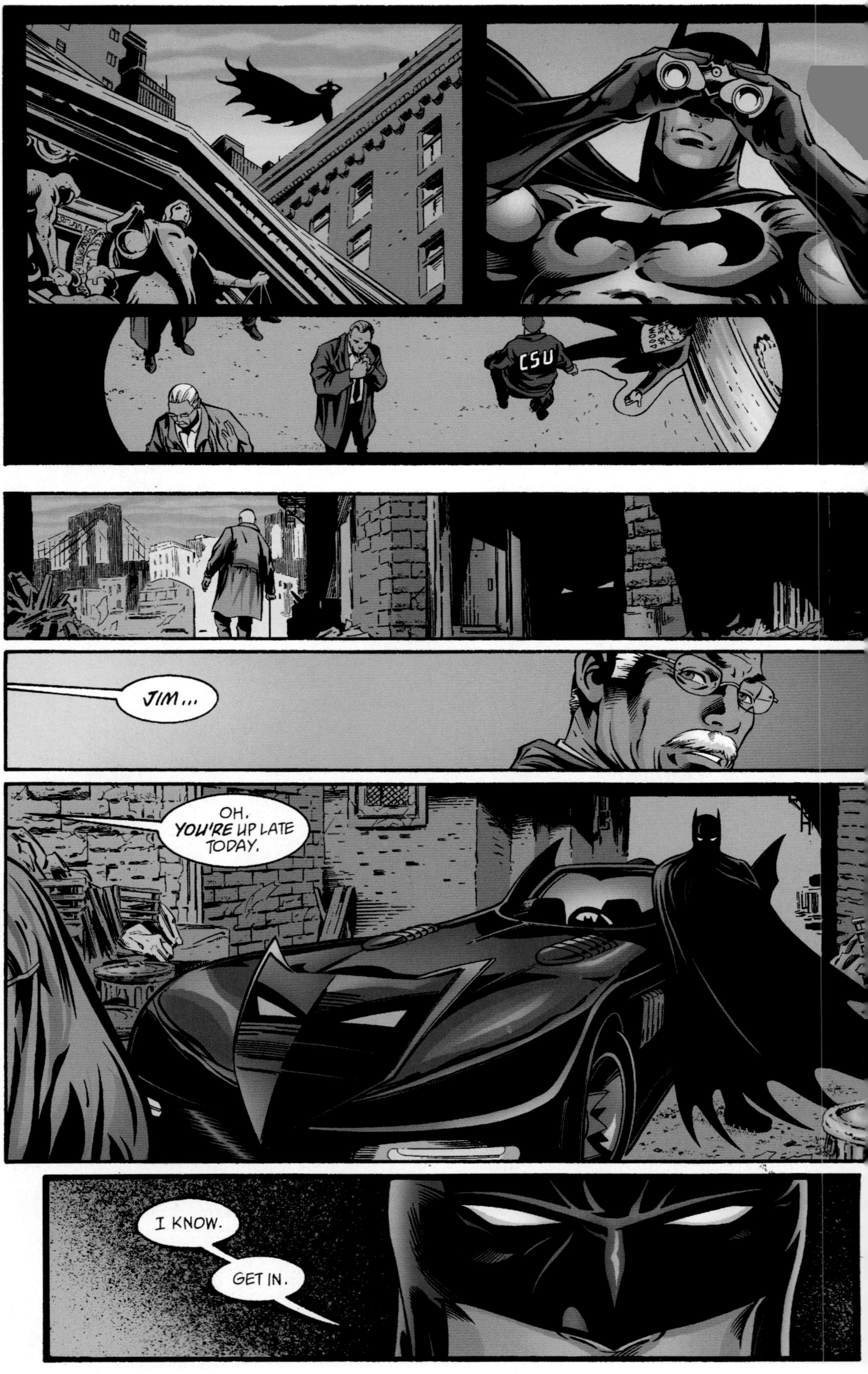
CSU
JIM...
OH. YOU'RE UP LATE TODAY.
I KNOW.
GET IN.

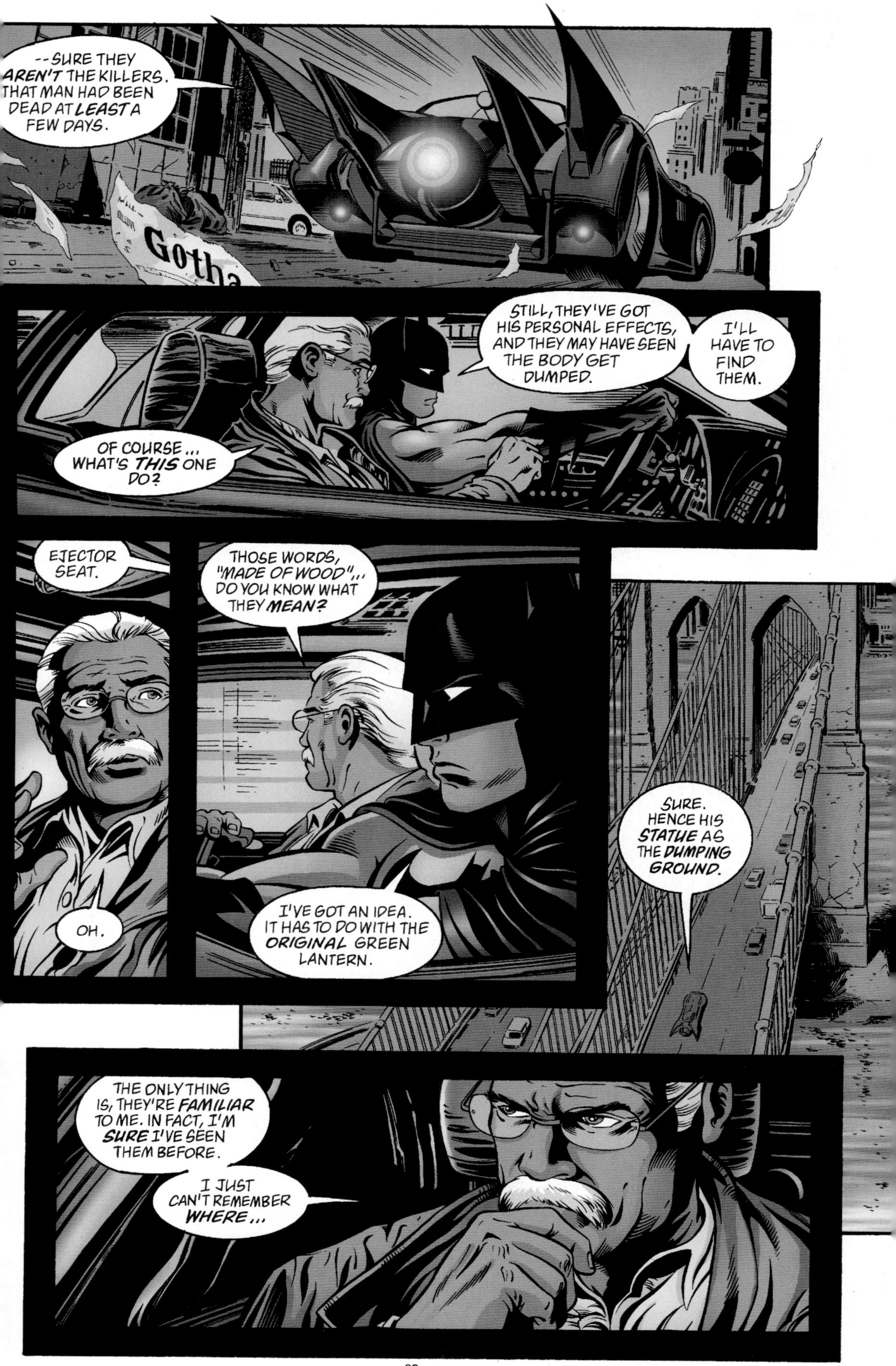
--SURE THEY AREN'T THE KILLERS. THAT MAN HAD BEEN DEAD AT LEAST A FEW DAYS.
Gotha
STILL, THEY'VE GOT HIS PERSONAL EFFECTS, AND THEY MAY HAVE SEEN THE BODY GET DUMPED.
I'LL HAVE TO FIND THEM.
OF COURSE... WHAT'S THIS ONE DO?
EJECTOR SEAT.
OH.
THOSE WORDS, "MADE OF WOOD"... DO YOU KNOW WHAT THEY MEAN?
I'VE GOT AN IDEA. IT HAS TO DO WITH THE ORIGINAL GREEN LANTERN.
SURE. HENCE HIS STATUE AS THE DUMPING GROUND.
THE ONLY THING IS, THEY'RE FAMILIAR TO ME. IN FACT, I'M SURE I'VE SEEN THEM BEFORE.
I JUST CAN'T REMEMBER WHERE...

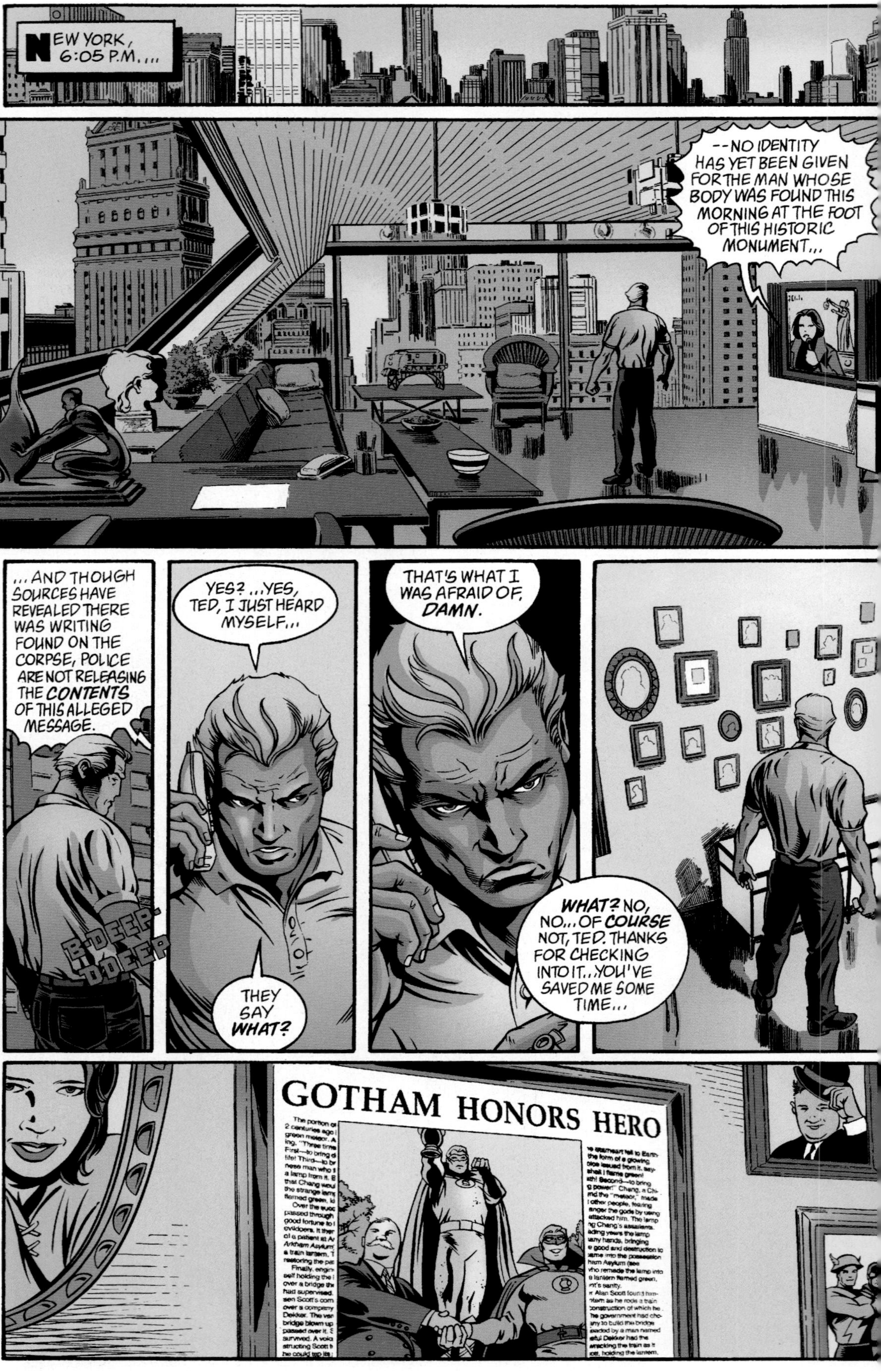
NEW YORK, 6:05 P.M....
--NO IDENTITY HAS YET BEEN GIVEN FOR THE MAN WHOSE BODY WAS FOUND THIS MORNING AT THE FOOT OF THIS HISTORIC MONUMENT...
...AND THOUGH SOURCES HAVE REVEALED THERE WAS WRITING FOUND ON THE CORPSE, POLICE ARE NOT RELEASING THE CONTENTS OF THIS ALLEGED MESSAGE.
B-DEEP-DEEP
YES? ...YES, TED, I JUST HEARD MYSELF...
THEY SAY WHAT?
THAT'S WHAT I WAS AFRAID OF, DAMN.
WHAT? NO, NO... OF COURSE NOT, TED. THANKS FOR CHECKING INTO IT.. YOU'VE SAVED ME SOME TIME...
GOTHAM HONORS HERO

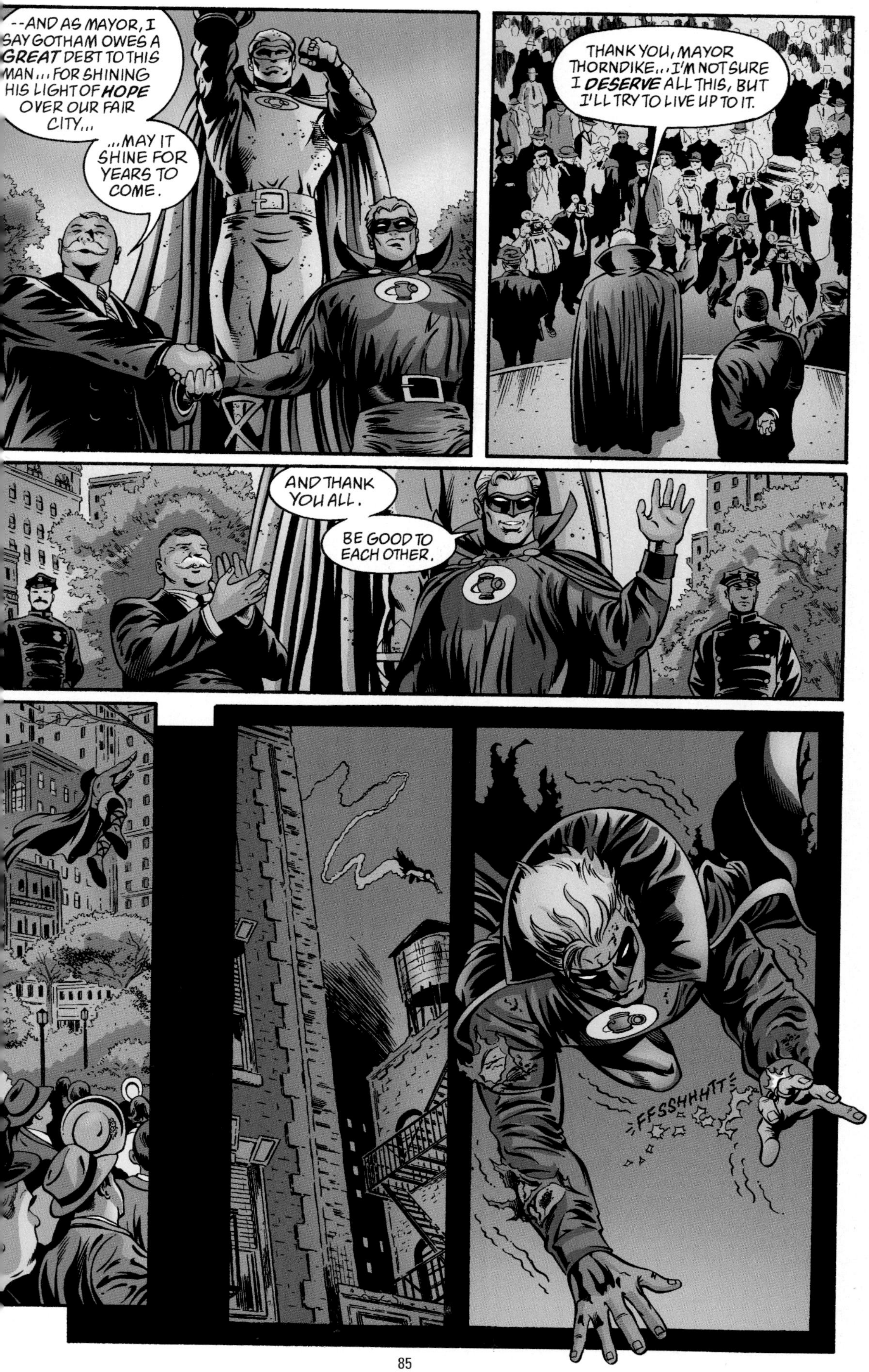
--AND AS MAYOR, I SAY GOTHAM OWES A GREAT DEBT TO THIS MAN... FOR SHINING HIS LIGHT OF HOPE OVER OUR FAIR CITY...
...MAY IT SHINE FOR YEARS TO COME.
THANK YOU, MAYOR THORNDIKE... I'M NOT SURE I DESERVE ALL THIS, BUT I'LL TRY TO LIVE UP TO IT.
AND THANK YOU ALL.
BE GOOD TO EACH OTHER.
FFSSHHHTT

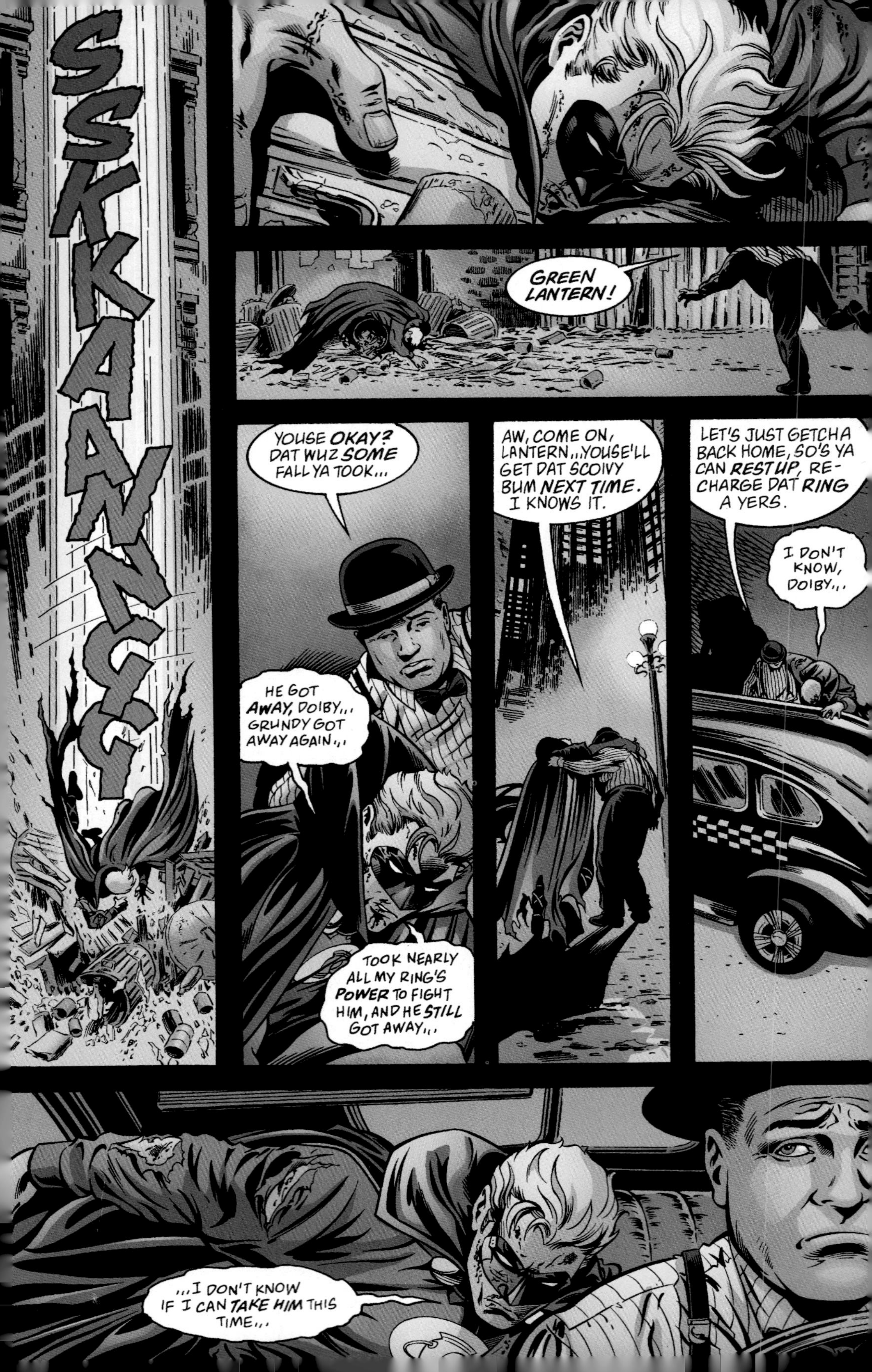
SSKKAANNGG
GREEN LANTERN!
YOUSE OKAY? DAT WUZ SOME FALL YA TOOK...
HE GOT AWAY, DOIBY... GRUNDY GOT AWAY AGAIN...
TOOK NEARLY ALL MY RING'S POWER TO FIGHT HIM, AND HE STILL GOT AWAY...
AW, COME ON, LANTERN... YOUSE'LL GET DAT SCOIVY BUM NEXT TIME. I KNOWS IT.
LET'S JUST GETCHA BACK HOME, SO'S YA CAN REST UP, RE-CHARGE DAT RING A YERS.
I DON'T KNOW, DOIBY...
...I DON'T KNOW IF I CAN TAKE HIM THIS TIME...

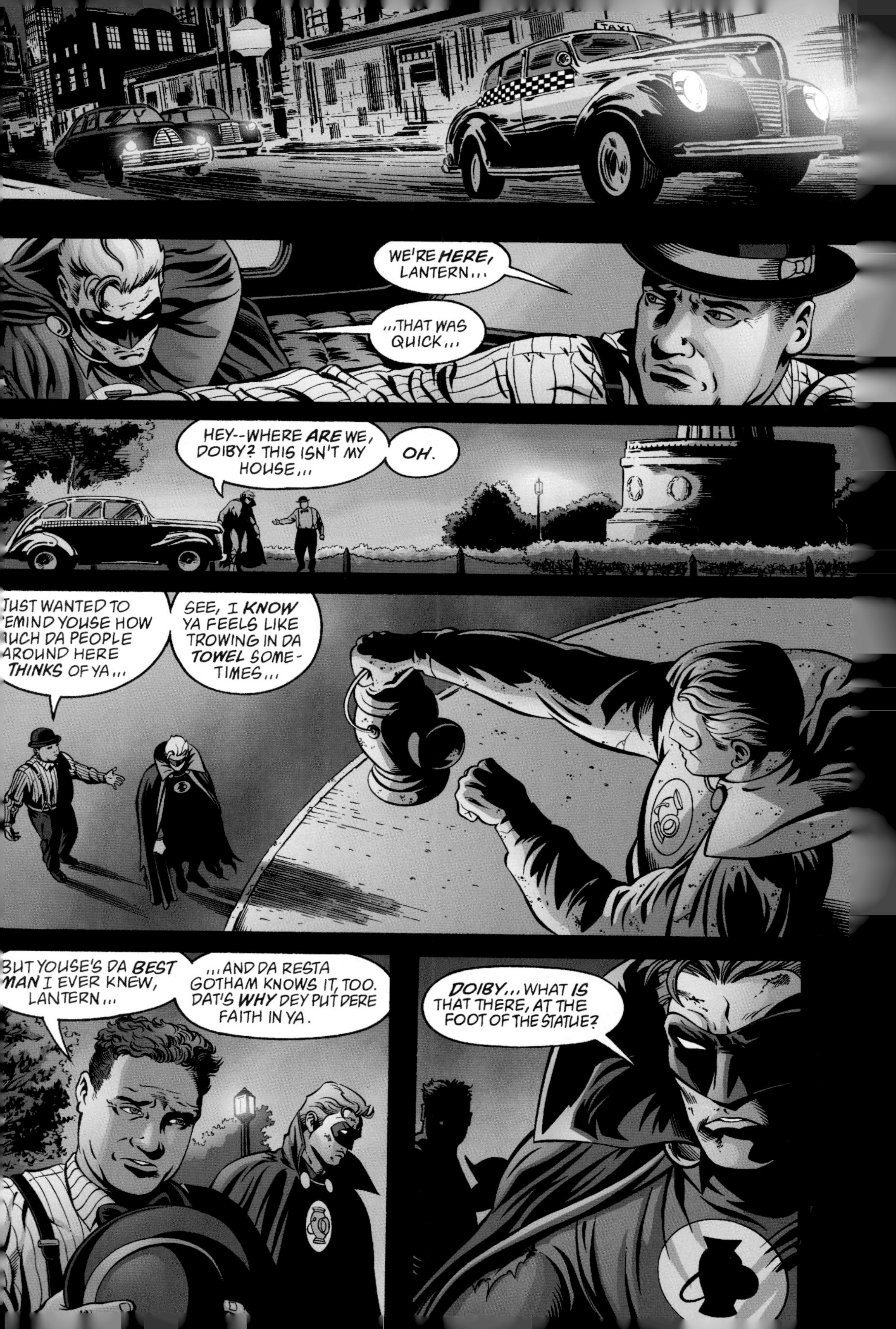
TAXI
WE'RE HERE, LANTERN...
...THAT WAS QUICK...
HEY--WHERE ARE WE, DOIBY? THIS ISN'T MY HOUSE...
OH.
JUST WANTED TO REMIND YOUSE HOW MUCH DA PEOPLE AROUND HERE THINKS OF YA...
SEE, I KNOW YA FEELS LIKE TROWING IN DA TOWEL SOME-TIMES...
BUT YOUSE'S DA BEST MAN I EVER KNEW, LANTERN...
...AND DA RESTA GOTHAM KNOWS IT, TOO. DAT'S WHY DEY PUT DERE FAITH IN YA.
DOIBY... WHAT IS THAT THERE, AT THE FOOT OF THE STATUE?

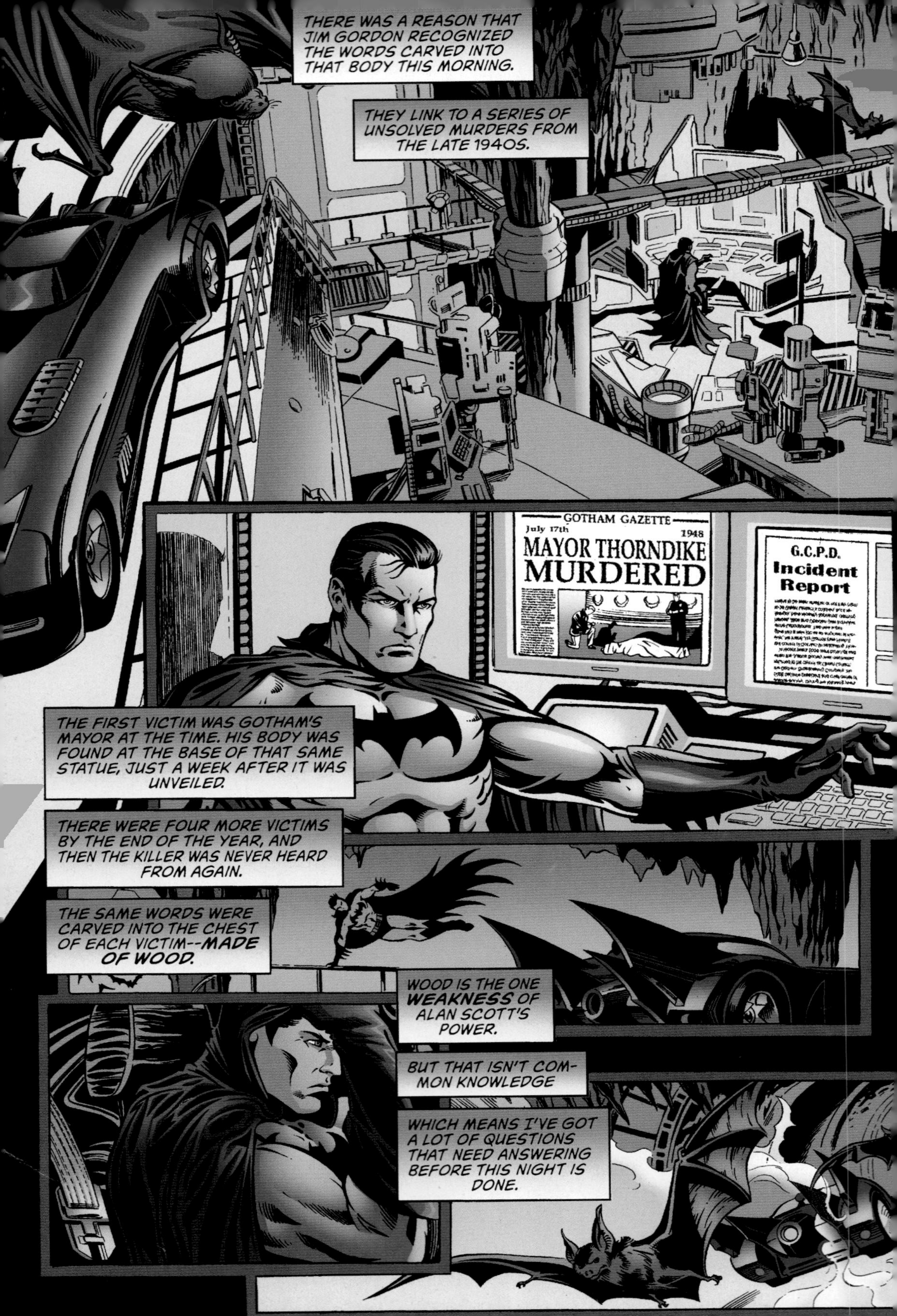
THERE WAS A REASON THAT JIM GORDON RECOGNIZED THE WORDS CARVED INTO THAT BODY THIS MORNING.
THEY LINK TO A SERIES OF UNSOLVED MURDERS FROM THE LATE 1940S.
GOTHAM GAZETTE
July 17th
1948
MAYOR THORNDIKE MURDERED
G.C.P.D.
Incident Report
THE FIRST VICTIM WAS GOTHAM'S MAYOR AT THE TIME. HIS BODY WAS FOUND AT THE BASE OF THAT SAME STATUE, JUST A WEEK AFTER IT WAS UNVEILED.
THERE WERE FOUR MORE VICTIMS BY THE END OF THE YEAR, AND THEN THE KILLER WAS NEVER HEARD FROM AGAIN.
THE SAME WORDS WERE CARVED INTO THE CHEST OF EACH VICTIM--MADE OF WOOD.
WOOD IS THE ONE WEAKNESS OF ALAN SCOTT'S POWER.
BUT THAT ISN'T COM-MON KNOWLEDGE
WHICH MEANS I'VE GOT A LOT OF QUESTIONS THAT NEED ANSWERING BEFORE THIS NIGHT IS DONE.

--AN' SOME OLD GIMP WUZ TRYIN' TO KEEP ME FROM HAVIN' A DECENT PAIR'A SHOES FOR ONCE...

I CUT HIM *GOOD*, THOUGH. NEED *TWO* CANES NOW.

DON'T FORGET THE *WALLET*, TOO, HEATHCLIFF... GOT ALMOST TWO HUNDRED *BUCKS.*

YOU'RE WEARING A *DEAD MAN'S* SHOES?

SURE. FOUND HIM ALL *CARVED UP*, FIGURE *HE* DON'T NEED 'EM NO MORE...

WHAT'S IT TO *YOU?*

I'M *TAKING* THEM.

THE *WALLET*, TOO.

WHAT?

WHO THE HELL'RE *YOU?*

I'M A MAN WHO'S GIVING YOU A CHANCE TO DO THE RIGHT THING.
YEAH, WHATEVER...I'LL PASS.
YOUR CHOICE.

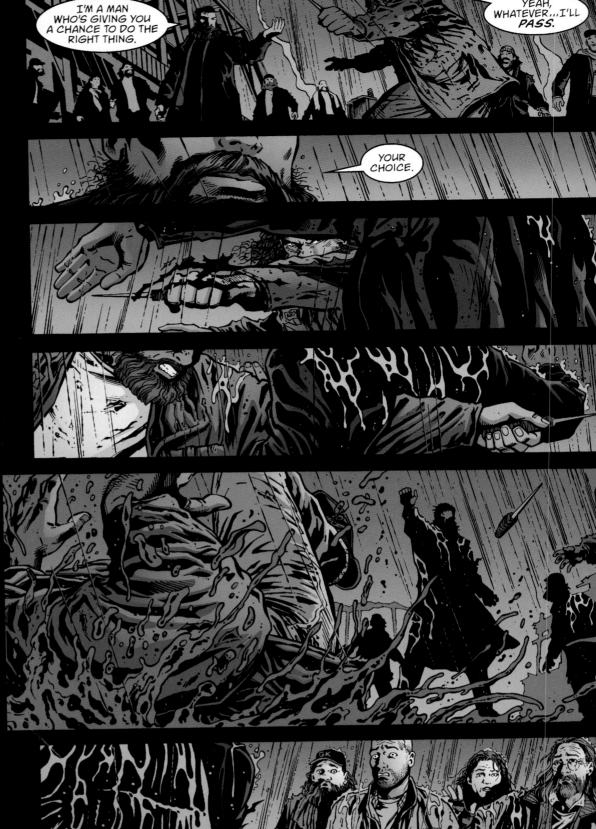

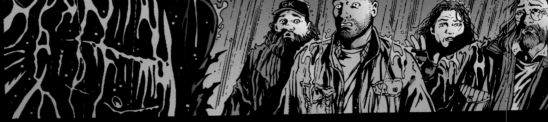

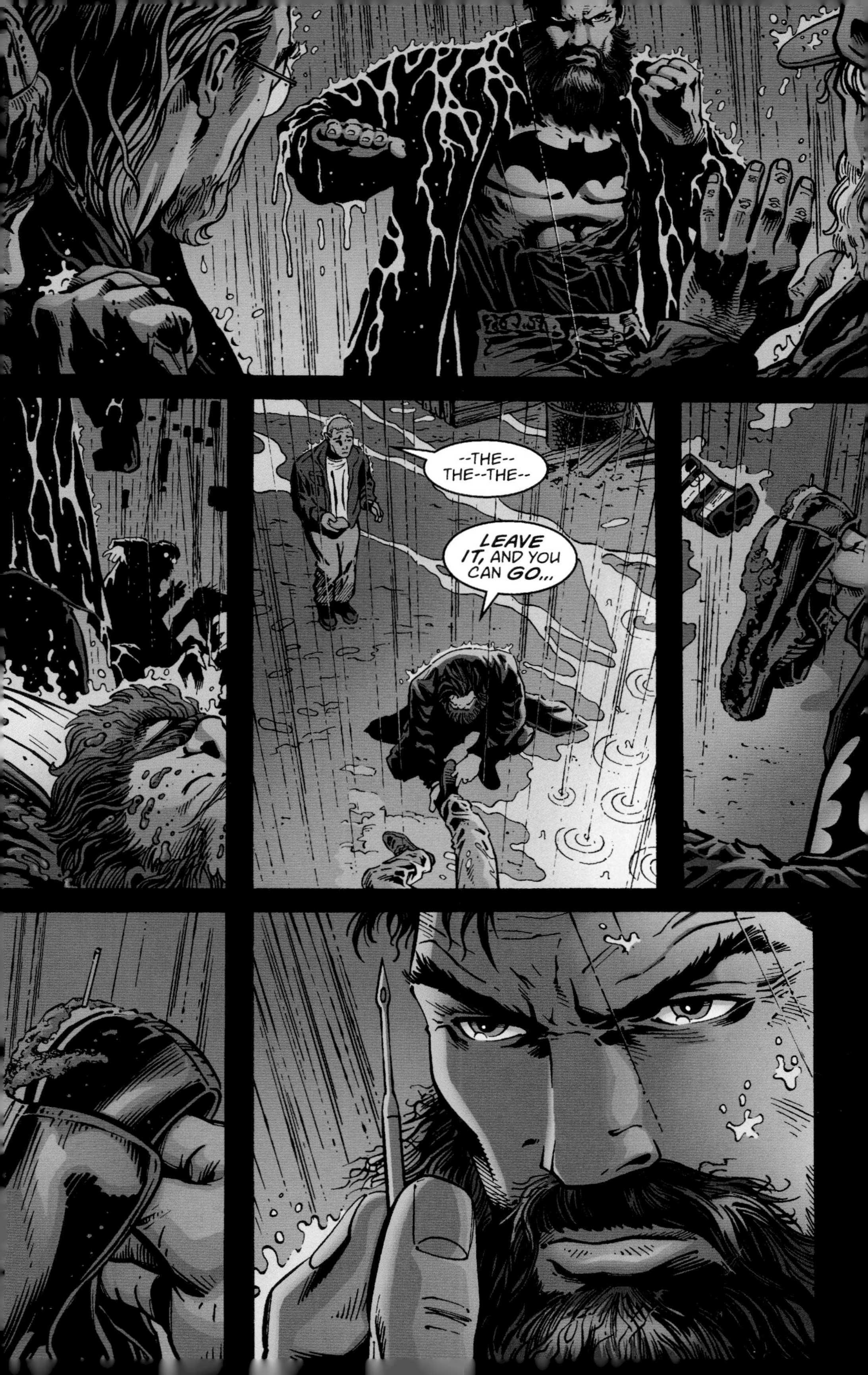
--THE--
THE--THE--
LEAVE IT, AND YOU CAN GO...

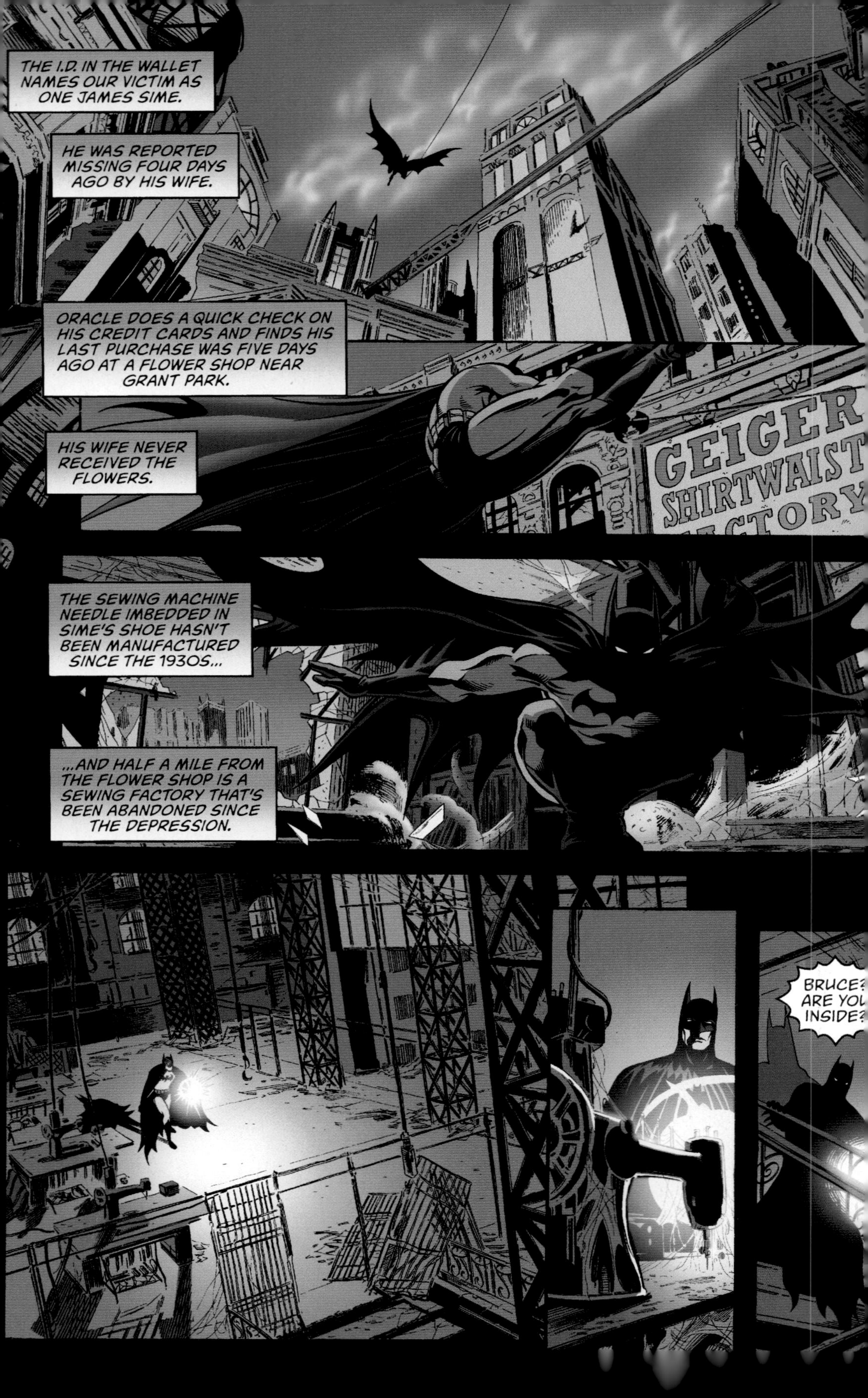
THE I.D. IN THE WALLET NAMES OUR VICTIM AS ONE JAMES SIME.
HE WAS REPORTED MISSING FOUR DAYS AGO BY HIS WIFE.
ORACLE DOES A QUICK CHECK ON HIS CREDIT CARDS AND FINDS HIS LAST PURCHASE WAS FIVE DAYS AGO AT A FLOWER SHOP NEAR GRANT PARK.
HIS WIFE NEVER RECEIVED THE FLOWERS.
GEIGER SHIRTWAIST
THE SEWING MACHINE NEEDLE IMBEDDED IN SIME'S SHOE HASN'T BEEN MANUFACTURED SINCE THE 1930S...
...AND HALF A MILE FROM THE FLOWER SHOP IS A SEWING FACTORY THAT'S BEEN ABANDONED SINCE THE DEPRESSION.
BRUCE? ARE YOU INSIDE?

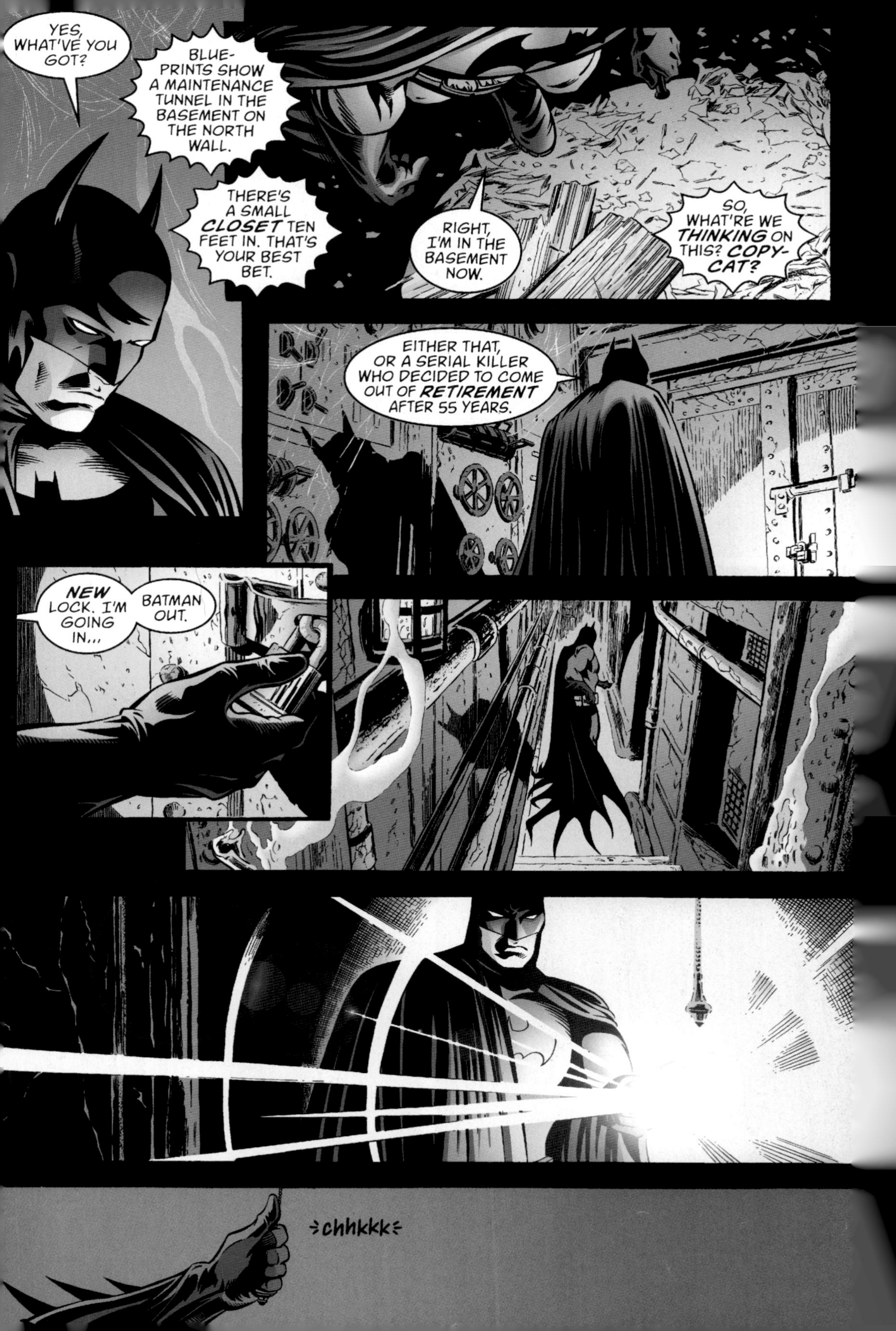
YES, WHAT'VE YOU GOT?
BLUE-PRINTS SHOW A MAINTENANCE TUNNEL IN THE BASEMENT ON THE NORTH WALL.
THERE'S A SMALL CLOSET TEN FEET IN. THAT'S YOUR BEST BET.
RIGHT, I'M IN THE BASEMENT NOW.
SO, WHAT'RE WE THINKING ON THIS? COPY-CAT?
EITHER THAT, OR A SERIAL KILLER WHO DECIDED TO COME OUT OF RETIREMENT AFTER 55 YEARS.
NEW LOCK. I'M GOING IN...
BATMAN OUT.
chhkkk

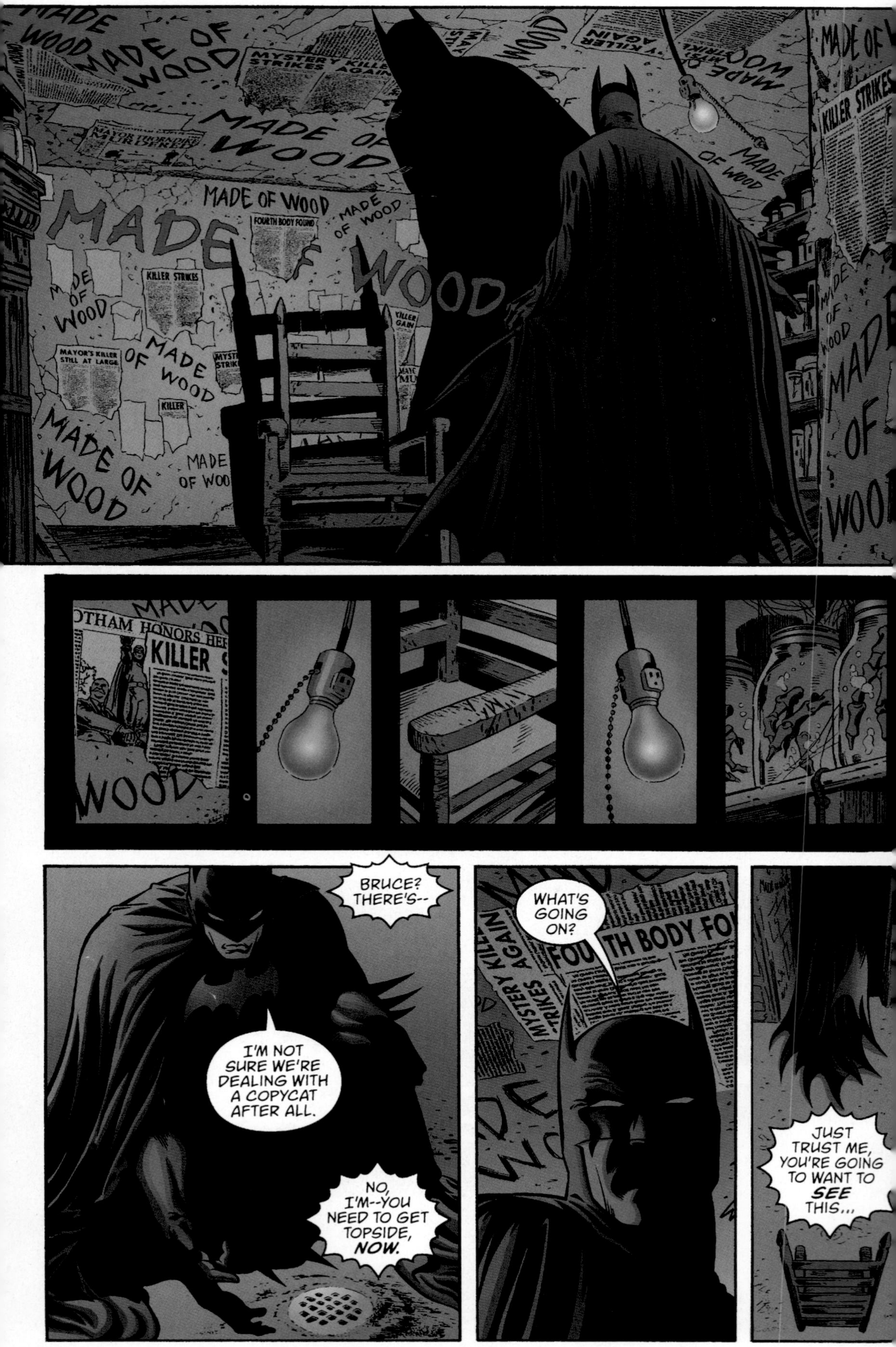
MADE OF WOOD
MYSTERY KILLER STRIKES AGAIN
FOURTH BODY FOUND
KILLER STRIKES
MAYOR'S KILLER STILL AT LARGE
BRUCE? THERE'S--
I'M NOT SURE WE'RE DEALING WITH A COPYCAT AFTER ALL.
NO, I'M--YOU NEED TO GET TOPSIDE, NOW.
WHAT'S GOING ON?
JUST TRUST ME, YOU'RE GOING TO WANT TO SEE THIS...

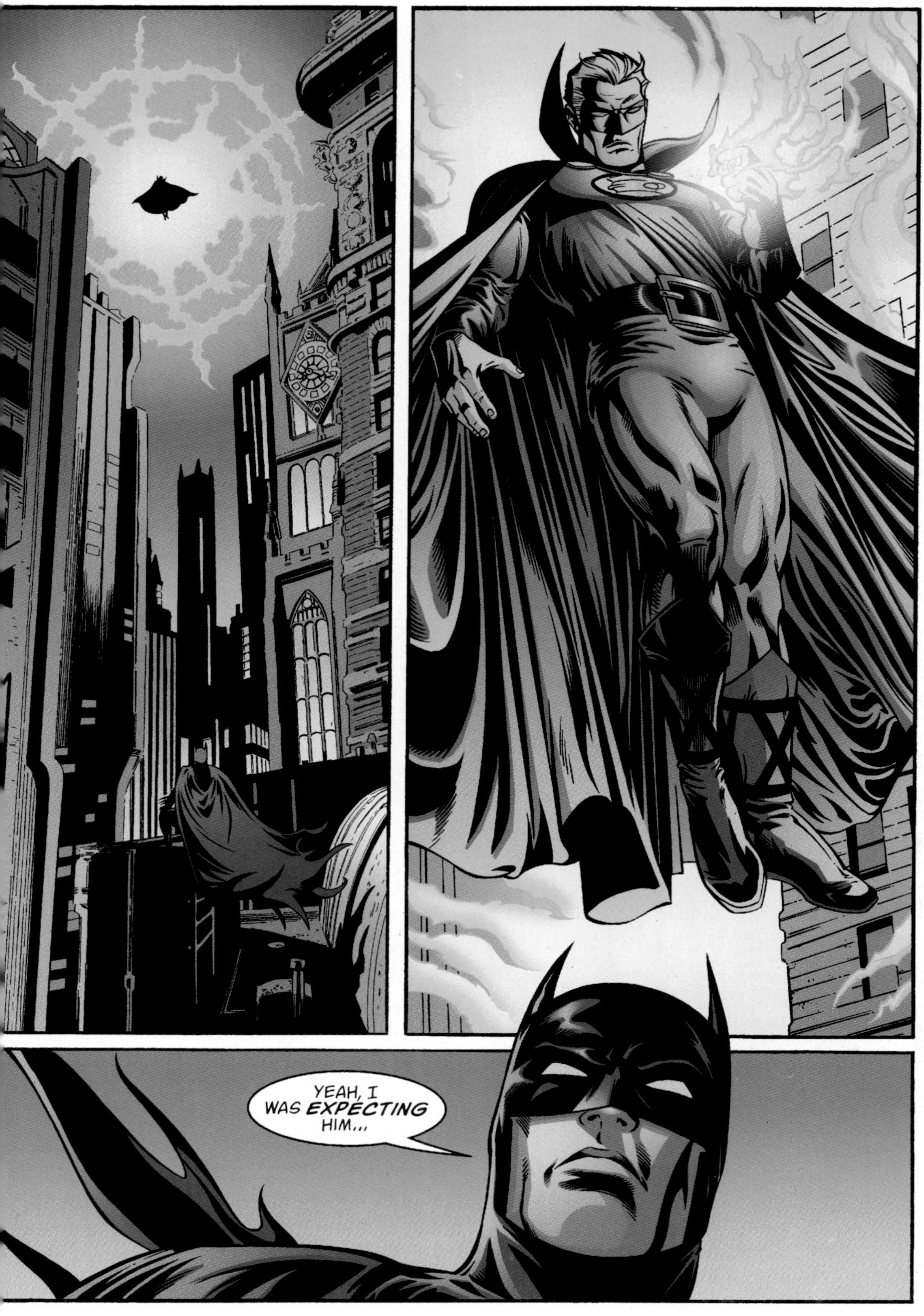
YEAH, I WAS EXPECTING HIM...

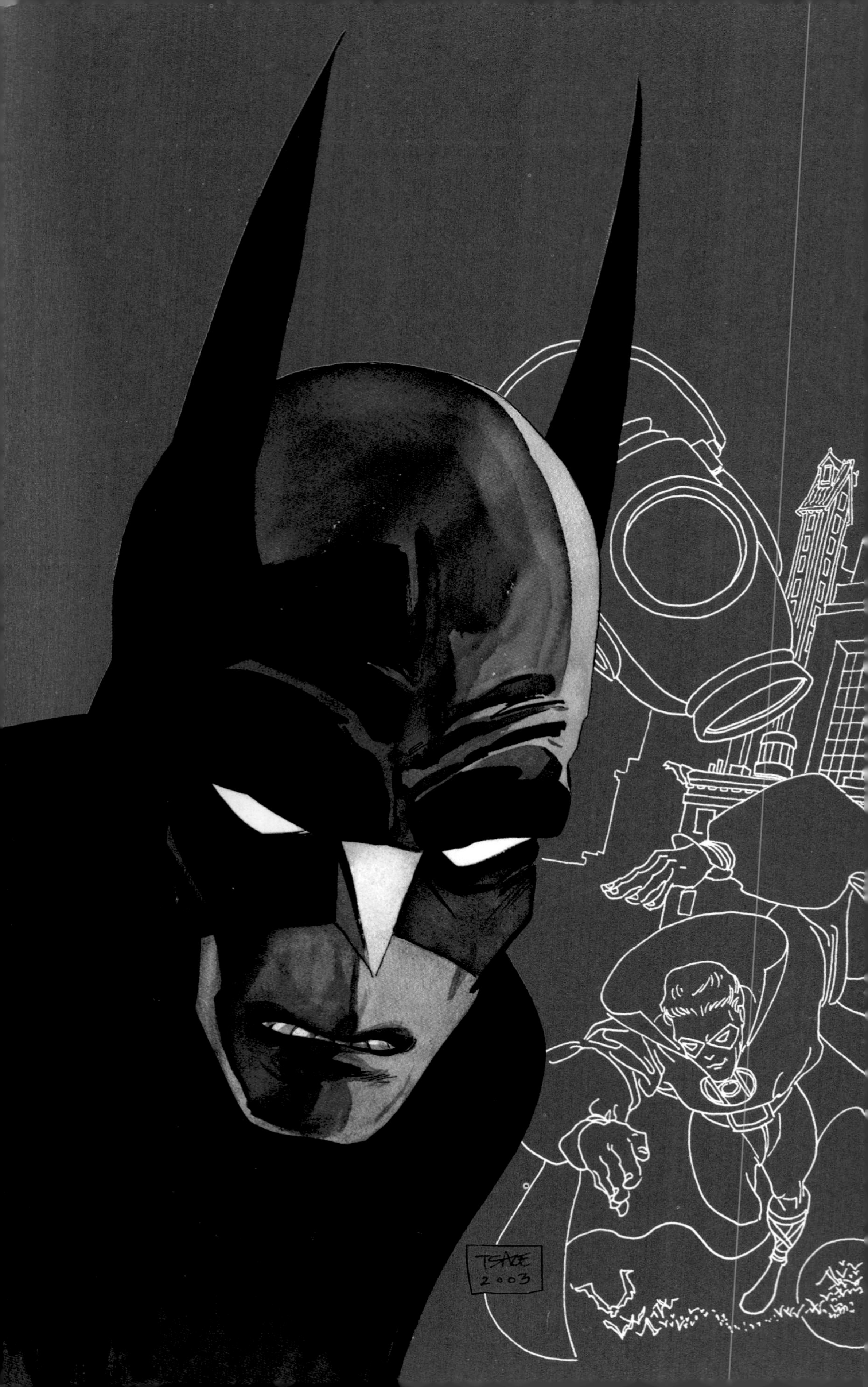
TSALE
2003

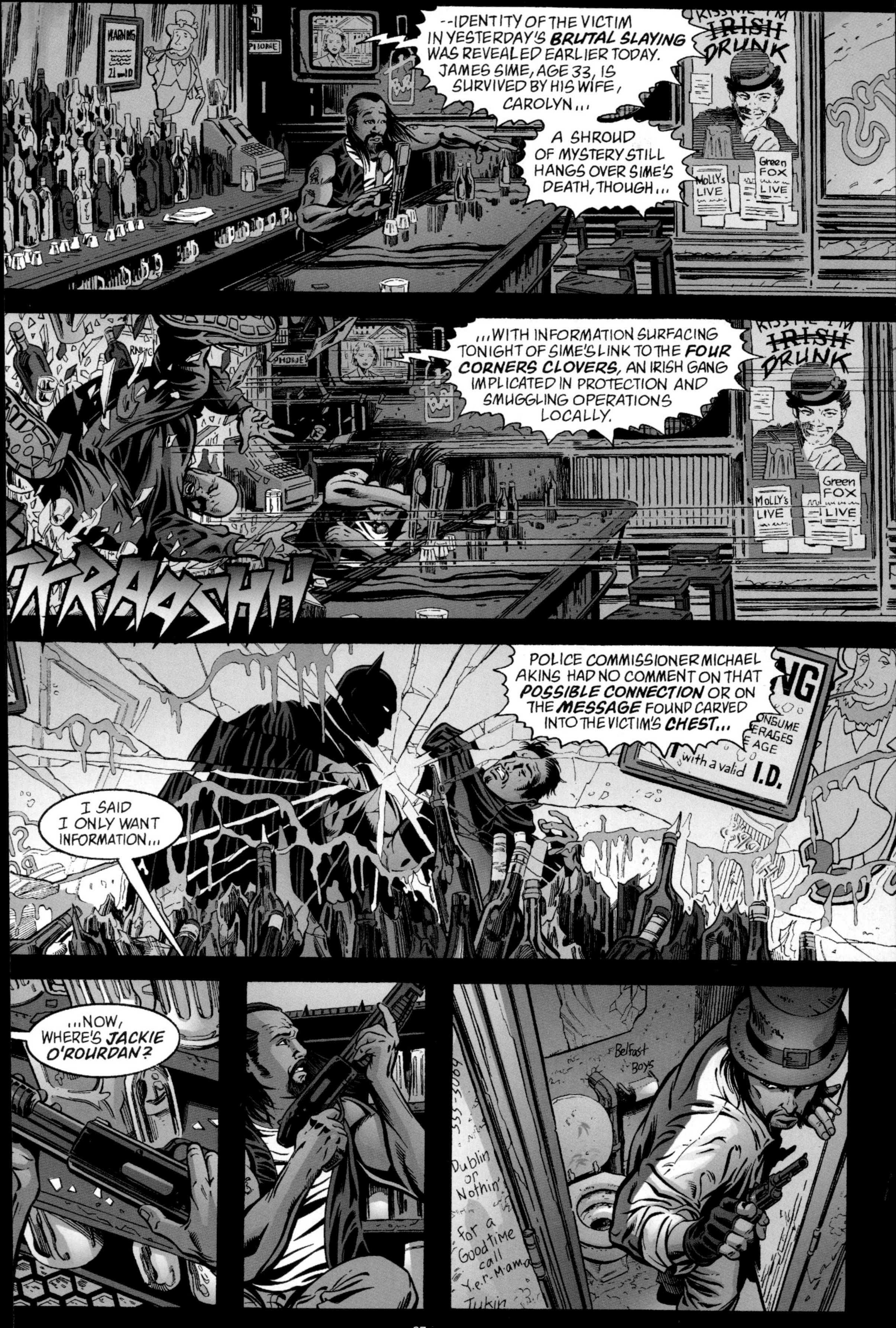
WARNING
PHONE
--IDENTITY OF THE VICTIM IN YESTERDAY'S BRUTAL SLAYING WAS REVEALED EARLIER TODAY. JAMES SIME, AGE 33, IS SURVIVED BY HIS WIFE, CAROLYN...
A SHROUD OF MYSTERY STILL HANGS OVER SIME'S DEATH, THOUGH...
IRISH DRUNK
MOLLY'S LIVE
Green FOX LIVE
...WITH INFORMATION SURFACING TONIGHT OF SIME'S LINK TO THE FOUR CORNERS CLOVERS, AN IRISH GANG IMPLICATED IN PROTECTION AND SMUGGLING OPERATIONS LOCALLY.
KRAASHH
POLICE COMMISSIONER MICHAEL AKINS HAD NO COMMENT ON THAT POSSIBLE CONNECTION OR ON THE MESSAGE FOUND CARVED INTO THE VICTIM'S CHEST...
with a valid I.D.
I SAID I ONLY WANT INFORMATION...
...NOW, WHERE'S JACKIE O'ROURDAN?
Belfast Boys
Dublin or Nothin'
for a Good time call Y.e.r. M.ama

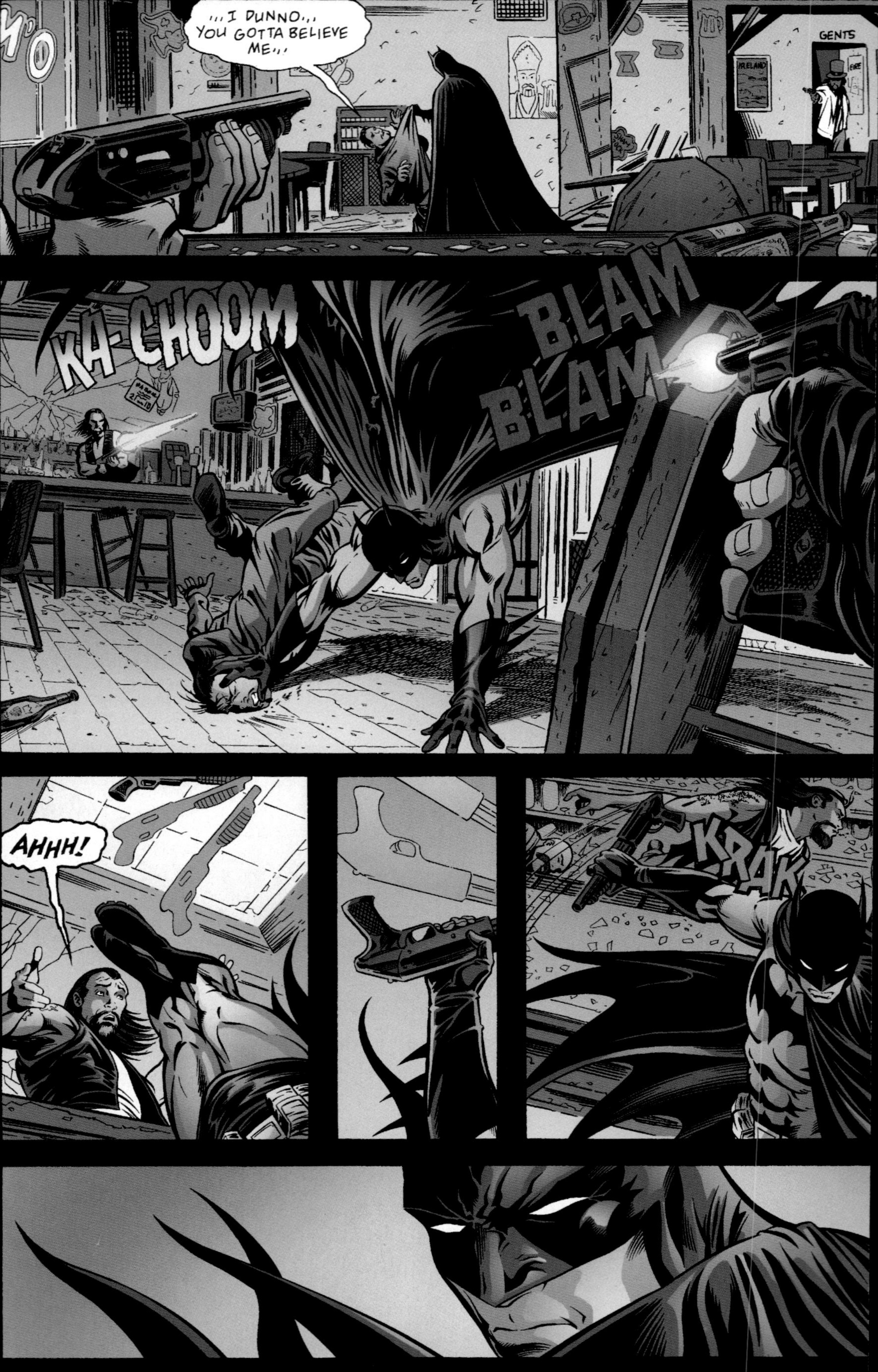

...I DUNNO... YOU GOTTA BELIEVE ME...
GENTS
IRELAND
KA-CHOOM
BLAM
BLAM
AHHH!
KRAK

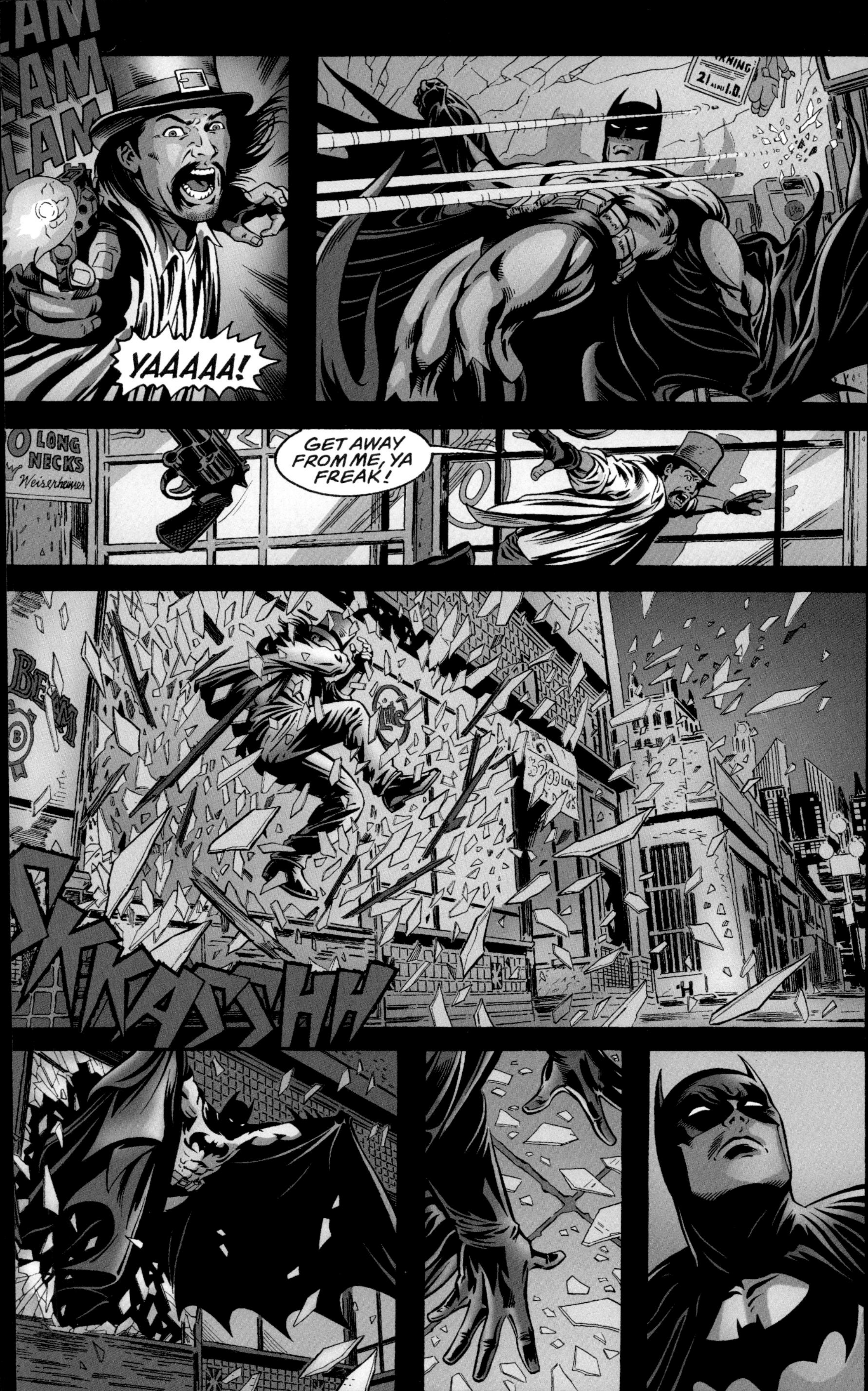
YAAAAA!
GET AWAY FROM ME, YA FREAK!
LONG NECKS

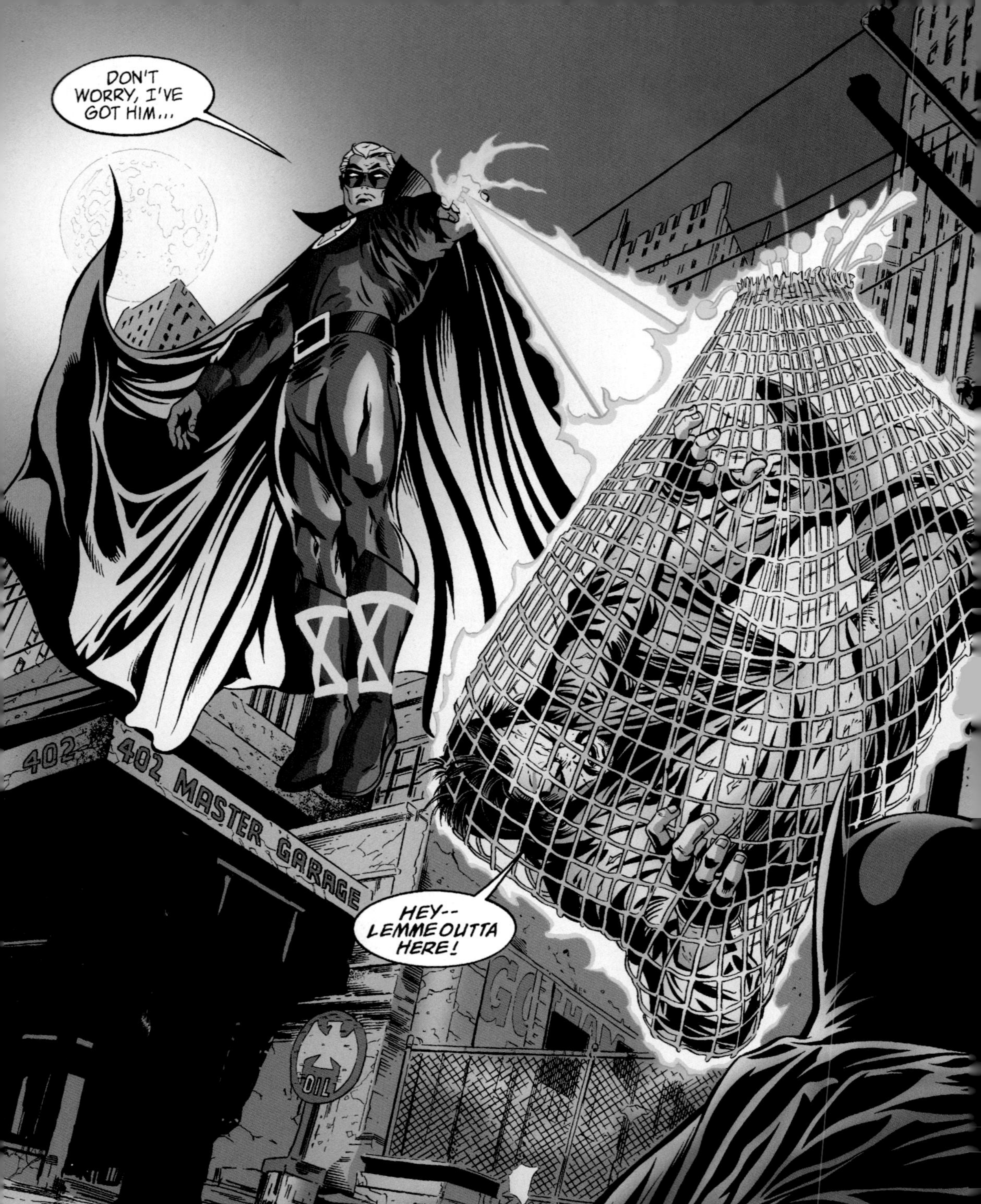
DON'T WORRY, I'VE GOT HIM...
402
402 MASTER GARAGE
HEY-- LEMME OUTTA HERE!
OIL
GOTHAM

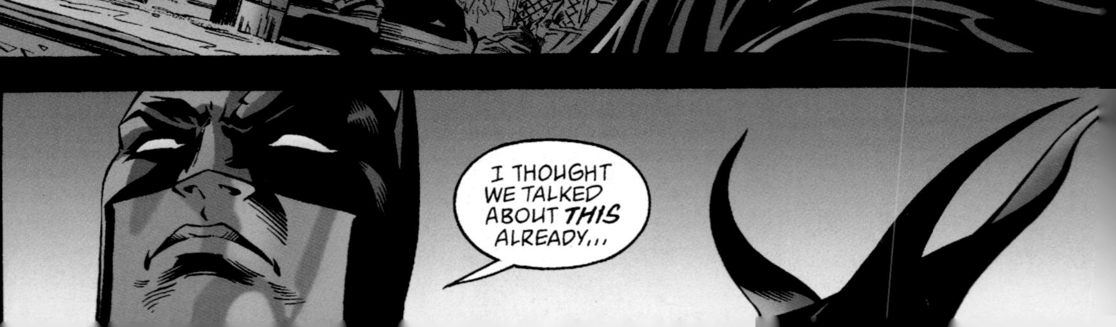
I THOUGHT WE TALKED ABOUT *THIS* ALREADY...

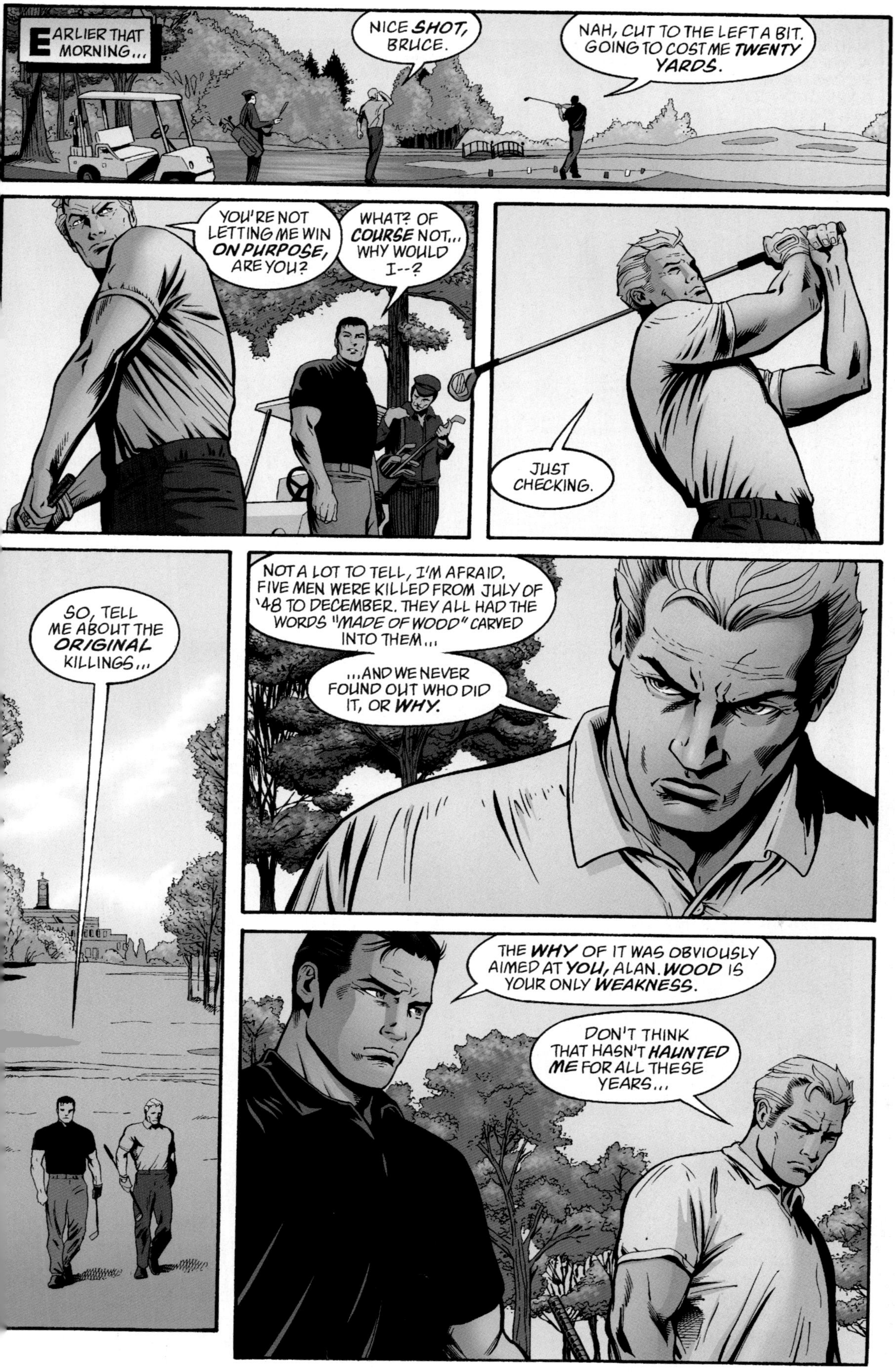
EARLIER THAT MORNING...
NICE SHOT, BRUCE.
NAH, CUT TO THE LEFT A BIT. GOING TO COST ME TWENTY YARDS.
YOU'RE NOT LETTING ME WIN ON PURPOSE, ARE YOU?
WHAT? OF COURSE NOT... WHY WOULD I--?
JUST CHECKING.
SO, TELL ME ABOUT THE ORIGINAL KILLINGS...
NOT A LOT TO TELL, I'M AFRAID. FIVE MEN WERE KILLED FROM JULY OF '48 TO DECEMBER. THEY ALL HAD THE WORDS "MADE OF WOOD" CARVED INTO THEM...
...AND WE NEVER FOUND OUT WHO DID IT, OR WHY.
THE WHY OF IT WAS OBVIOUSLY AIMED AT YOU, ALAN. WOOD IS YOUR ONLY WEAKNESS.
DON'T THINK THAT HASN'T HAUNTED ME FOR ALL THESE YEARS...

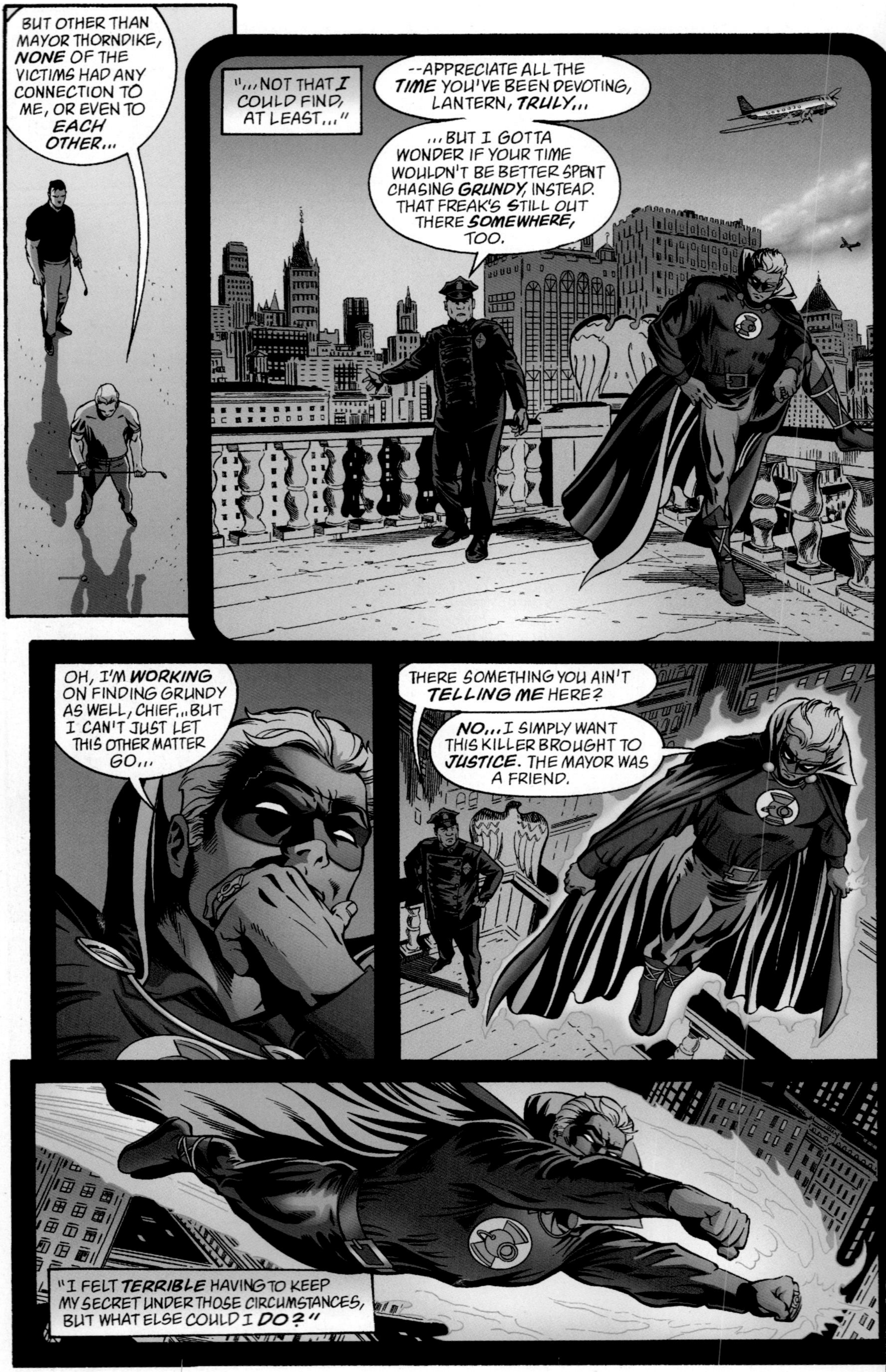
BUT OTHER THAN MAYOR THORNDIKE, NONE OF THE VICTIMS HAD ANY CONNECTION TO ME, OR EVEN TO EACH OTHER...
"...NOT THAT I COULD FIND, AT LEAST..."
--APPRECIATE ALL THE TIME YOU'VE BEEN DEVOTING, LANTERN, TRULY...
...BUT I GOTTA WONDER IF YOUR TIME WOULDN'T BE BETTER SPENT CHASING GRUNDY, INSTEAD. THAT FREAK'S STILL OUT THERE SOMEWHERE, TOO.
OH, I'M WORKING ON FINDING GRUNDY AS WELL, CHIEF...BUT I CAN'T JUST LET THIS OTHER MATTER GO...
THERE SOMETHING YOU AIN'T TELLING ME HERE?
NO...I SIMPLY WANT THIS KILLER BROUGHT TO JUSTICE. THE MAYOR WAS A FRIEND.
"I FELT TERRIBLE HAVING TO KEEP MY SECRET UNDER THOSE CIRCUMSTANCES, BUT WHAT ELSE COULD I DO?"

"MY **FAMILY'S** SAFETY, MY **CITY'S** SAFETY, ALL DEPENDED ON **ME**. ON MY POWER, AND MY SECRET.

"I CAN ONLY IMAGINE HOW BAD IT WOULD'VE BEEN IF ONE OF MY ADVERSARIES HAD DISCOVERED MY WEAKNESS.

"MY BATTLES WERE HARD ENOUGH ALREADY.

"SO I TRIED TO PURSUE HIS MURDERER ON MY OWN, KNOWING THAT HIS MESSAGE WASN'T TO THE POLICE OR THE REST OF THE CITY...

"...IT WAS TO ME."

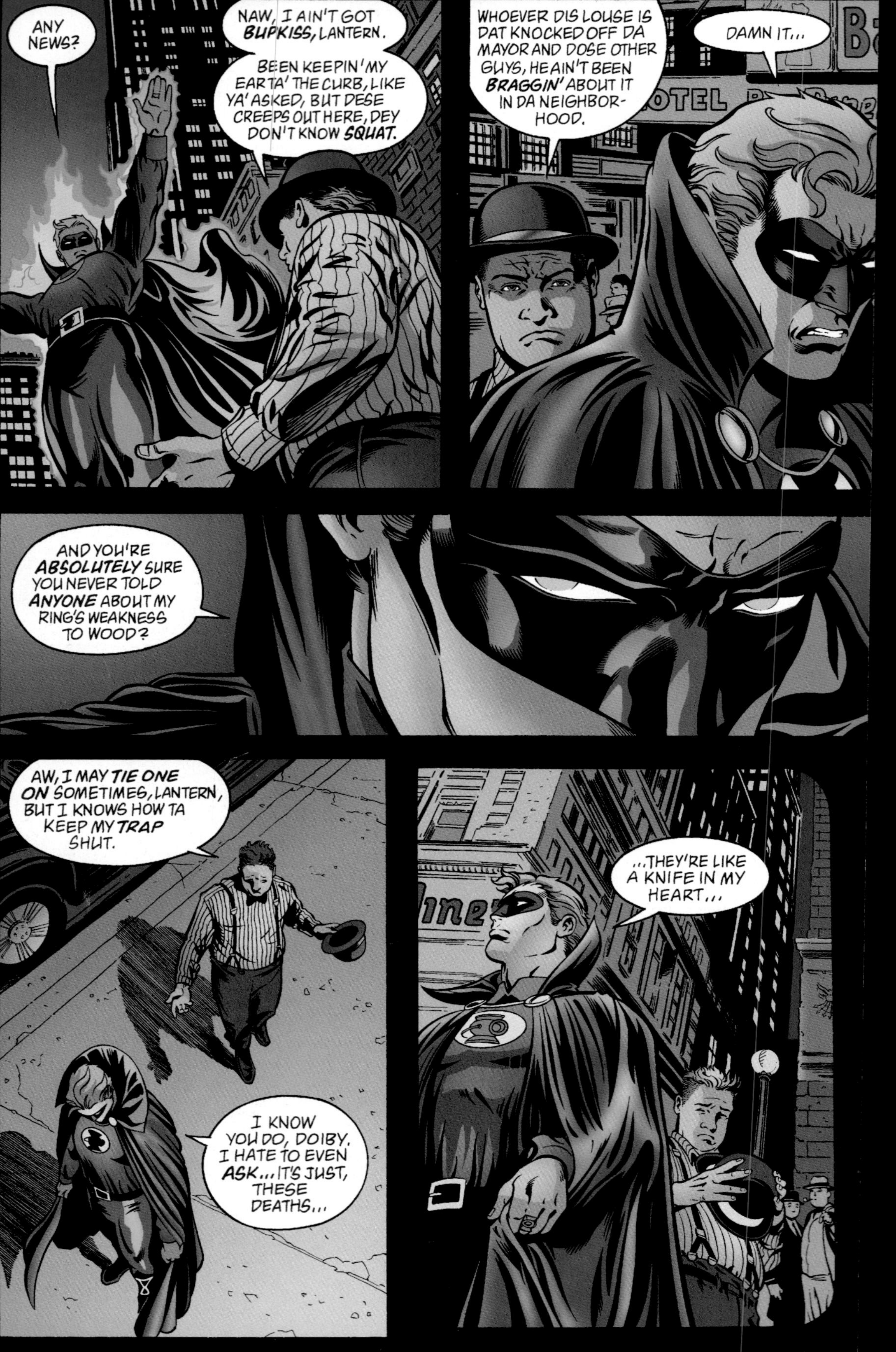
ANY NEWS?
NAW, I AIN'T GOT BUPKISS, LANTERN.
BEEN KEEPIN' MY EAR TA' THE CURB, LIKE YA' ASKED, BUT DESE CREEPS OUT HERE, DEY DON'T KNOW SQUAT.
WHOEVER DIS LOUSE IS DAT KNOCKED OFF DA MAYOR AND DOSE OTHER GUYS, HE AIN'T BEEN BRAGGIN' ABOUT IT IN DA NEIGHBOR-HOOD.
DAMN IT...
HOTEL
AND YOU'RE ABSOLUTELY SURE YOU NEVER TOLD ANYONE ABOUT MY RING'S WEAKNESS TO WOOD?
AW, I MAY TIE ONE ON SOMETIMES, LANTERN, BUT I KNOWS HOW TA KEEP MY TRAP SHUT.
I KNOW YOU DO, DOIBY. I HATE TO EVEN ASK... IT'S JUST, THESE DEATHS...
...THEY'RE LIKE A KNIFE IN MY HEART...

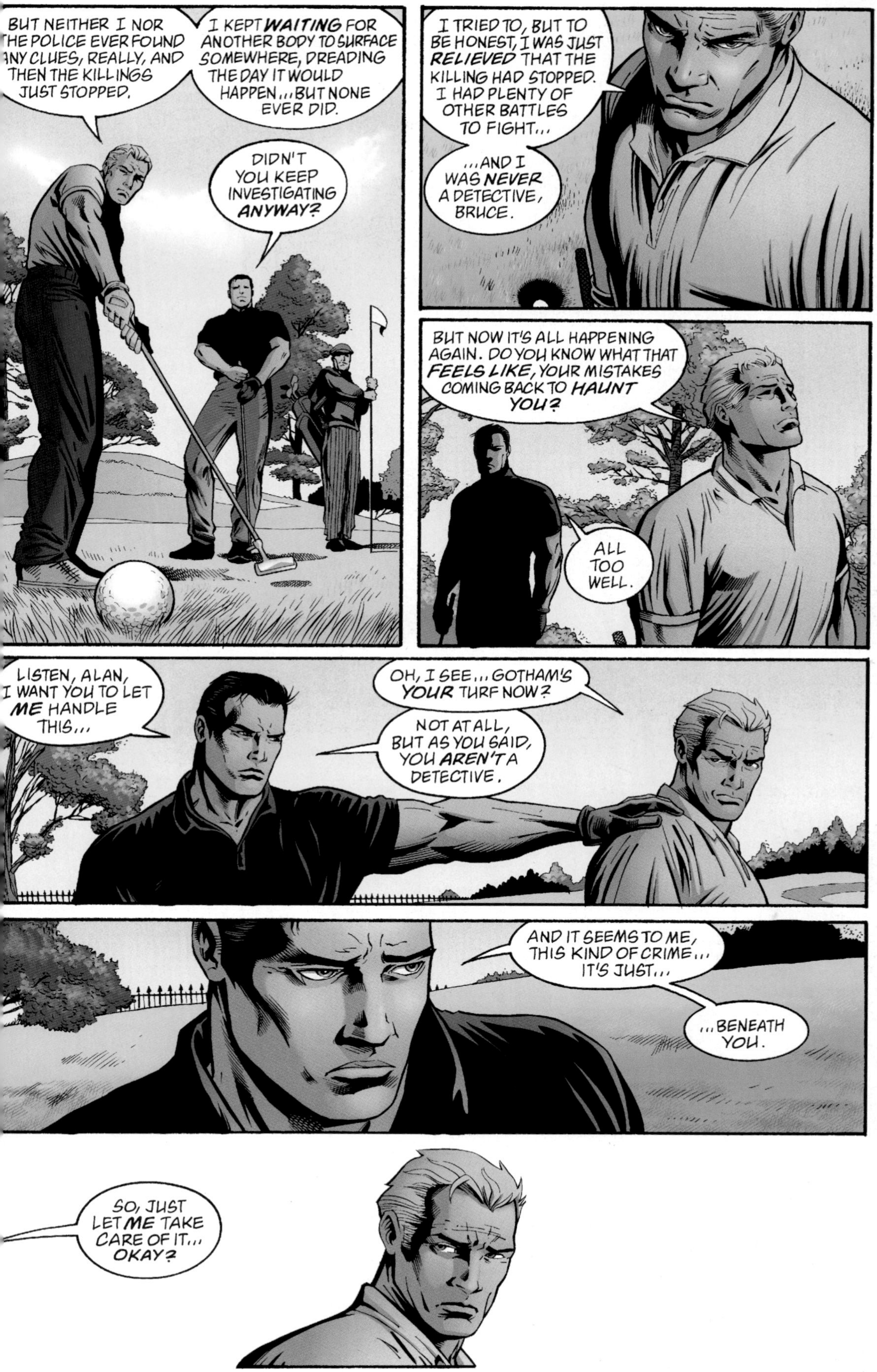

BUT NEITHER I NOR THE POLICE EVER FOUND ANY CLUES, REALLY, AND THEN THE KILLINGS JUST STOPPED.
I KEPT WAITING FOR ANOTHER BODY TO SURFACE SOMEWHERE, DREADING THE DAY IT WOULD HAPPEN... BUT NONE EVER DID.
DIDN'T YOU KEEP INVESTIGATING ANYWAY?
I TRIED TO, BUT TO BE HONEST, I WAS JUST RELIEVED THAT THE KILLING HAD STOPPED. I HAD PLENTY OF OTHER BATTLES TO FIGHT...
...AND I WAS NEVER A DETECTIVE, BRUCE.
BUT NOW IT'S ALL HAPPENING AGAIN. DO YOU KNOW WHAT THAT FEELS LIKE, YOUR MISTAKES COMING BACK TO HAUNT YOU?
ALL TOO WELL.
LISTEN, ALAN, I WANT YOU TO LET ME HANDLE THIS...
OH, I SEE... GOTHAM'S YOUR TURF NOW?
NOT AT ALL, BUT AS YOU SAID, YOU AREN'T A DETECTIVE.
AND IT SEEMS TO ME, THIS KIND OF CRIME... IT'S JUST...
...BENEATH YOU.
SO, JUST LET ME TAKE CARE OF IT... OKAY?

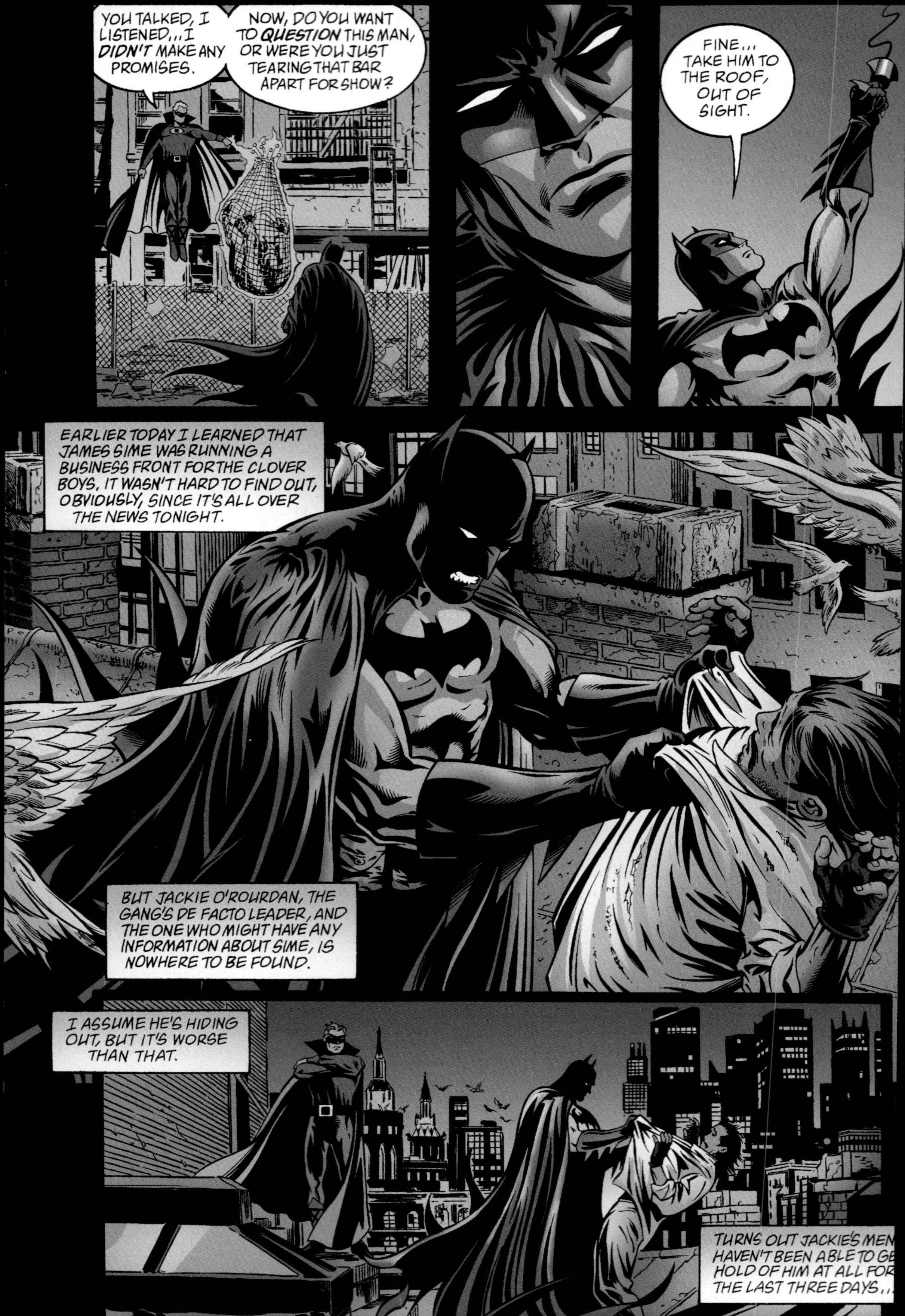
YOU TALKED, I LISTENED... I **DIDN'T** MAKE ANY PROMISES.
NOW, DO YOU WANT TO **QUESTION** THIS MAN, OR WERE YOU JUST TEARING THAT BAR APART FOR SHOW?
FINE... TAKE HIM TO THE ROOF, OUT OF SIGHT.
EARLIER TODAY I LEARNED THAT JAMES SIME WAS RUNNING A BUSINESS FRONT FOR THE CLOVER BOYS. IT WASN'T HARD TO FIND OUT, OBVIOUSLY, SINCE IT'S ALL OVER THE NEWS TONIGHT.
BUT JACKIE O'ROURDAN, THE GANG'S DE FACTO LEADER, AND THE ONE WHO MIGHT HAVE ANY INFORMATION ABOUT SIME, IS NOWHERE TO BE FOUND.
I ASSUME HE'S HIDING OUT, BUT IT'S WORSE THAN THAT.
TURNS OUT JACKIE'S MEN HAVEN'T BEEN ABLE TO GE HOLD OF HIM AT ALL FOR THE LAST THREE DAYS...

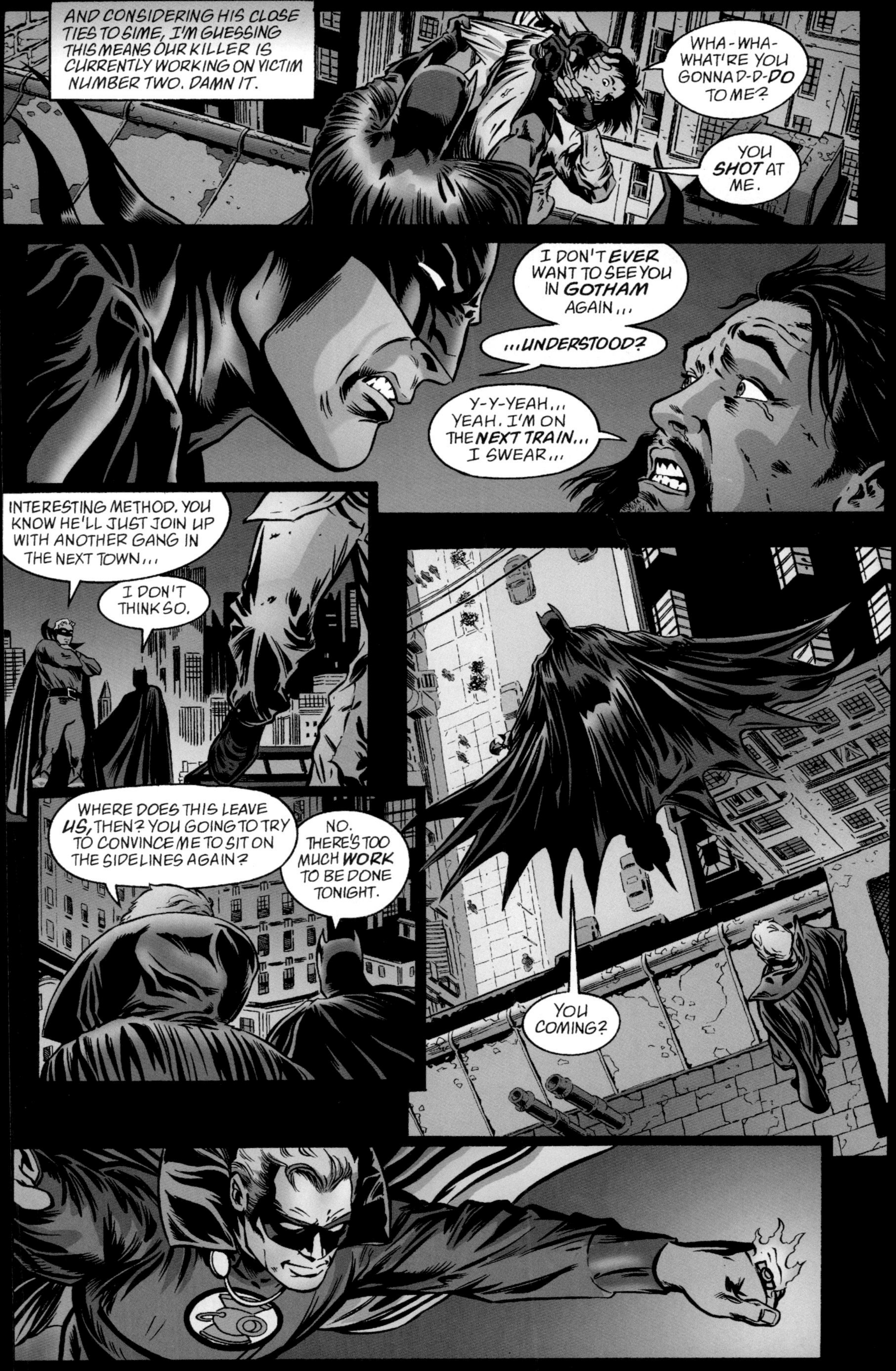
AND CONSIDERING HIS CLOSE TIES TO SIME, I'M GUESSING THIS MEANS OUR KILLER IS CURRENTLY WORKING ON VICTIM NUMBER TWO. DAMN IT.
WHA-WHA-WHAT'RE YOU GONNA D-D-DO TO ME?
YOU SHOT AT ME.
I DON'T EVER WANT TO SEE YOU IN GOTHAM AGAIN...
...UNDERSTOOD?
Y-Y-YEAH... YEAH. I'M ON THE NEXT TRAIN... I SWEAR...
INTERESTING METHOD. YOU KNOW HE'LL JUST JOIN UP WITH ANOTHER GANG IN THE NEXT TOWN...
I DON'T THINK SO.
WHERE DOES THIS LEAVE US, THEN? YOU GOING TO TRY TO CONVINCE ME TO SIT ON THE SIDELINES AGAIN?
NO. THERE'S TOO MUCH WORK TO BE DONE TONIGHT.
YOU COMING?

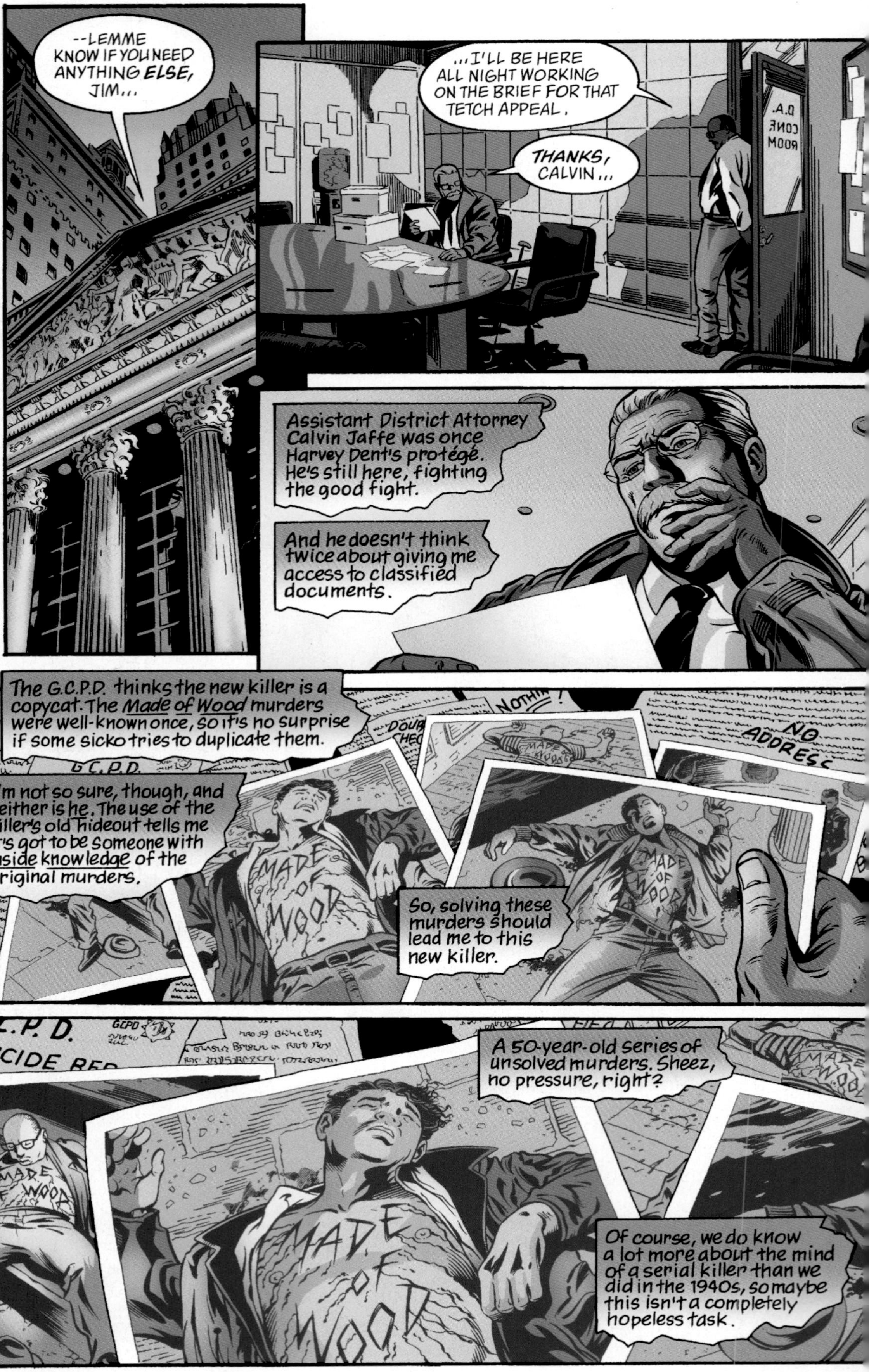
--LEMME KNOW IF YOU NEED ANYTHING ELSE, JIM...
...I'LL BE HERE ALL NIGHT WORKING ON THE BRIEF FOR THAT TETCH APPEAL.
THANKS, CALVIN...
D.A. CONF ROOM
Assistant District Attorney Calvin Jaffe was once Harvey Dent's protégé. He's still here, fighting the good fight.
And he doesn't think twice about giving me access to classified documents.
The G.C.P.D. thinks the new killer is a copycat. The Made of Wood murders were well-known once, so it's no surprise if some sicko tries to duplicate them.
I'm not so sure, though, and neither is he. The use of the killer's old hideout tells me it's got to be someone with inside knowledge of the original murders.
So, solving these murders should lead me to this new killer.
A 50-year-old series of unsolved murders. Sheez, no pressure, right?
Of course, we do know a lot more about the mind of a serial killer than we did in the 1940s, so maybe this isn't a completely hopeless task.

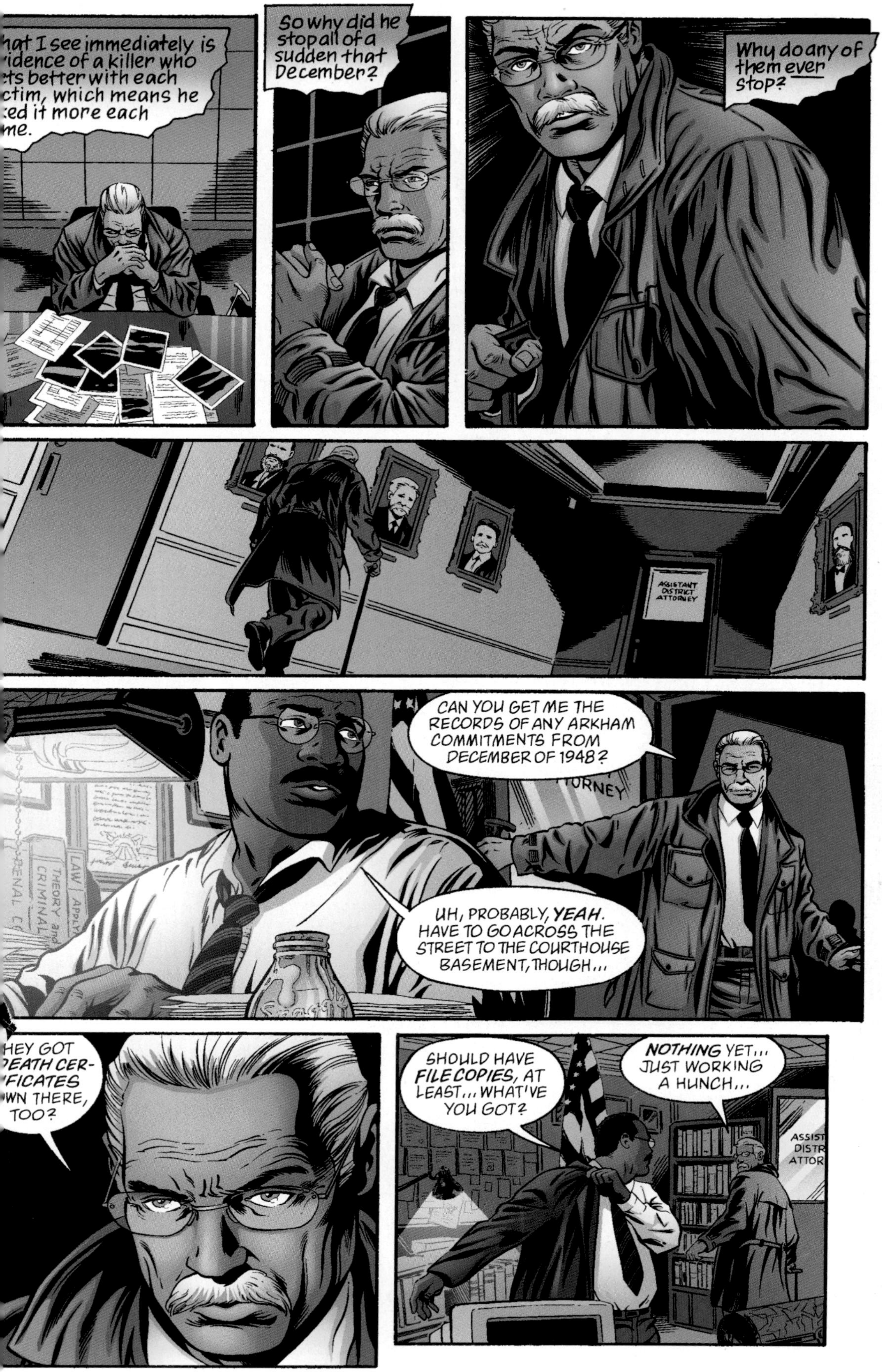
hat I see immediately is
vidence of a killer who
ts better with each
ctim, which means he
ked it more each
me.
So why did he stop all of a sudden that December?
Why do any of them *ever* stop?
ASSISTANT DISTRICT ATTORNEY
CAN YOU GET ME THE RECORDS OF ANY ARKHAM COMMITMENTS FROM DECEMBER OF 1948?
UH, PROBABLY, **YEAH**. HAVE TO GO ACROSS THE STREET TO THE COURTHOUSE BASEMENT, THOUGH...
HEY GOT
EATH CER-
FICATES
WN THERE,
TOO?
SHOULD HAVE **FILE COPIES**, AT LEAST... WHAT'VE YOU GOT?
NOTHING YET... JUST WORKING A HUNCH...

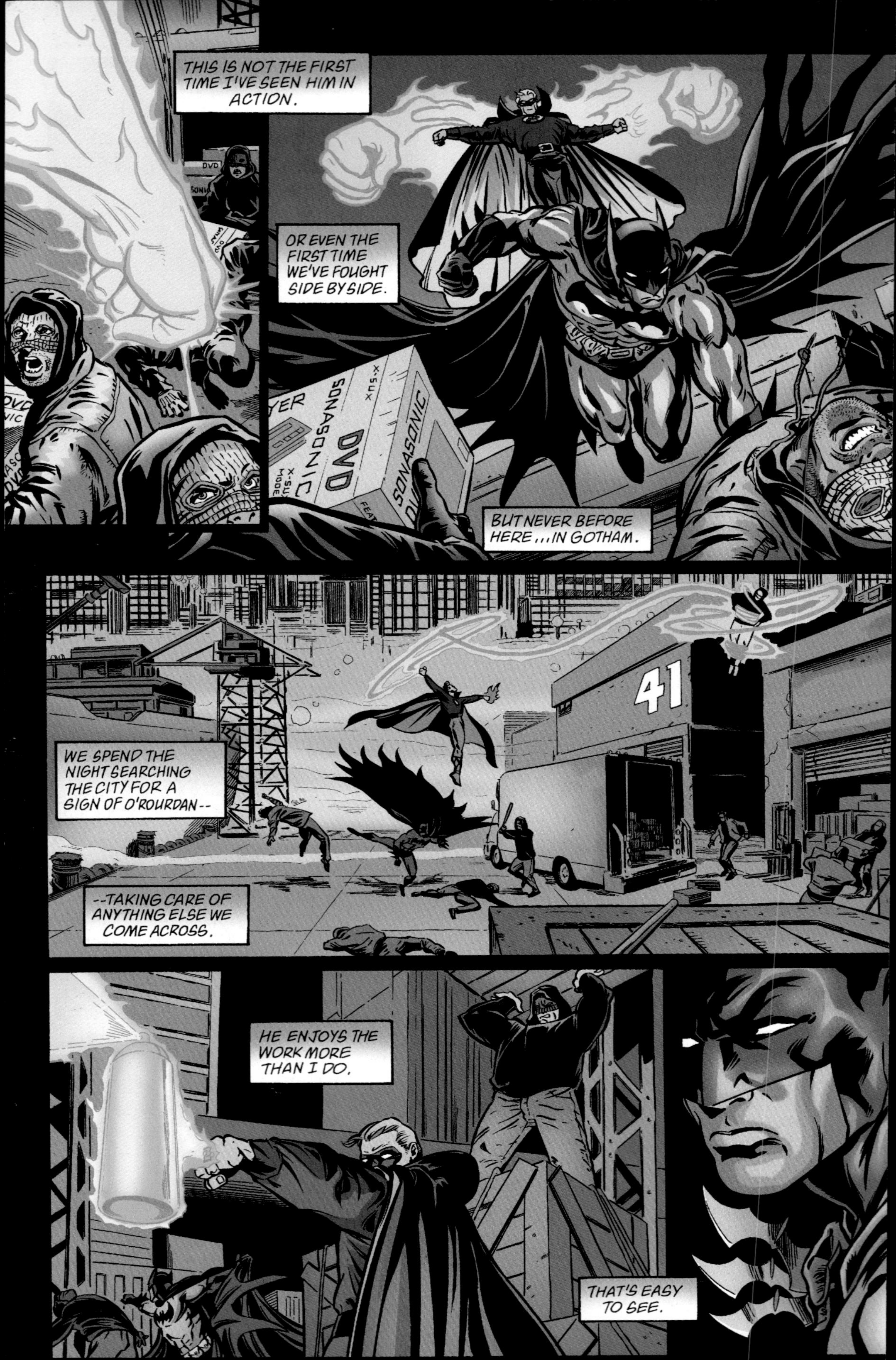
THIS IS NOT THE FIRST TIME I'VE SEEN HIM IN ACTION.
DVD
SONASONIC
DVD
OR EVEN THE FIRST TIME WE'VE FOUGHT SIDE BY SIDE.
X-SUX
DVD
SONASONIC
SONASONIC
BUT NEVER BEFORE HERE,,, IN GOTHAM.
41
WE SPEND THE NIGHT SEARCHING THE CITY FOR A SIGN OF O'ROURDAN--
--TAKING CARE OF ANYTHING ELSE WE COME ACROSS.
HE ENJOYS THE WORK MORE THAN I DO.
THAT'S EASY TO SEE.

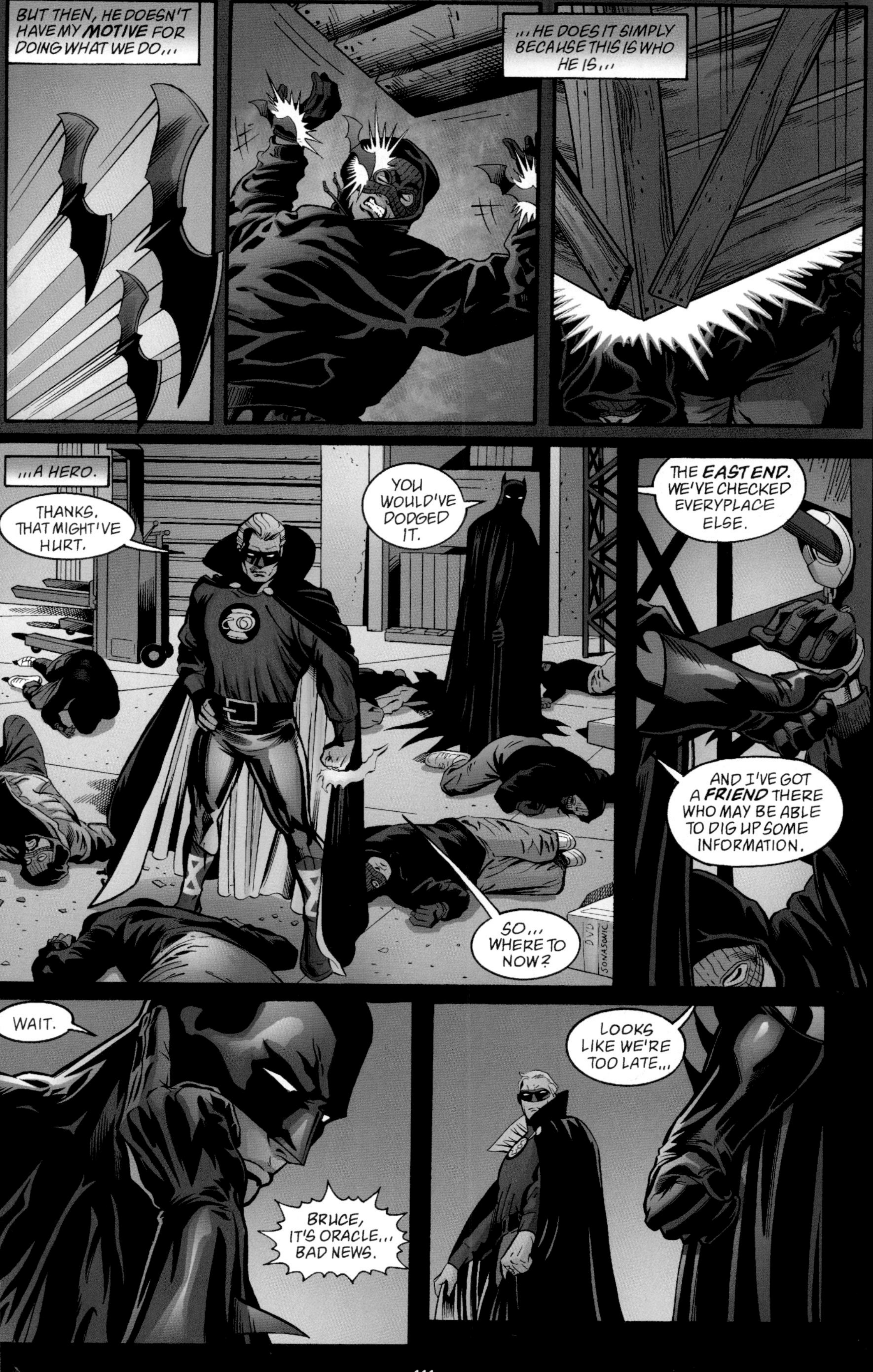
BUT THEN, HE DOESN'T HAVE MY MOTIVE FOR DOING WHAT WE DO,,,
,,,HE DOES IT SIMPLY BECAUSE THIS IS WHO HE IS,,,
,,,A HERO.
THANKS. THAT MIGHT'VE HURT.
YOU WOULD'VE DODGED IT.
SO,,, WHERE TO NOW?
THE EAST END. WE'VE CHECKED EVERYPLACE ELSE.
AND I'VE GOT A FRIEND THERE WHO MAY BE ABLE TO DIG UP SOME INFORMATION.
WAIT.
BRUCE, IT'S ORACLE,,, BAD NEWS.
LOOKS LIKE WE'RE TOO LATE,,,

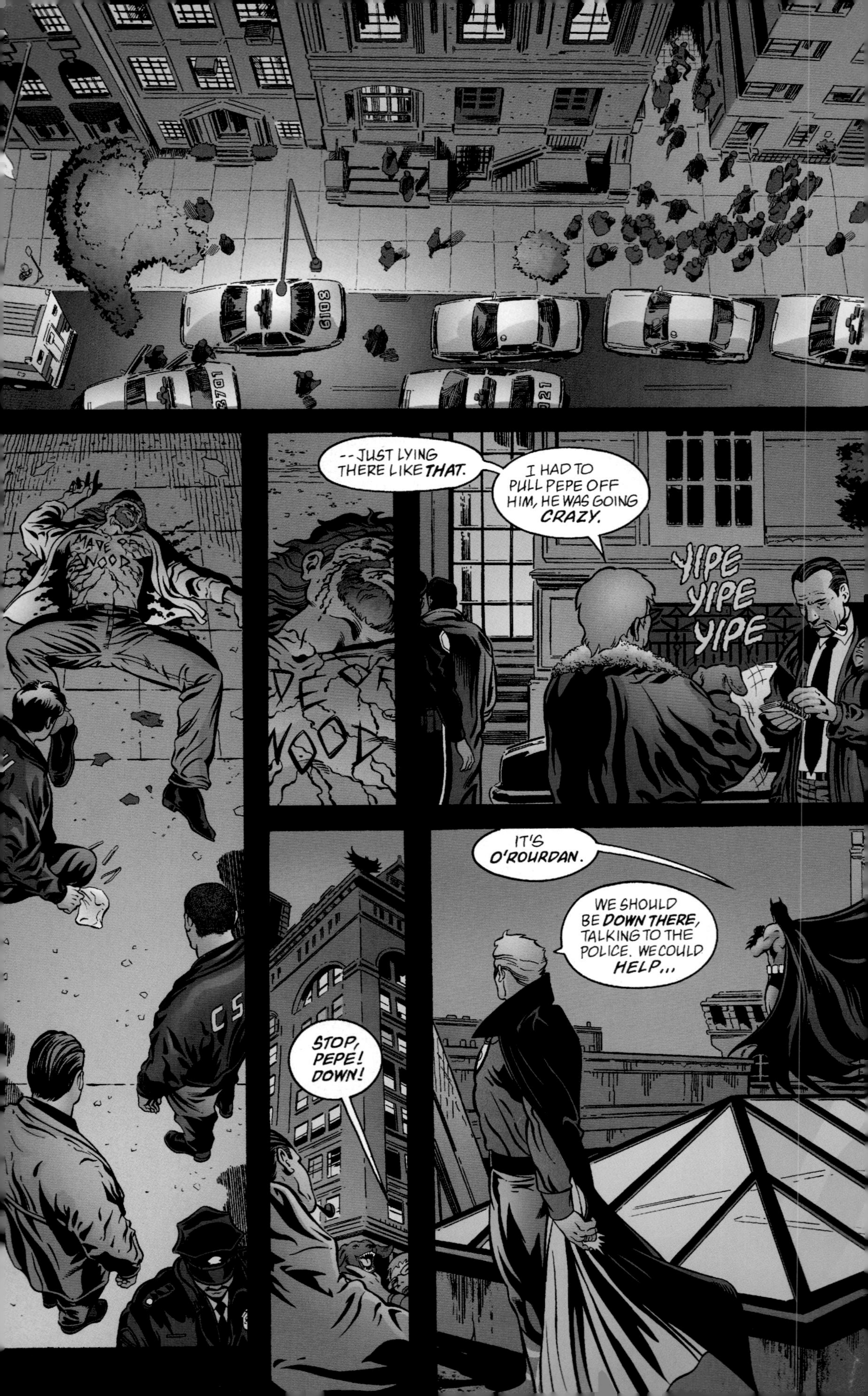
MADE OF WOOD
MADE OF WOOD
--JUST LYING THERE LIKE THAT.
I HAD TO PULL PEPE OFF HIM, HE WAS GOING CRAZY.
YIPE YIPE YIPE
IT'S O'ROURDAN.
WE SHOULD BE DOWN THERE, TALKING TO THE POLICE. WE COULD HELP...
STOP, PEPE! DOWN!

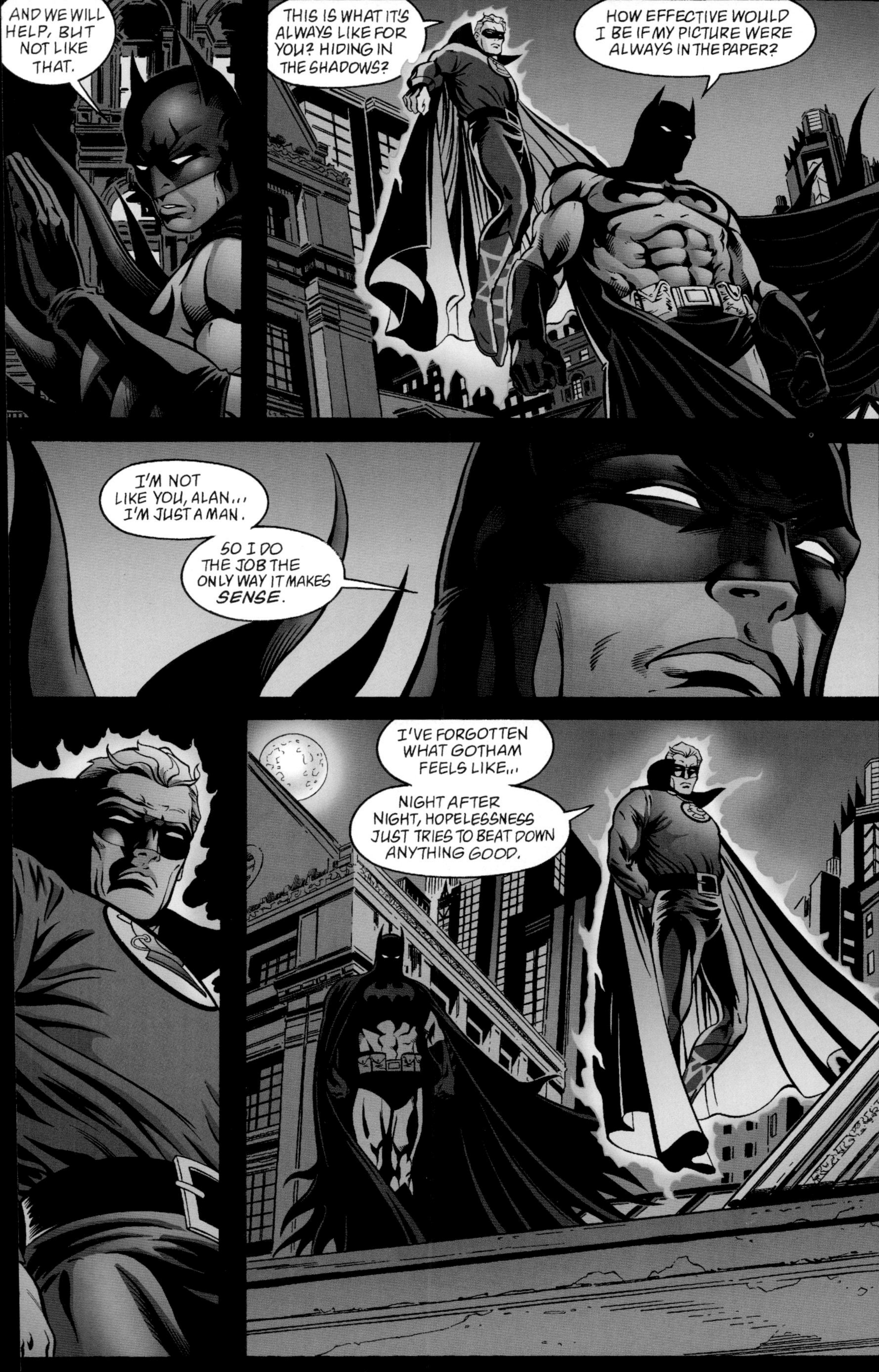
AND WE WILL HELP, BUT NOT LIKE THAT.
THIS IS WHAT IT'S ALWAYS LIKE FOR YOU? HIDING IN THE SHADOWS?
HOW EFFECTIVE WOULD I BE IF MY PICTURE WERE ALWAYS IN THE PAPER?
I'M NOT LIKE YOU, ALAN... I'M JUST A MAN.
SO I DO THE JOB THE ONLY WAY IT MAKES SENSE.
I'VE FORGOTTEN WHAT GOTHAM FEELS LIKE...
NIGHT AFTER NIGHT, HOPELESSNESS JUST TRIES TO BEAT DOWN ANYTHING GOOD.

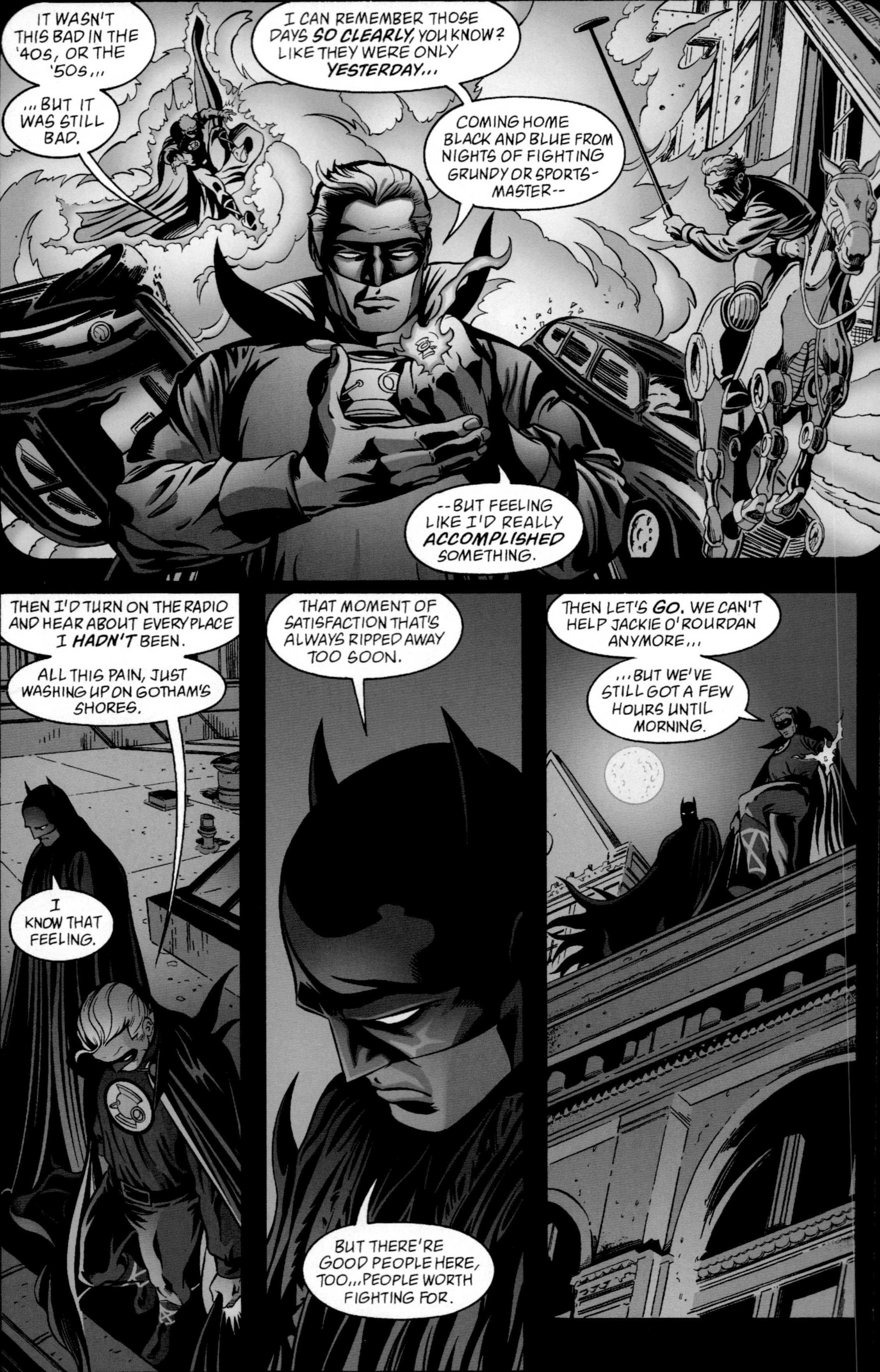
IT WASN'T THIS BAD IN THE '40S, OR THE '50S...
...BUT IT WAS STILL BAD.
I CAN REMEMBER THOSE DAYS SO CLEARLY, YOU KNOW? LIKE THEY WERE ONLY YESTERDAY...
COMING HOME BLACK AND BLUE FROM NIGHTS OF FIGHTING GRUNDY OR SPORTSMASTER--
--BUT FEELING LIKE I'D REALLY ACCOMPLISHED SOMETHING.
THEN I'D TURN ON THE RADIO AND HEAR ABOUT EVERY PLACE I HADN'T BEEN.
ALL THIS PAIN, JUST WASHING UP ON GOTHAM'S SHORES.
I KNOW THAT FEELING.
THAT MOMENT OF SATISFACTION THAT'S ALWAYS RIPPED AWAY TOO SOON.
BUT THERE'RE GOOD PEOPLE HERE, TOO...PEOPLE WORTH FIGHTING FOR.
THEN LET'S GO. WE CAN'T HELP JACKIE O'ROURDAN ANYMORE...
...BUT WE'VE STILL GOT A FEW HOURS UNTIL MORNING.

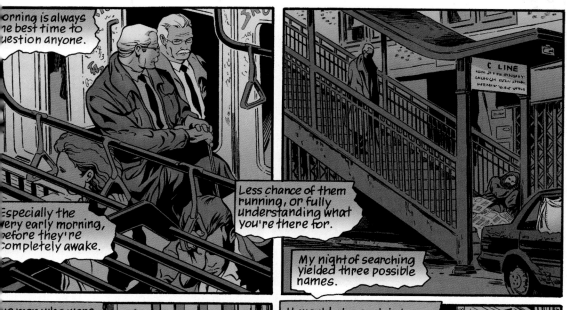

orning is always ne best time to uestion anyone.

Especially the very early morning, before they're completely awake.

Less chance of them running, or fully understanding what you're there for.

My night of searching yielded three possible names.

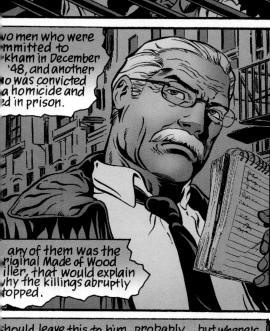

wo men who were mmitted to rkham in December '48, and another o was convicted a homicide and d in prison.

any of them was the riginal Made of Wood iller, that would explain hy the killings abruptly topped.

It would also explain how a new murderer might know the intimate details of those crimes. Things the police never knew.

Because these men were alive for a long time after the crimes stopped, and they could have told relatives or even cellmates.

should leave this to him, probably... but where's e danger in asking a few questions?

o have the ining, and I n't just sit my hands day long.

My first stop, an old cellmate of a homicidal maniac, is a dead end.

The man can barely walk, and he swears he doesn't know anything about any killings. I believe him.

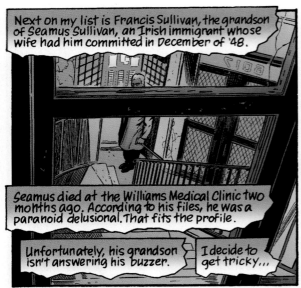

Next on my list is Francis Sullivan, the grandson of Seamus Sullivan, an Irish immigrant whose wife had him committed in December of '48.

Seamus died at the Williams Medical Clinic two months ago. According to his files, he was a paranoid delusional. That fits the profile.

Unfortunately, his grandson isn't answering his buzzer.

I decide to get tricky...

...and buzz the super to see if he'll let me into the building... never hurts to ask, as long as you have a decent lie.

RICHARD DILLIN

D. L. NEWTON

H. EUGENE DAY

ELI KATZ

OFFICE: BUILDING SUPERINTENDENT

MORTIMER

YEAH?

SORRY TO BOTHER YOU. I'M SUPPOSED TO MEET FRANCIS SULLIVAN...

HIS GRANDFATHER PASSED AWAY A FEW MONTHS AGO AND FRANCIS IS THE SOLE BENEFICIARY OF HIS WILL.

REALLY? THAT LITTLE SCUMBALL'S GONNA BE RICH ALL OF A SUDDEN?

JEEZ, WHAT KIND OF JUSTICE IS THAT?

WELL, IN ANY CASE, I NEED HIM TO SIGN SOME DOCUMENTS, AND I WAS WONDERING IF I COULD WAIT INSIDE?

SURE, I GUESS SO...MAYBE OLD FRANNY'LL THROW ME A FINDER'S FEE, YOU THINK?

IT'S BEEN KNOWN TO HAPPEN.

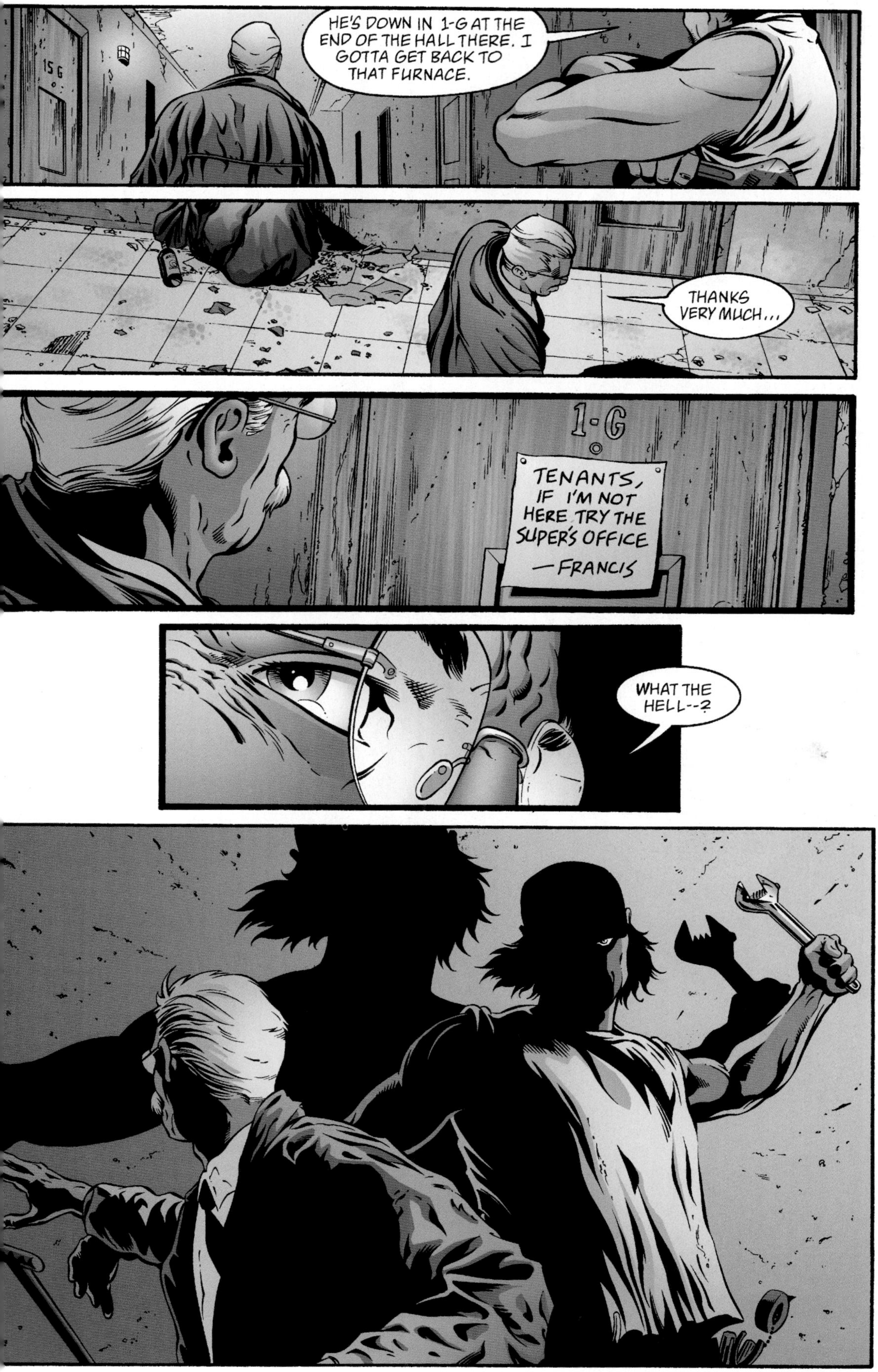
HE'S DOWN IN 1-G AT THE END OF THE HALL THERE. I GOTTA GET BACK TO THAT FURNACE.
15 G
THANKS VERY MUCH...
1-G
TENANTS, IF I'M NOT HERE TRY THE SUPER'S OFFICE —FRANCIS
WHAT THE HELL--?

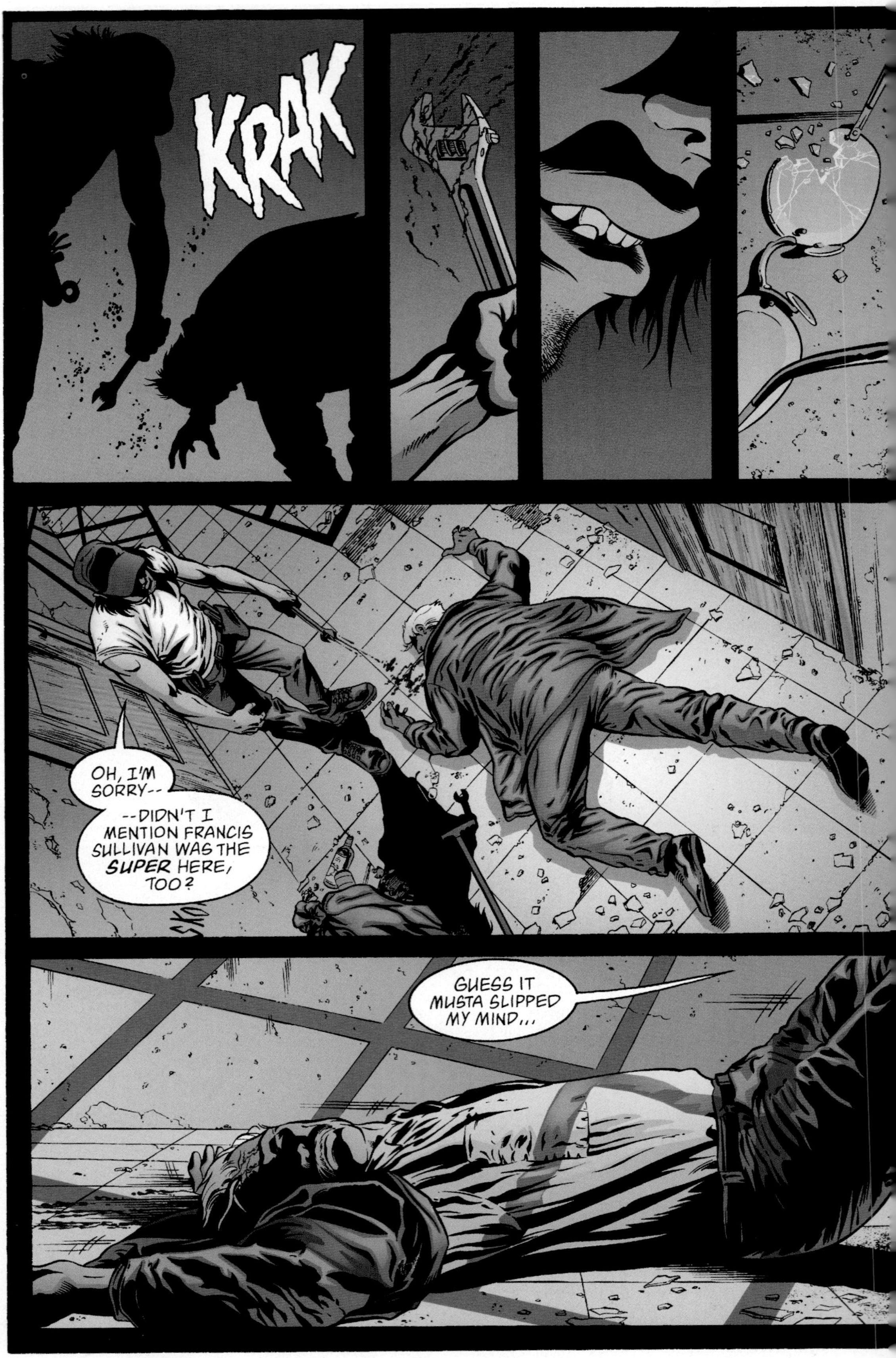
KRAK
OH, I'M SORRY--
--DIDN'T I MENTION FRANCIS SULLIVAN WAS THE SUPER HERE, TOO?
GUESS IT MUSTA SLIPPED MY MIND...

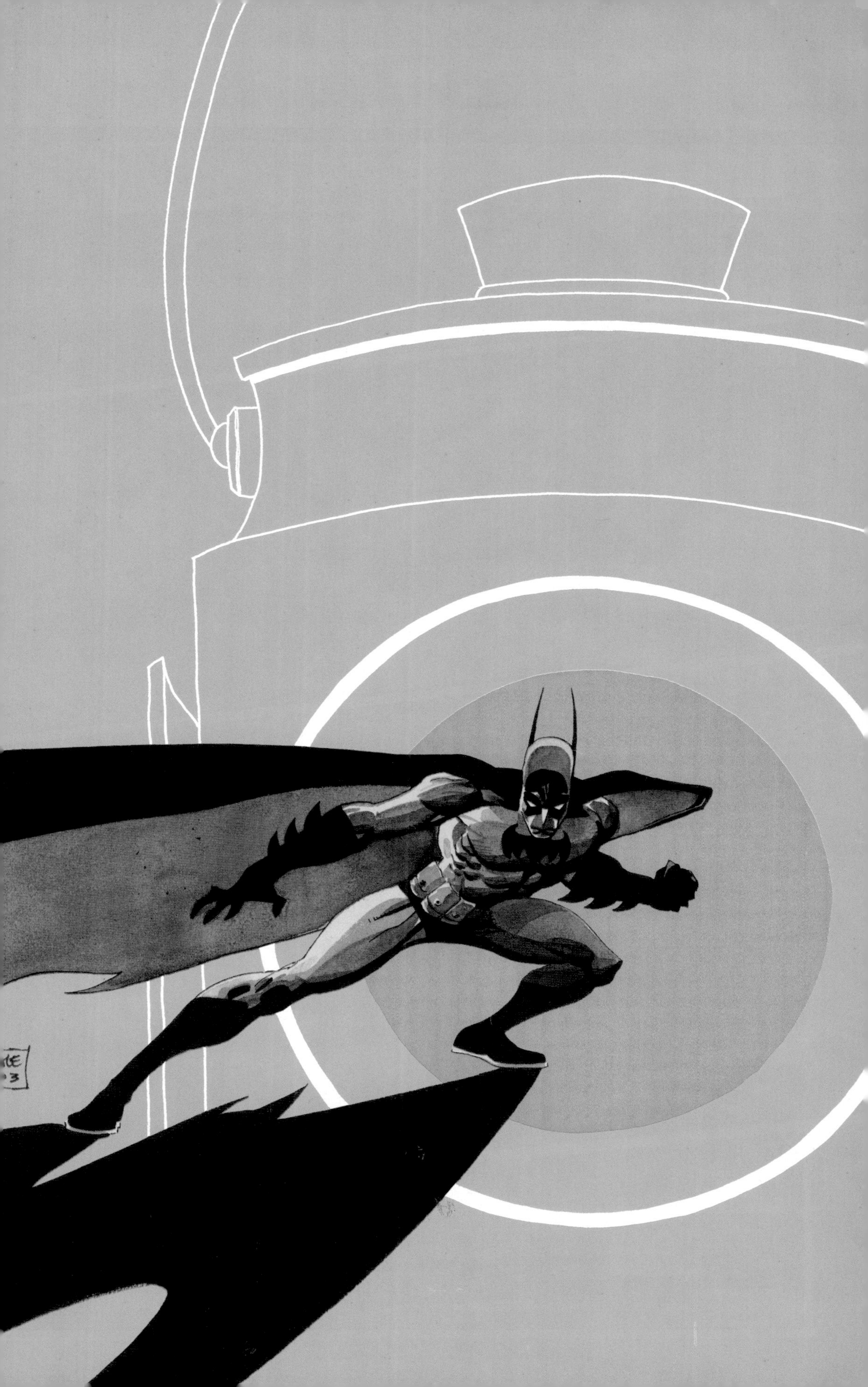

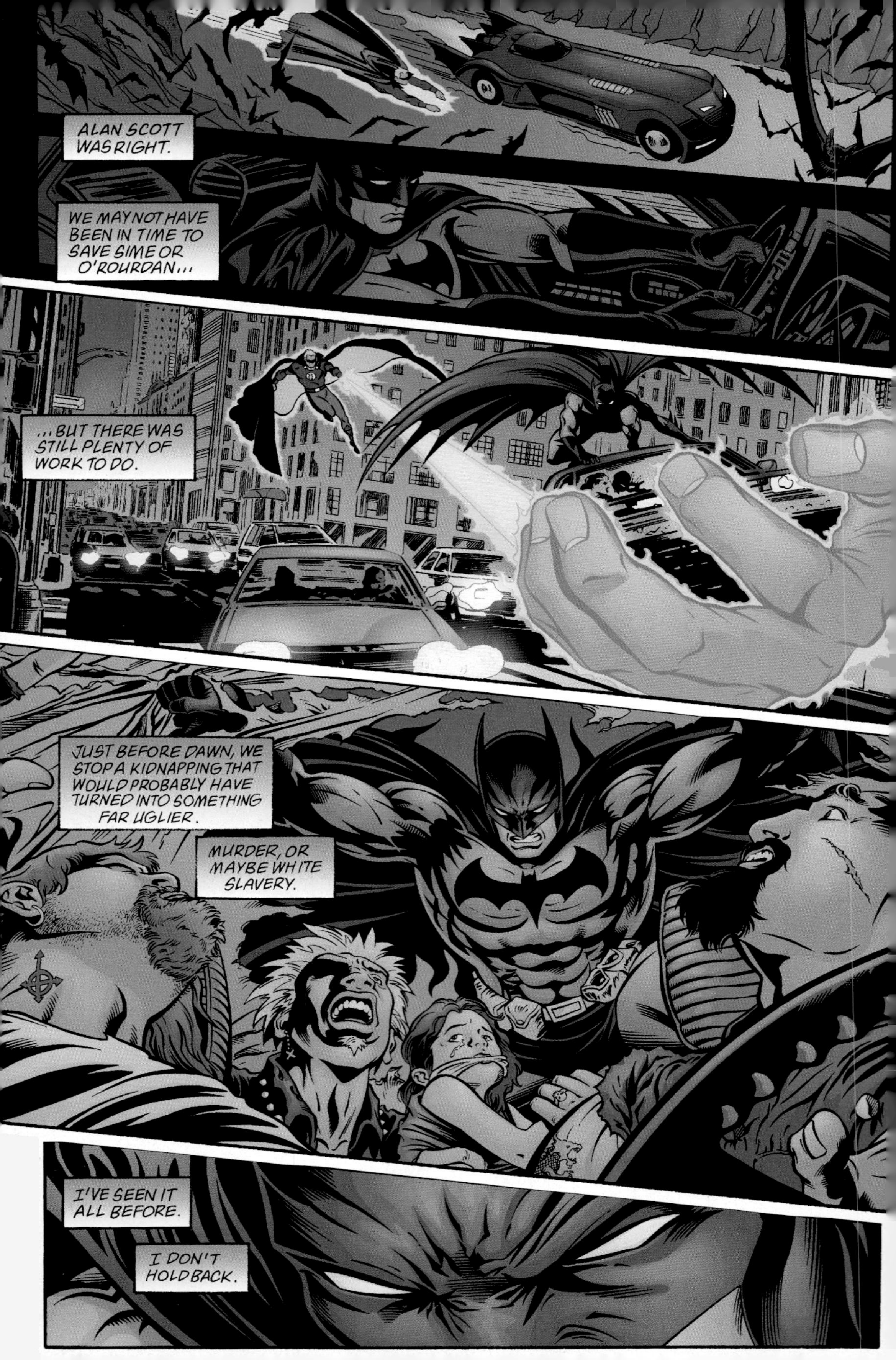
ALAN SCOTT WAS RIGHT.
WE MAY NOT HAVE BEEN IN TIME TO SAVE SIME OR O'ROURDAN...
...BUT THERE WAS STILL PLENTY OF WORK TO DO.
JUST BEFORE DAWN, WE STOP A KIDNAPPING THAT WOULD PROBABLY HAVE TURNED INTO SOMETHING FAR UGLIER.
MURDER, OR MAYBE WHITE SLAVERY.
I'VE SEEN IT ALL BEFORE.
I DON'T HOLD BACK.

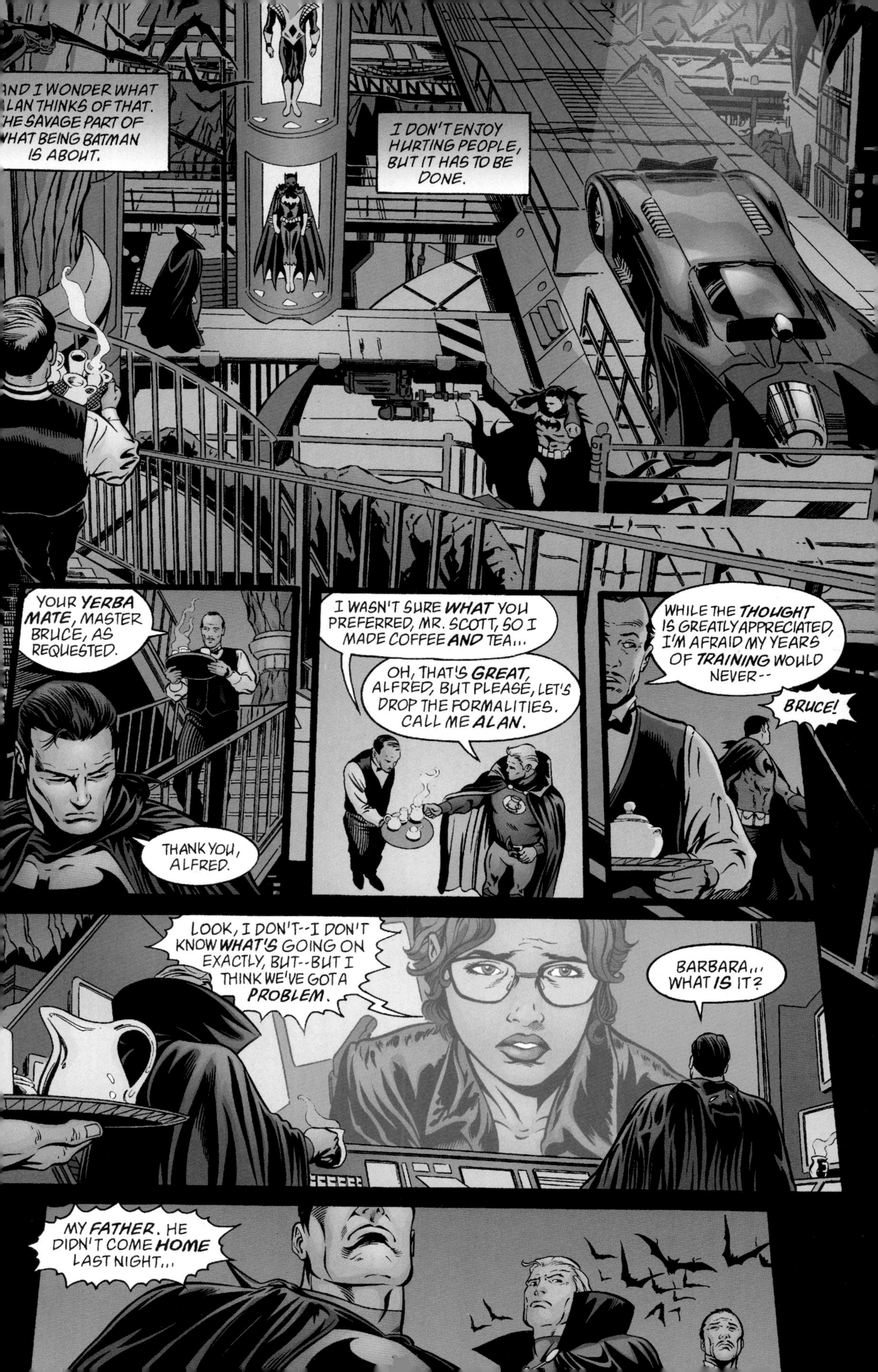
AND I WONDER WHAT ALAN THINKS OF THAT. THE SAVAGE PART OF WHAT BEING BATMAN IS ABOUT.
I DON'T ENJOY HURTING PEOPLE, BUT IT HAS TO BE DONE.
YOUR YERBA MATE, MASTER BRUCE, AS REQUESTED.
THANK YOU, ALFRED.
I WASN'T SURE WHAT YOU PREFERRED, MR. SCOTT, SO I MADE COFFEE AND TEA...
OH, THAT'S GREAT, ALFRED, BUT PLEASE, LET'S DROP THE FORMALITIES. CALL ME ALAN.
WHILE THE THOUGHT IS GREATLY APPRECIATED, I'M AFRAID MY YEARS OF TRAINING WOULD NEVER--
BRUCE!
LOOK, I DON'T--I DON'T KNOW WHAT'S GOING ON EXACTLY, BUT--BUT I THINK WE'VE GOT A PROBLEM.
BARBARA... WHAT IS IT?
MY FATHER. HE DIDN'T COME HOME LAST NIGHT...

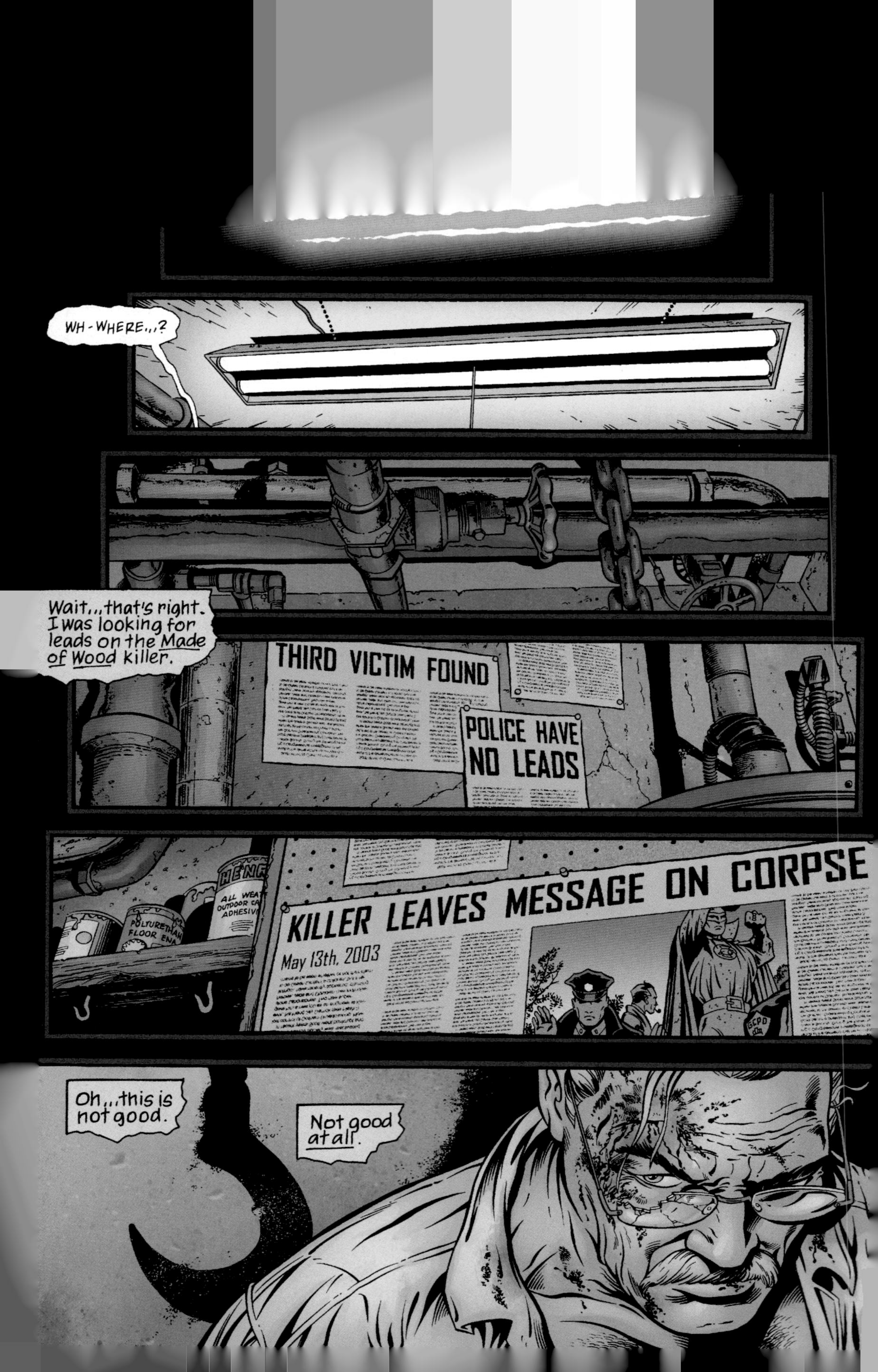

WH-WHERE...?
Wait...that's right. I was looking for leads on the Made of Wood killer.
THIRD VICTIM FOUND
POLICE HAVE NO LEADS
KILLER LEAVES MESSAGE ON CORPSE
May 13th, 2003
POLYURETHAN FLOOR ENA
ALL WEAT OUTDOOR CA ADHESIV
Oh...this is not good.
Not good at all.

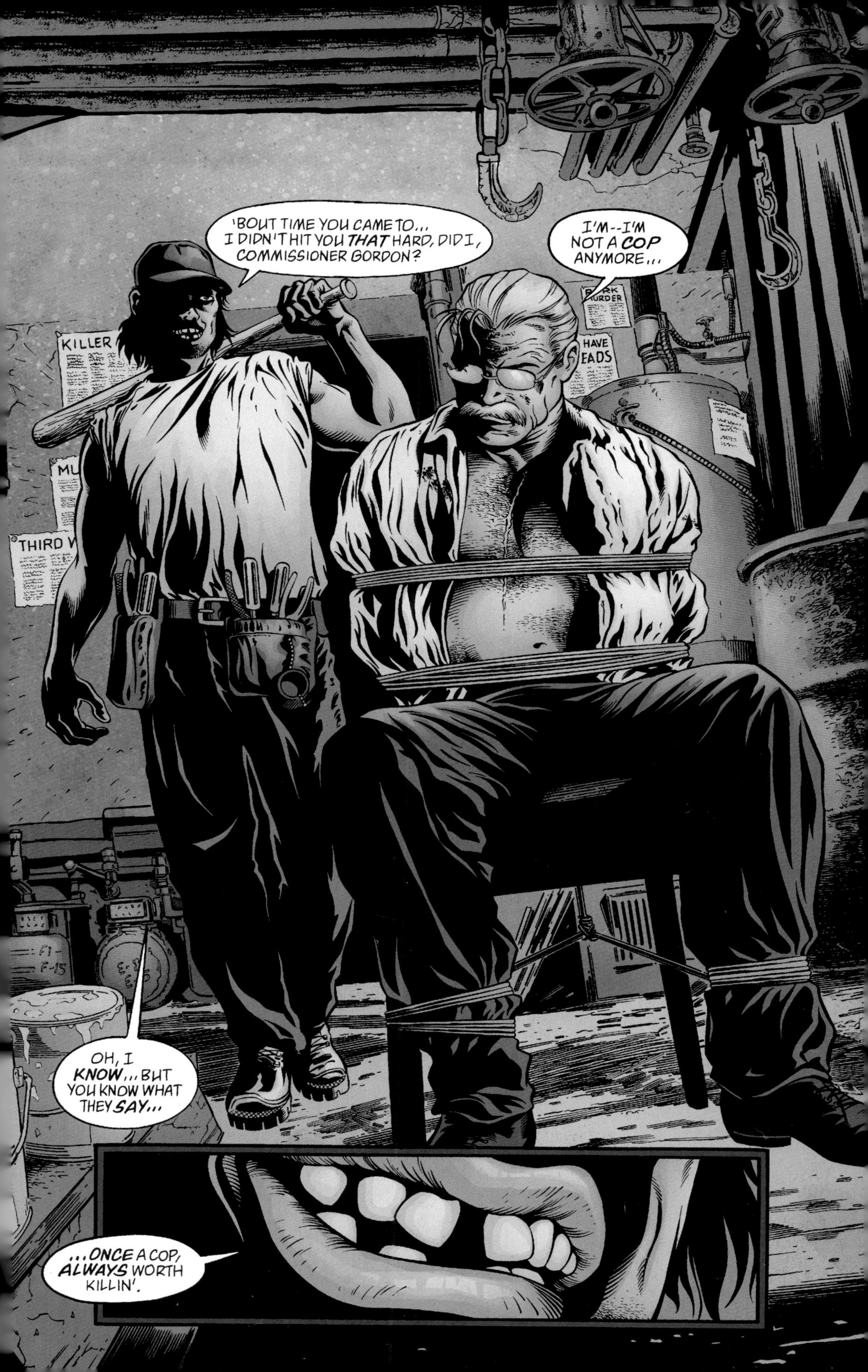
'BOUT TIME YOU CAME TO... I DIDN'T HIT YOU THAT HARD, DID I, COMMISSIONER GORDON?
I'M--I'M NOT A COP ANYMORE...
OH, I KNOW... BUT YOU KNOW WHAT THEY SAY...
...ONCE A COP, ALWAYS WORTH KILLIN'.

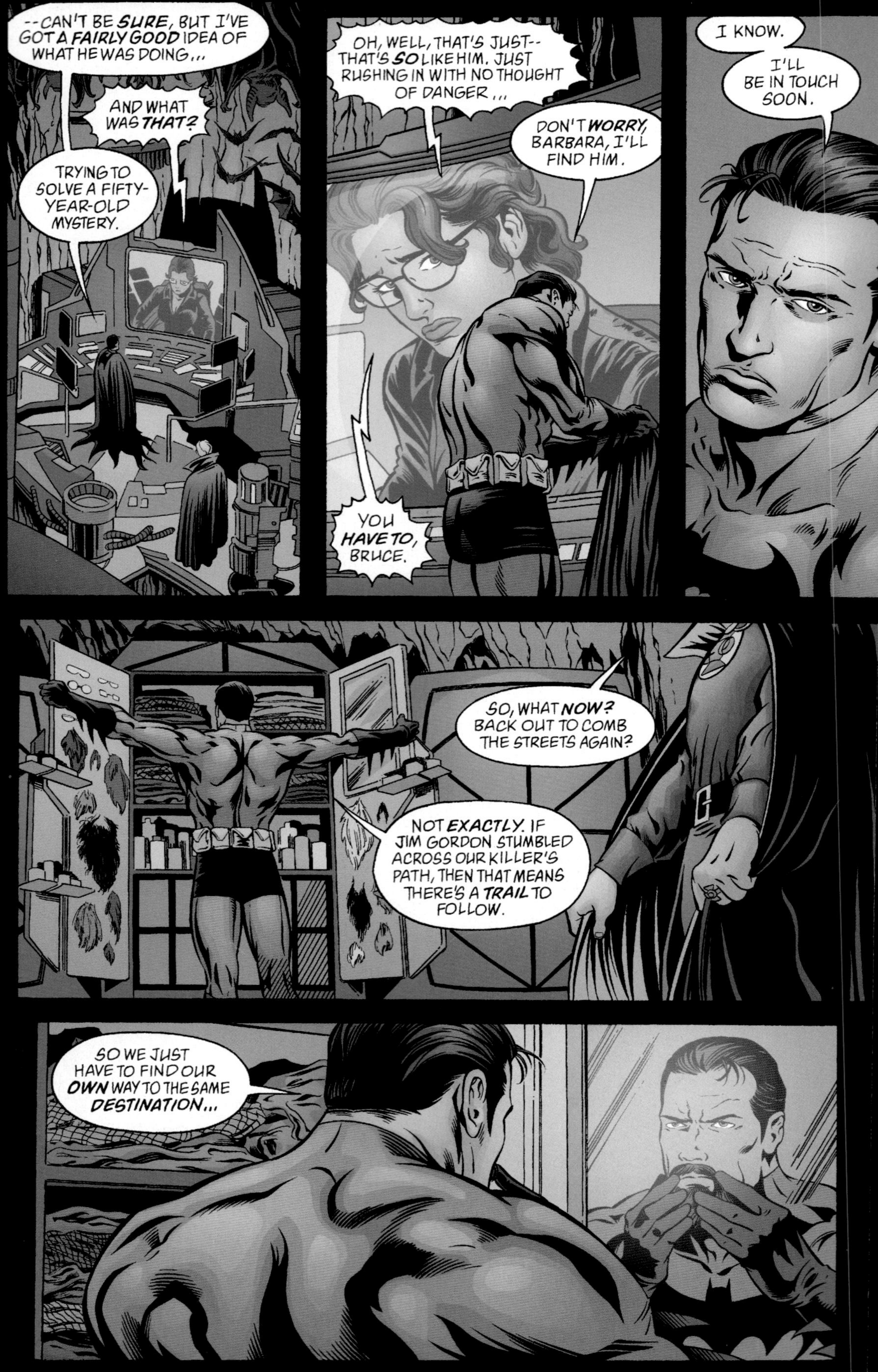
--CAN'T BE SURE, BUT I'VE GOT A FAIRLY GOOD IDEA OF WHAT HE WAS DOING...
AND WHAT WAS THAT?
TRYING TO SOLVE A FIFTY-YEAR-OLD MYSTERY.
OH, WELL, THAT'S JUST-- THAT'S SO LIKE HIM. JUST RUSHING IN WITH NO THOUGHT OF DANGER...
DON'T WORRY, BARBARA, I'LL FIND HIM.
YOU HAVE TO, BRUCE.
I KNOW.
I'LL BE IN TOUCH SOON.
SO, WHAT NOW? BACK OUT TO COMB THE STREETS AGAIN?
NOT EXACTLY. IF JIM GORDON STUMBLED ACROSS OUR KILLER'S PATH, THEN THAT MEANS THERE'S A TRAIL TO FOLLOW.
SO WE JUST HAVE TO FIND OUR OWN WAY TO THE SAME DESTINATION...

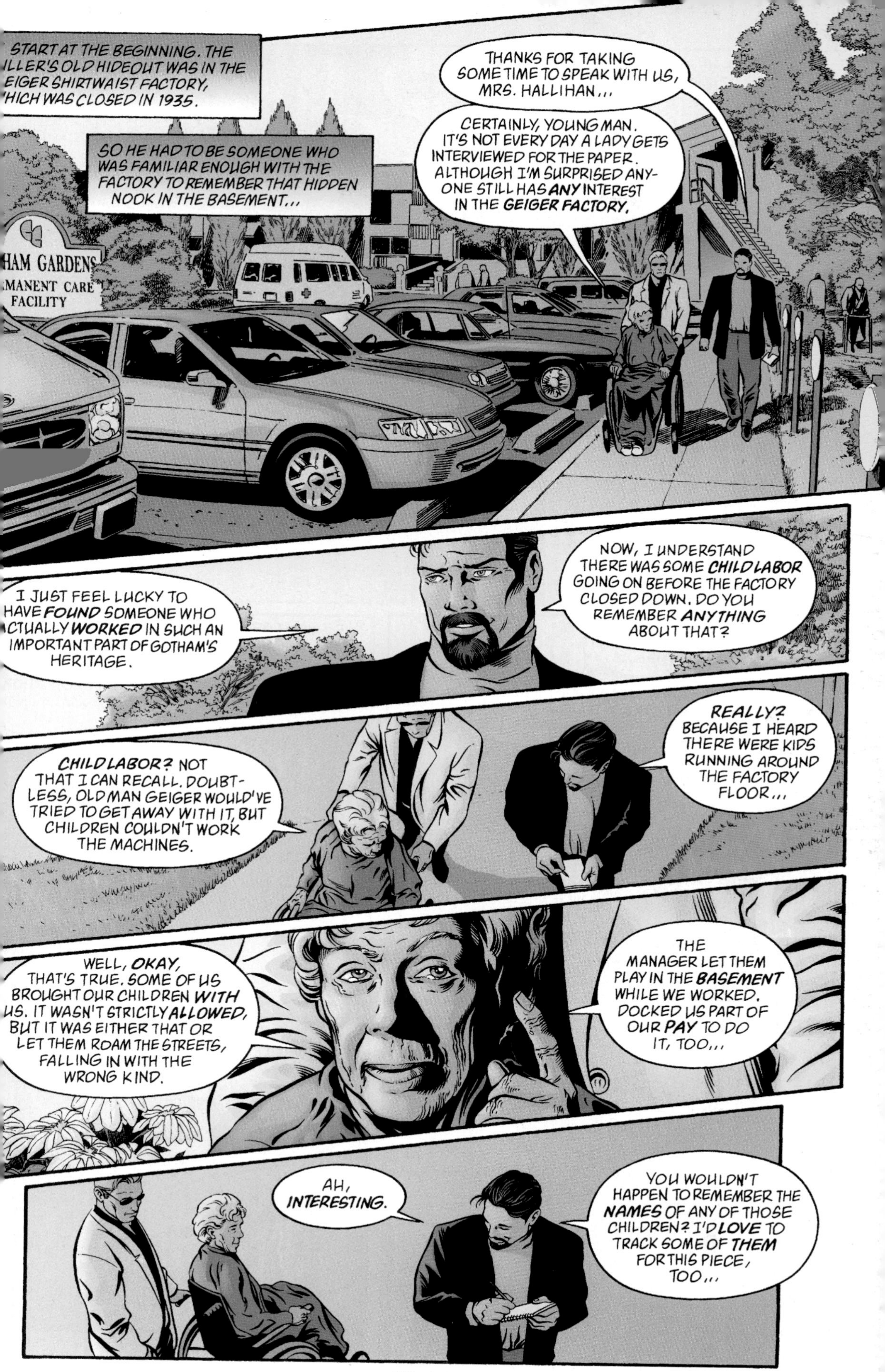
START AT THE BEGINNING. THE ILLER'S OLD HIDEOUT WAS IN THE EIGER SHIRTWAIST FACTORY, HICH WAS CLOSED IN 1935.
SO HE HAD TO BE SOMEONE WHO WAS FAMILIAR ENOUGH WITH THE FACTORY TO REMEMBER THAT HIDDEN NOOK IN THE BASEMENT...
THANKS FOR TAKING SOME TIME TO SPEAK WITH US, MRS. HALLIHAN...
CERTAINLY, YOUNG MAN. IT'S NOT EVERY DAY A LADY GETS INTERVIEWED FOR THE PAPER. ALTHOUGH I'M SURPRISED ANYONE STILL HAS ANY INTEREST IN THE GEIGER FACTORY.
HAM GARDENS
MANENT CARE
FACILITY
I JUST FEEL LUCKY TO HAVE FOUND SOMEONE WHO CTUALLY WORKED IN SUCH AN IMPORTANT PART OF GOTHAM'S HERITAGE.
NOW, I UNDERSTAND THERE WAS SOME CHILD LABOR GOING ON BEFORE THE FACTORY CLOSED DOWN. DO YOU REMEMBER ANYTHING ABOUT THAT?
CHILD LABOR? NOT THAT I CAN RECALL. DOUBTLESS, OLD MAN GEIGER WOULD'VE TRIED TO GET AWAY WITH IT, BUT CHILDREN COULDN'T WORK THE MACHINES.
REALLY? BECAUSE I HEARD THERE WERE KIDS RUNNING AROUND THE FACTORY FLOOR...
WELL, OKAY, THAT'S TRUE. SOME OF US BROUGHT OUR CHILDREN WITH US. IT WASN'T STRICTLY ALLOWED, BUT IT WAS EITHER THAT OR LET THEM ROAM THE STREETS, FALLING IN WITH THE WRONG KIND.
THE MANAGER LET THEM PLAY IN THE BASEMENT WHILE WE WORKED. DOCKED US PART OF OUR PAY TO DO IT, TOO...
AH, INTERESTING.
YOU WOULDN'T HAPPEN TO REMEMBER THE NAMES OF ANY OF THOSE CHILDREN? I'D LOVE TO TRACK SOME OF THEM FOR THIS PIECE, TOO...

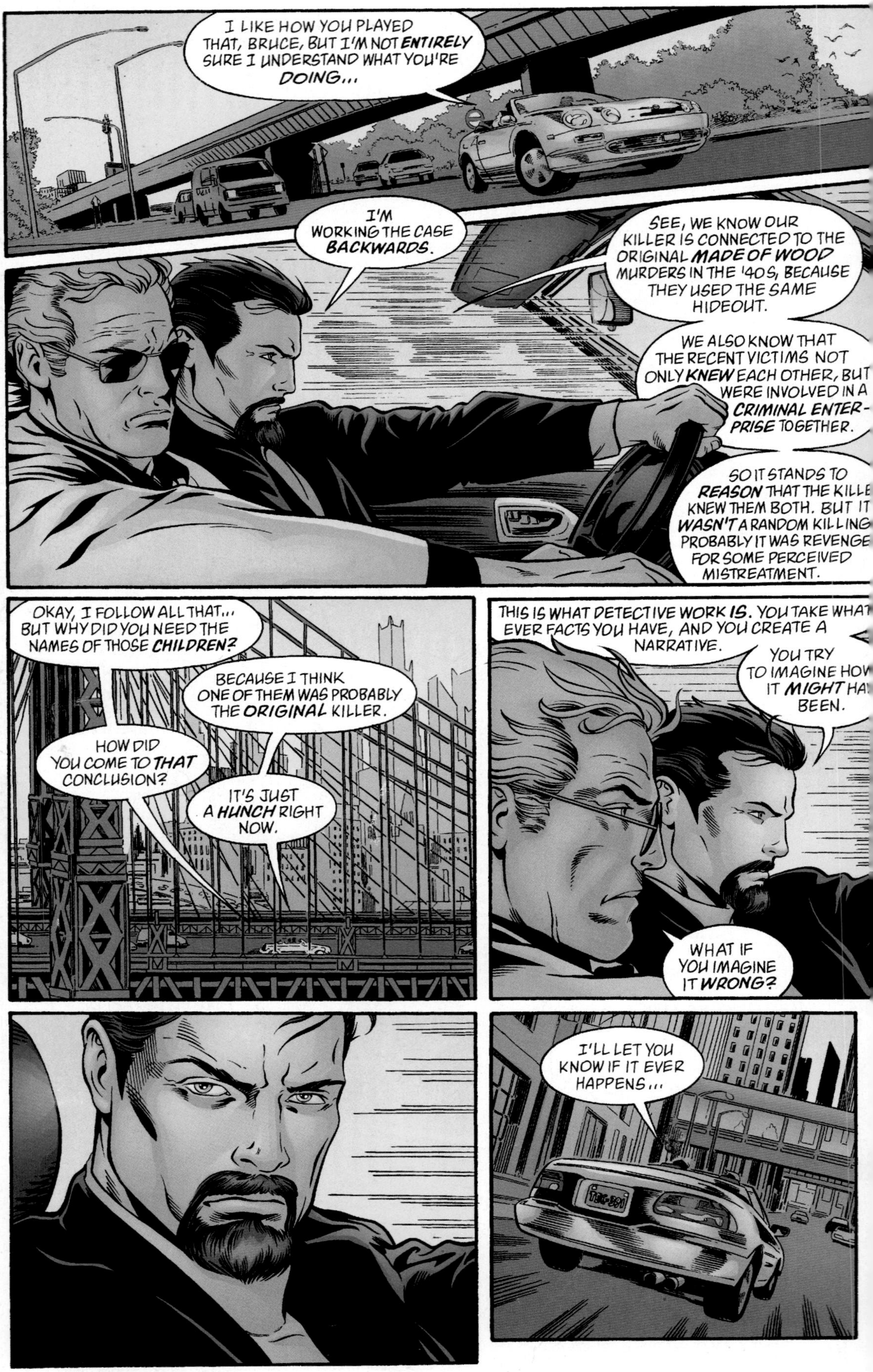

I LIKE HOW YOU PLAYED THAT, BRUCE, BUT I'M NOT ENTIRELY SURE I UNDERSTAND WHAT YOU'RE DOING...
I'M WORKING THE CASE BACKWARDS.
SEE, WE KNOW OUR KILLER IS CONNECTED TO THE ORIGINAL MADE OF WOOD MURDERS IN THE '40S, BECAUSE THEY USED THE SAME HIDEOUT.
WE ALSO KNOW THAT THE RECENT VICTIMS NOT ONLY KNEW EACH OTHER, BUT WERE INVOLVED IN A CRIMINAL ENTERPRISE TOGETHER.
SO IT STANDS TO REASON THAT THE KILLE KNEW THEM BOTH. BUT IT WASN'T A RANDOM KILLING PROBABLY IT WAS REVENGE FOR SOME PERCEIVED MISTREATMENT.
OKAY, I FOLLOW ALL THAT... BUT WHY DID YOU NEED THE NAMES OF THOSE CHILDREN?
BECAUSE I THINK ONE OF THEM WAS PROBABLY THE ORIGINAL KILLER.
HOW DID YOU COME TO THAT CONCLUSION?
IT'S JUST A HUNCH RIGHT NOW.
THIS IS WHAT DETECTIVE WORK IS. YOU TAKE WHAT EVER FACTS YOU HAVE, AND YOU CREATE A NARRATIVE.
YOU TRY TO IMAGINE HOW IT MIGHT HA BEEN.
WHAT IF YOU IMAGINE IT WRONG?
I'LL LET YOU KNOW IF IT EVER HAPPENS...

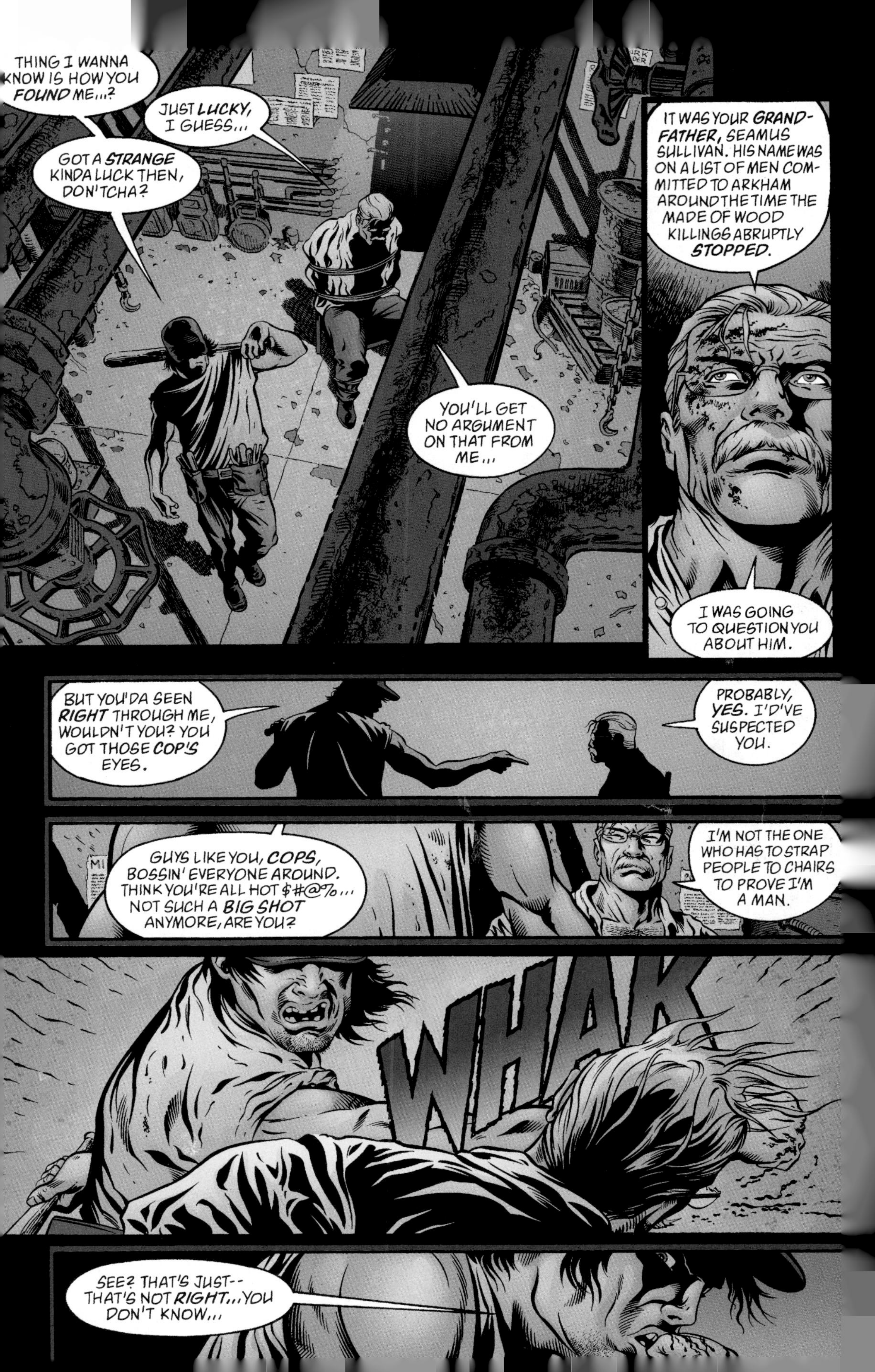
THING I WANNA KNOW IS HOW YOU FOUND ME...?
JUST LUCKY, I GUESS...
GOT A STRANGE KINDA LUCK THEN, DON'TCHA?
YOU'LL GET NO ARGUMENT ON THAT FROM ME...
IT WAS YOUR GRAND-FATHER, SEAMUS SULLIVAN. HIS NAME WAS ON A LIST OF MEN COM-MITTED TO ARKHAM AROUND THE TIME THE MADE OF WOOD KILLINGS ABRUPTLY STOPPED.
I WAS GOING TO QUESTION YOU ABOUT HIM.
BUT YOU'DA SEEN RIGHT THROUGH ME, WOULDN'T YOU? YOU GOT THOSE COP'S EYES.
PROBABLY, YES. I'D'VE SUSPECTED YOU.
GUYS LIKE YOU, COPS, BOSSIN' EVERYONE AROUND. THINK YOU'RE ALL HOT $#@%... NOT SUCH A BIG SHOT ANYMORE, ARE YOU?
I'M NOT THE ONE WHO HAS TO STRAP PEOPLE TO CHAIRS TO PROVE I'M A MAN.
WHAK
SEE? THAT'S JUST-- THAT'S NOT RIGHT...YOU DON'T KNOW...

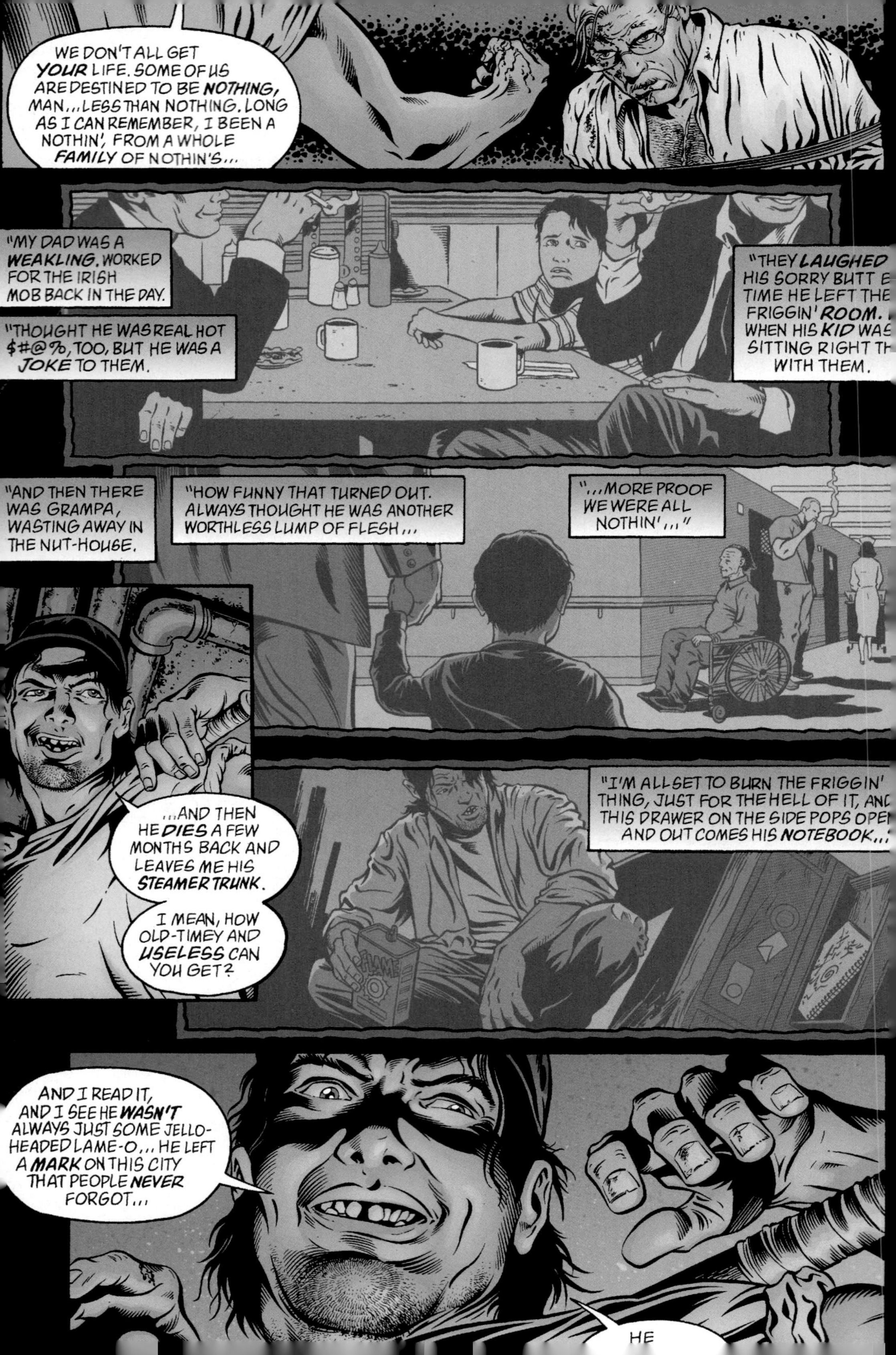

WE DON'T ALL GET YOUR LIFE. SOME OF US ARE DESTINED TO BE NOTHING, MAN... LESS THAN NOTHING. LONG AS I CAN REMEMBER, I BEEN A NOTHIN', FROM A WHOLE FAMILY OF NOTHIN'S...
"MY DAD WAS A WEAKLING. WORKED FOR THE IRISH MOB BACK IN THE DAY.
"THOUGHT HE WAS REAL HOT $#@%, TOO, BUT HE WAS A JOKE TO THEM.
"THEY LAUGHED HIS SORRY BUTT E TIME HE LEFT THE FRIGGIN' ROOM. WHEN HIS KID WAS SITTING RIGHT TH WITH THEM.
"AND THEN THERE WAS GRAMPA, WASTING AWAY IN THE NUT-HOUSE.
"HOW FUNNY THAT TURNED OUT. ALWAYS THOUGHT HE WAS ANOTHER WORTHLESS LUMP OF FLESH...
"...MORE PROOF WE WERE ALL NOTHIN'..."
...AND THEN HE DIES A FEW MONTHS BACK AND LEAVES ME HIS STEAMER TRUNK.
I MEAN, HOW OLD-TIMEY AND USELESS CAN YOU GET?
"I'M ALL SET TO BURN THE FRIGGIN' THING, JUST FOR THE HELL OF IT, AND THIS DRAWER ON THE SIDE POPS OPEN AND OUT COMES HIS NOTEBOOK...
FLAME
AND I READ IT, AND I SEE HE WASN'T ALWAYS JUST SOME JELLO-HEADED LAME-O... HE LEFT A MARK ON THIS CITY THAT PEOPLE NEVER FORGOT...
HE

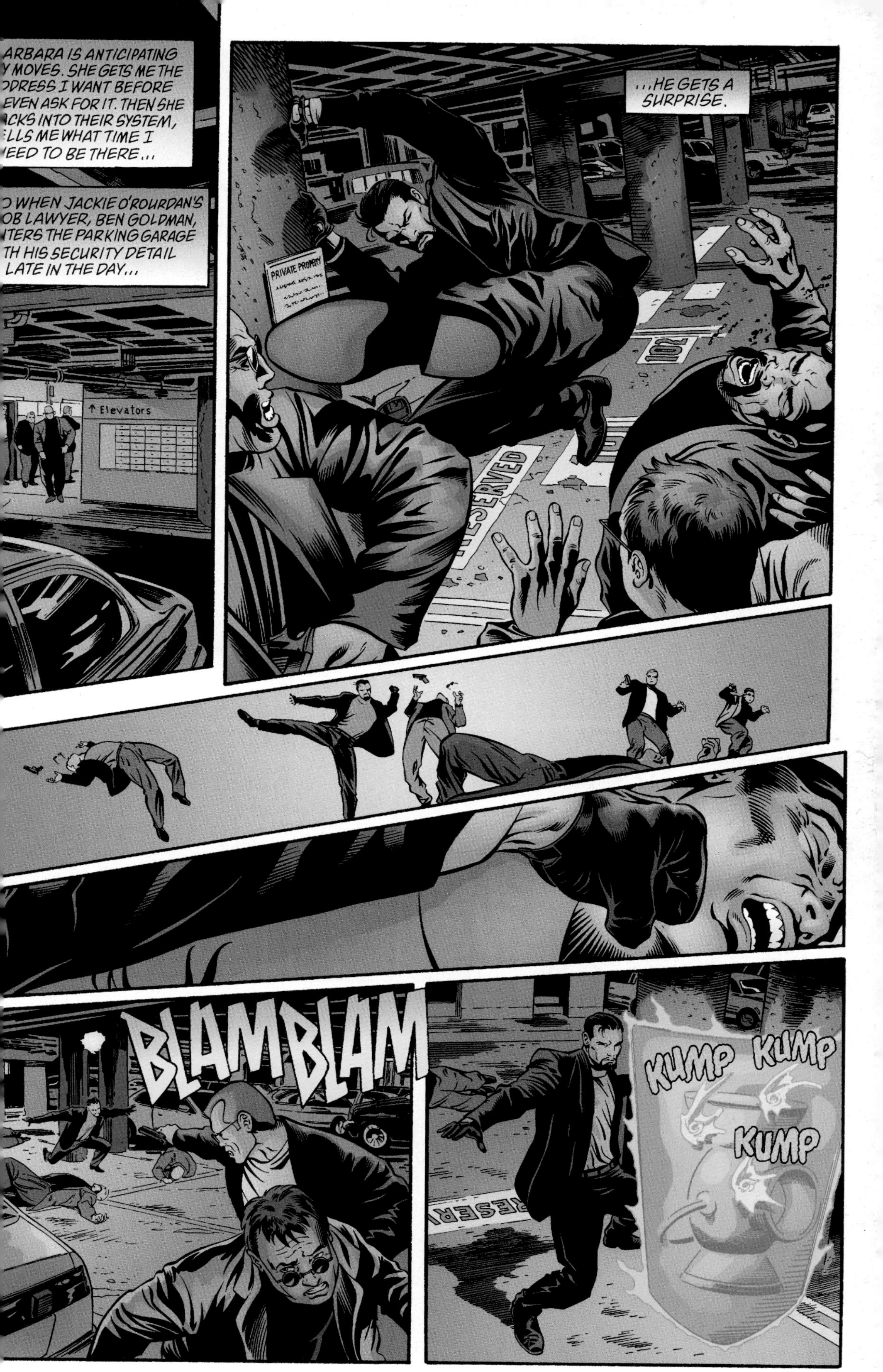
ARBARA IS ANTICIPATING Y MOVES. SHE GETS ME THE DDRESS I WANT BEFORE EVEN ASK FOR IT. THEN SHE CKS INTO THEIR SYSTEM, ELLS ME WHAT TIME I EED TO BE THERE...
O WHEN JACKIE O'ROURDAN'S OB LAWYER, BEN GOLDMAN, NTERS THE PARKING GARAGE TH HIS SECURITY DETAIL LATE IN THE DAY...
↑ Elevators
...HE GETS A SURPRISE.
PRIVATE PROPERTY
101
RESERVED
BLAMBLAM
KUMP KUMP
KUMP
RESER

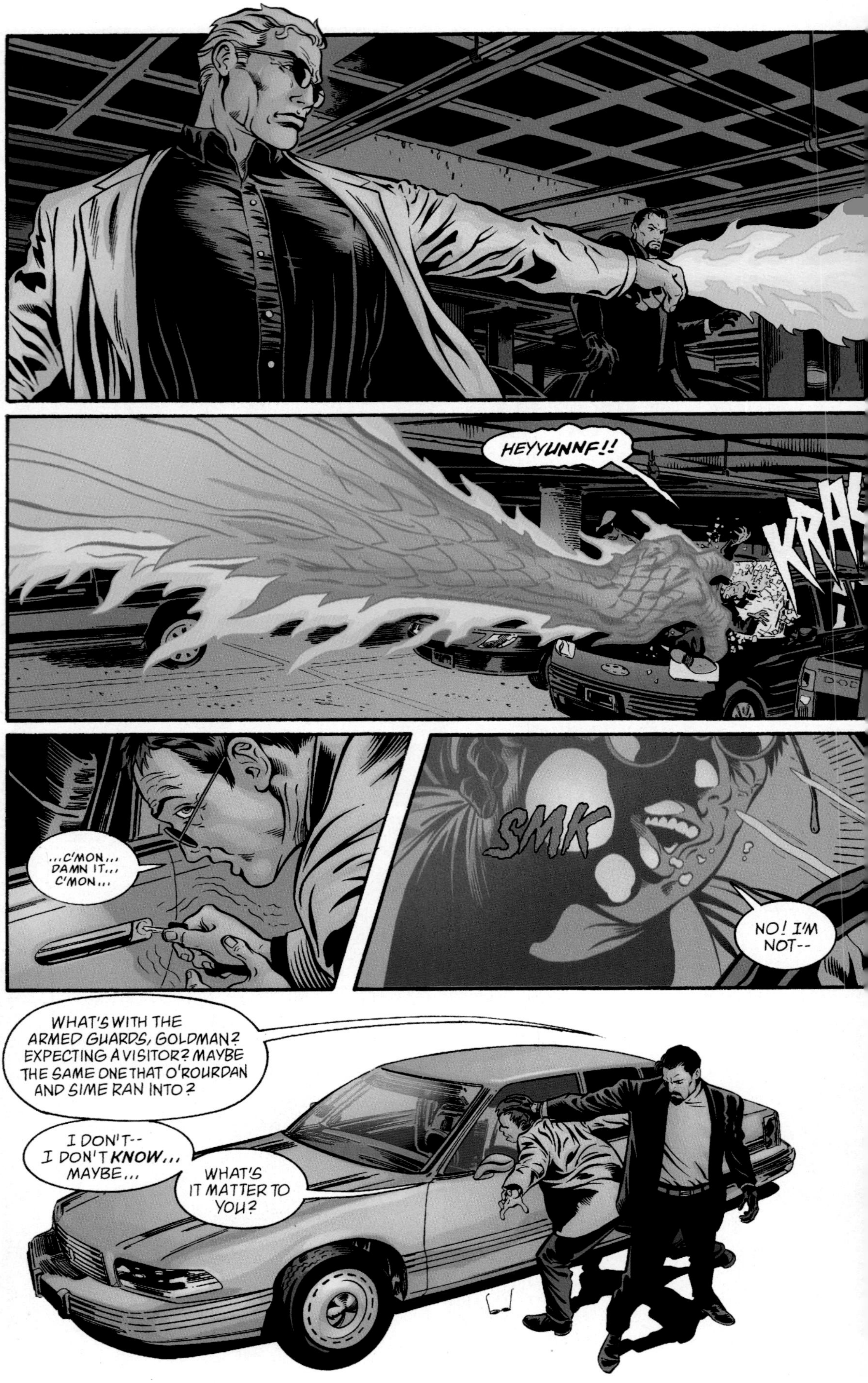
HEYYUNNF!!
KRA
...C'MON... DAMN IT... C'MON...
SMK
NO! I'M NOT--
WHAT'S WITH THE ARMED GUARDS, GOLDMAN? EXPECTING A VISITOR? MAYBE THE SAME ONE THAT O'ROURDAN AND SIME RAN INTO?
I DON'T-- I DON'T KNOW... MAYBE...
WHAT'S IT MATTER TO YOU?

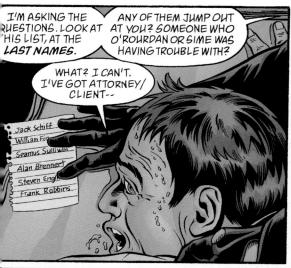

I'M ASKING THE QUESTIONS. LOOK AT THIS LIST, AT THE **LAST NAMES**.

ANY OF THEM JUMP OUT AT YOU? SOMEONE WHO O'ROURDAN OR SIME WAS HAVING TROUBLE WITH?

WHAT? I CAN'T. I'VE GOT ATTORNEY/CLIENT--

Jack Schiff
William Fin...
Seamus Sullivan
Alan Brennert
Steven Engl...
Frank Robbins

TRY AGAIN. LOOK AT THE LIST.

SMAK

OKAY, OKAY... **STOP!**

SULLIVAN. I DON'T KNOW WHO THIS SEAMUS GUY IS, BUT I KNOW A **FRANCIS** SULLIVAN. HE AND O'ROURDAN HAD A **BIG** FALLING OUT A WHILE **BACK**.

SULLIVAN WAS SUPPOSED TO WORK SOME OF THE FRONT BUSINESSES THAT **SIME** ENDED UP RUNNING...

WAIT! ARE YOU TRYING TO TELL ME THAT--?

WHO THE HELL **ARE** YOU?

OH... OH, **GOD**...

...OH, GOD PLEASE DON'T KILL ME... PLEASE...

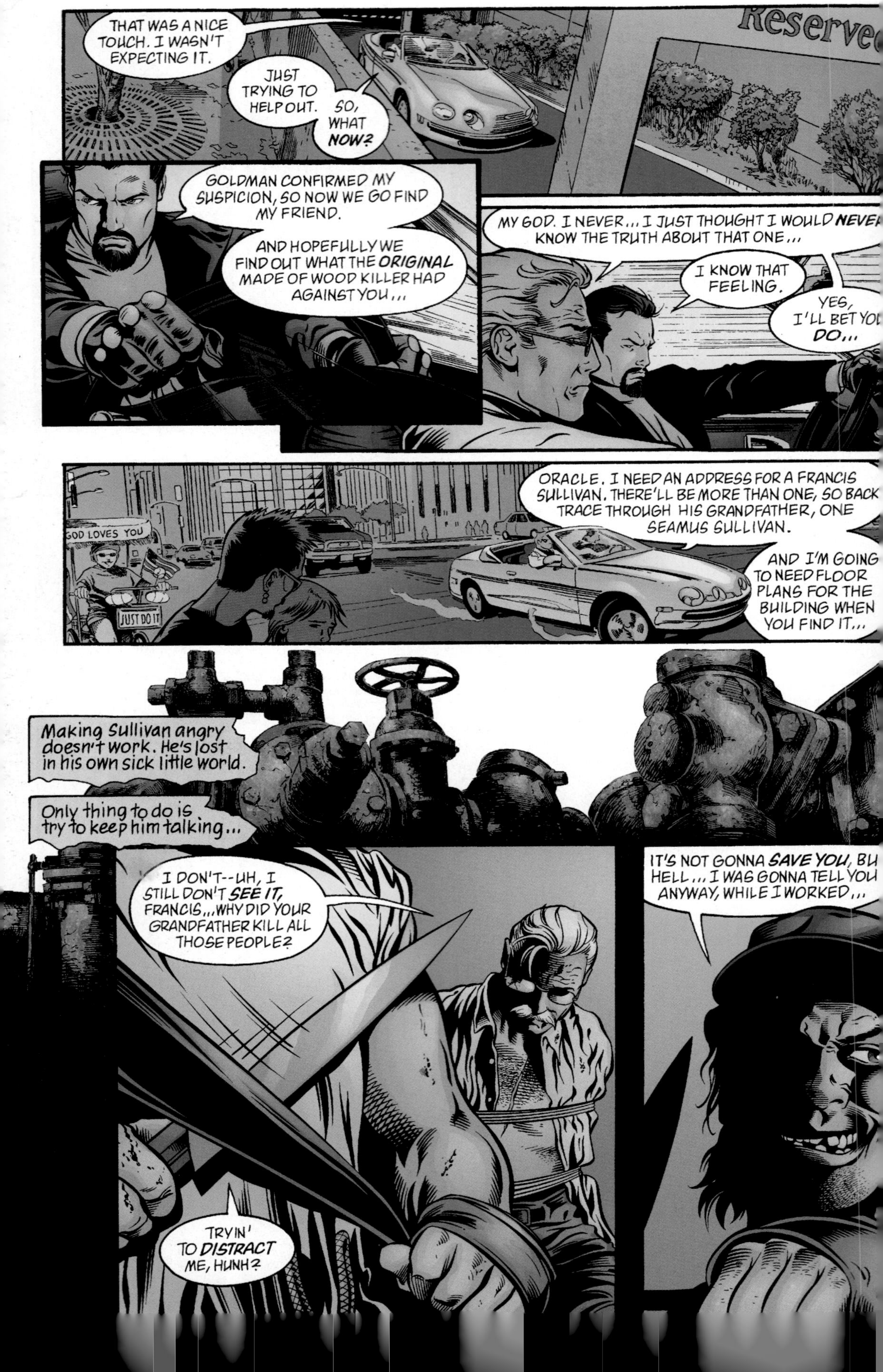
THAT WAS A NICE TOUCH. I WASN'T EXPECTING IT.
JUST TRYING TO HELP OUT.
SO, WHAT NOW?
Reserved
GOLDMAN CONFIRMED MY SUSPICION, SO NOW WE GO FIND MY FRIEND.
AND HOPEFULLY WE FIND OUT WHAT THE ORIGINAL MADE OF WOOD KILLER HAD AGAINST YOU...
MY GOD. I NEVER... I JUST THOUGHT I WOULD NEVER KNOW THE TRUTH ABOUT THAT ONE...
I KNOW THAT FEELING.
YES, I'LL BET YOU DO...
GOD LOVES YOU
JUST DO IT
ORACLE. I NEED AN ADDRESS FOR A FRANCIS SULLIVAN. THERE'LL BE MORE THAN ONE, SO BACK TRACE THROUGH HIS GRANDFATHER, ONE SEAMUS SULLIVAN.
AND I'M GOING TO NEED FLOOR PLANS FOR THE BUILDING WHEN YOU FIND IT...
Making Sullivan angry doesn't work. He's lost in his own sick little world.
Only thing to do is try to keep him talking...
I DON'T--UH, I STILL DON'T SEE IT, FRANCIS... WHY DID YOUR GRANDFATHER KILL ALL THOSE PEOPLE?
TRYIN' TO DISTRACT ME, HUNH?
IT'S NOT GONNA SAVE YOU, BUT HELL... I WAS GONNA TELL YOU ANYWAY, WHILE I WORKED...

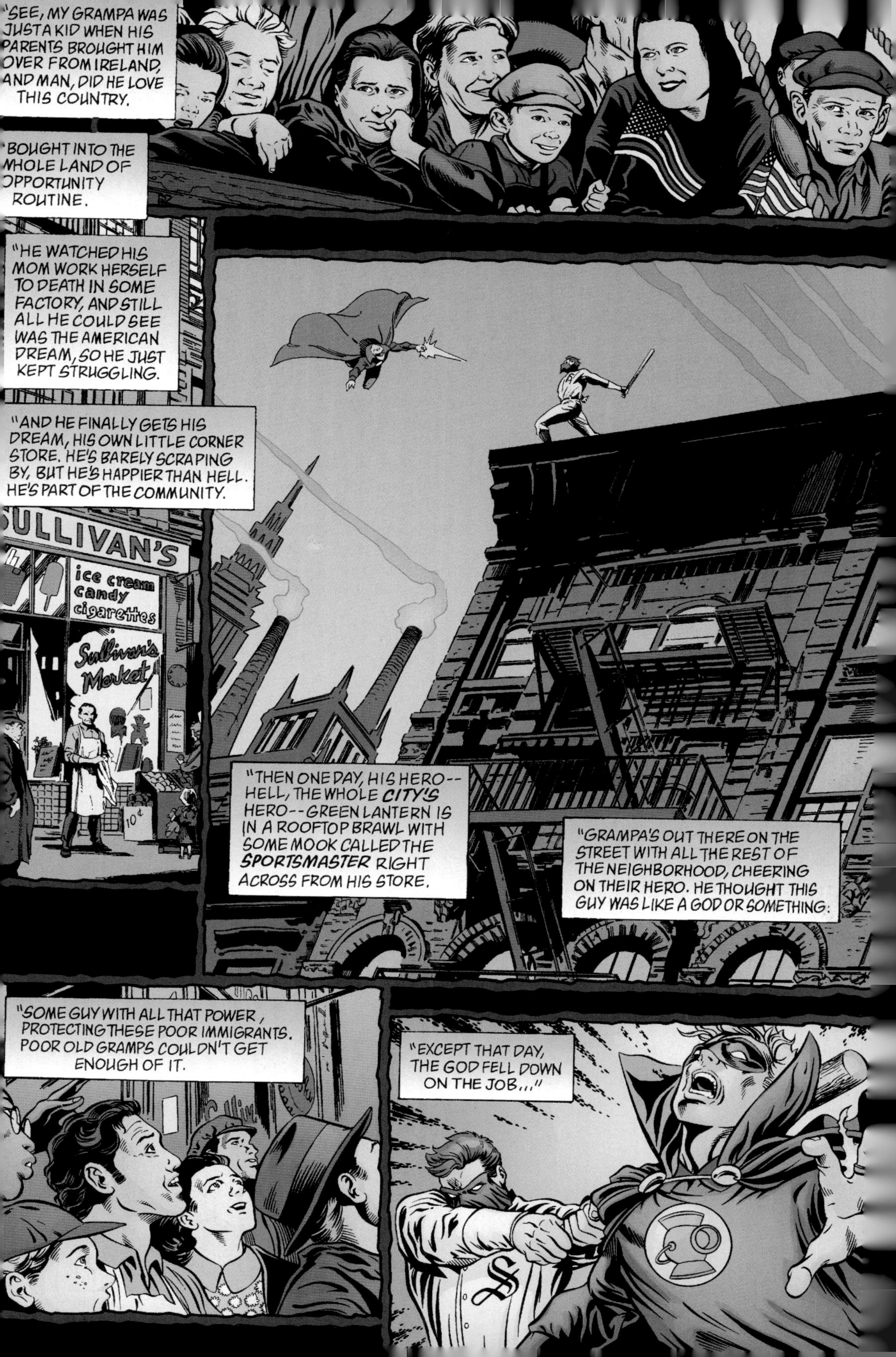
"SEE, MY GRAMPA WAS JUST A KID WHEN HIS PARENTS BROUGHT HIM OVER FROM IRELAND, AND MAN, DID HE LOVE THIS COUNTRY.
"BOUGHT INTO THE WHOLE LAND OF OPPORTUNITY ROUTINE.
"HE WATCHED HIS MOM WORK HERSELF TO DEATH IN SOME FACTORY, AND STILL ALL HE COULD SEE WAS THE AMERICAN DREAM, SO HE JUST KEPT STRUGGLING.
"AND HE FINALLY GETS HIS DREAM, HIS OWN LITTLE CORNER STORE. HE'S BARELY SCRAPING BY, BUT HE'S HAPPIER THAN HELL. HE'S PART OF THE COMMUNITY.
SULLIVAN'S
ice cream
candy
cigarettes
Sullivan's Market
10¢
"THEN ONE DAY, HIS HERO-- HELL, THE WHOLE CITY'S HERO--GREEN LANTERN IS IN A ROOFTOP BRAWL WITH SOME MOOK CALLED THE SPORTSMASTER RIGHT ACROSS FROM HIS STORE.
"GRAMPA'S OUT THERE ON THE STREET WITH ALL THE REST OF THE NEIGHBORHOOD, CHEERING ON THEIR HERO. HE THOUGHT THIS GUY WAS LIKE A GOD OR SOMETHING.
"SOME GUY WITH ALL THAT POWER, PROTECTING THESE POOR IMMIGRANTS. POOR OLD GRAMPS COULDN'T GET ENOUGH OF IT.
"EXCEPT THAT DAY, THE GOD FELL DOWN ON THE JOB..."

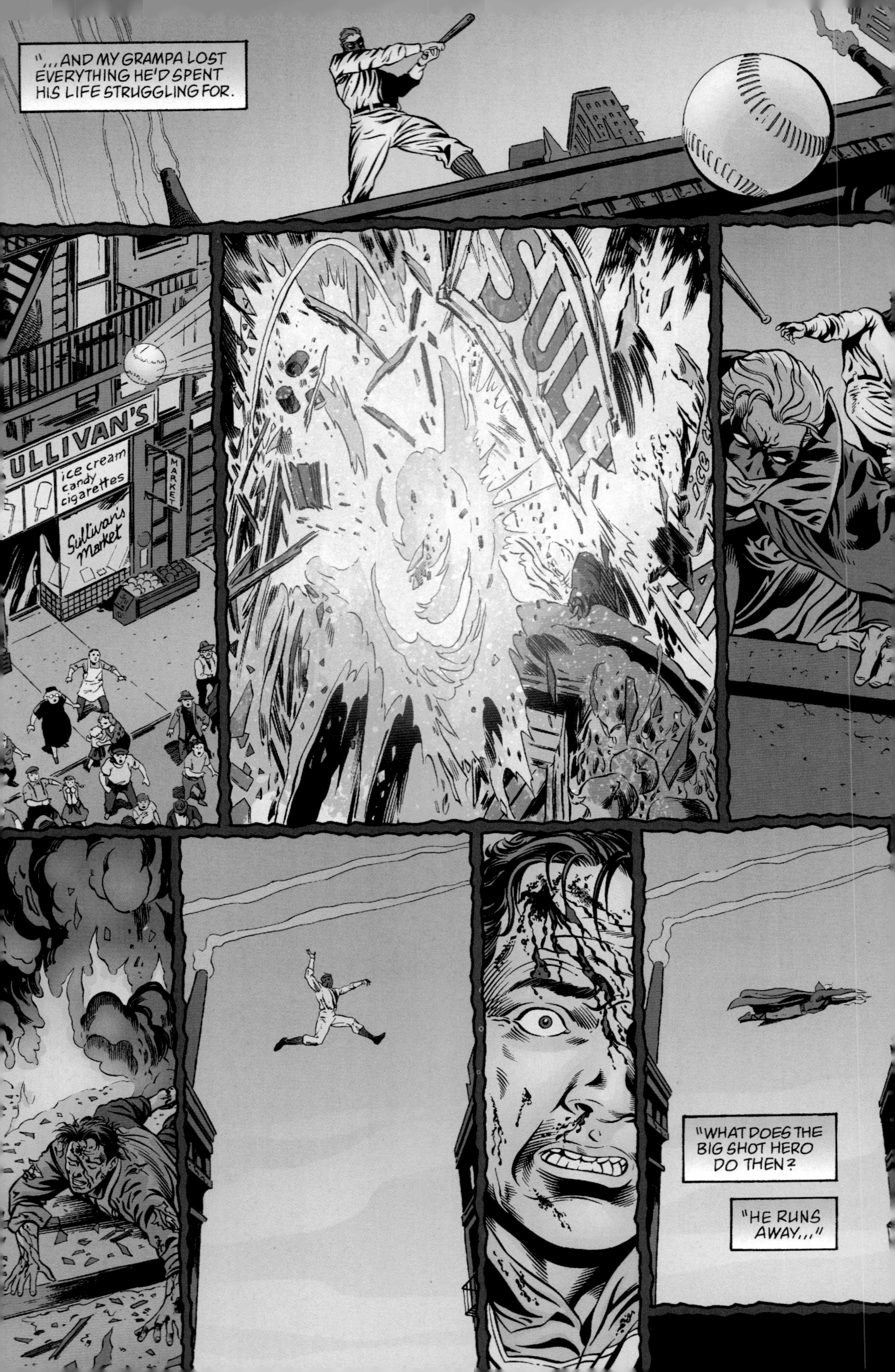
"...AND MY GRAMPA LOST EVERYTHING HE'D SPENT HIS LIFE STRUGGLING FOR.
SULLIVAN'S
SULLIVAN'S
ice cream
candy
cigarettes
Sullivan's Market
MARKET
"WHAT DOES THE BIG SHOT HERO DO THEN?
"HE RUNS AWAY..."

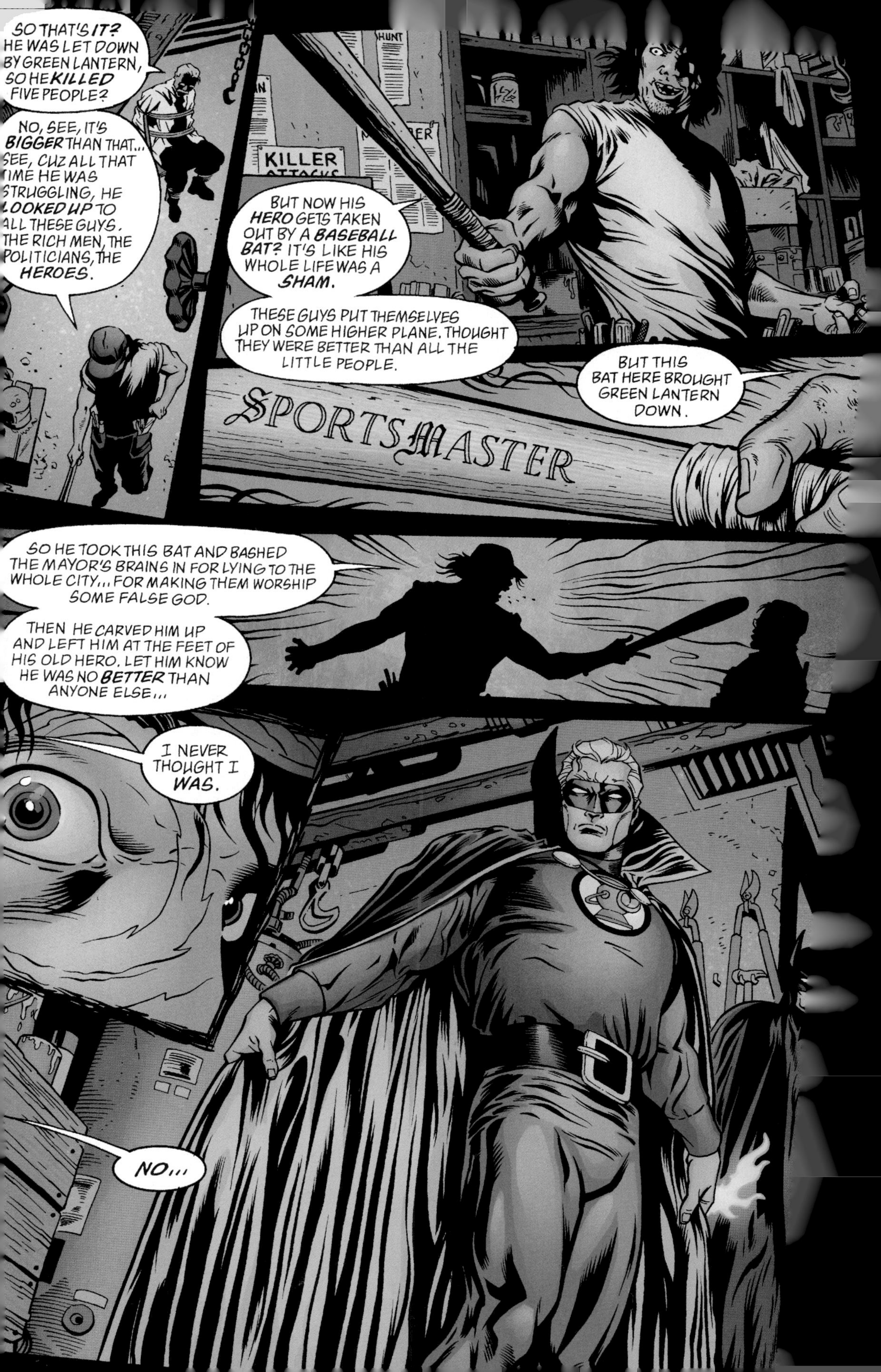
SO THAT'S IT? HE WAS LET DOWN BY GREEN LANTERN, SO HE KILLED FIVE PEOPLE?
NO, SEE, IT'S BIGGER THAN THAT... SEE, CUZ ALL THAT TIME HE WAS STRUGGLING, HE LOOKED UP TO ALL THESE GUYS. THE RICH MEN, THE POLITICIANS, THE HEROES.
KILLER ATTACKS
BUT NOW HIS HERO GETS TAKEN OUT BY A BASEBALL BAT? IT'S LIKE HIS WHOLE LIFE WAS A SHAM.
THESE GUYS PUT THEMSELVES UP ON SOME HIGHER PLANE. THOUGHT THEY WERE BETTER THAN ALL THE LITTLE PEOPLE.
BUT THIS BAT HERE BROUGHT GREEN LANTERN DOWN.
SPORTSMASTER
SO HE TOOK THIS BAT AND BASHED THE MAYOR'S BRAINS IN FOR LYING TO THE WHOLE CITY... FOR MAKING THEM WORSHIP SOME FALSE GOD.
THEN HE CARVED HIM UP AND LEFT HIM AT THE FEET OF HIS OLD HERO. LET HIM KNOW HE WAS NO BETTER THAN ANYONE ELSE...
I NEVER THOUGHT I WAS.
NO...

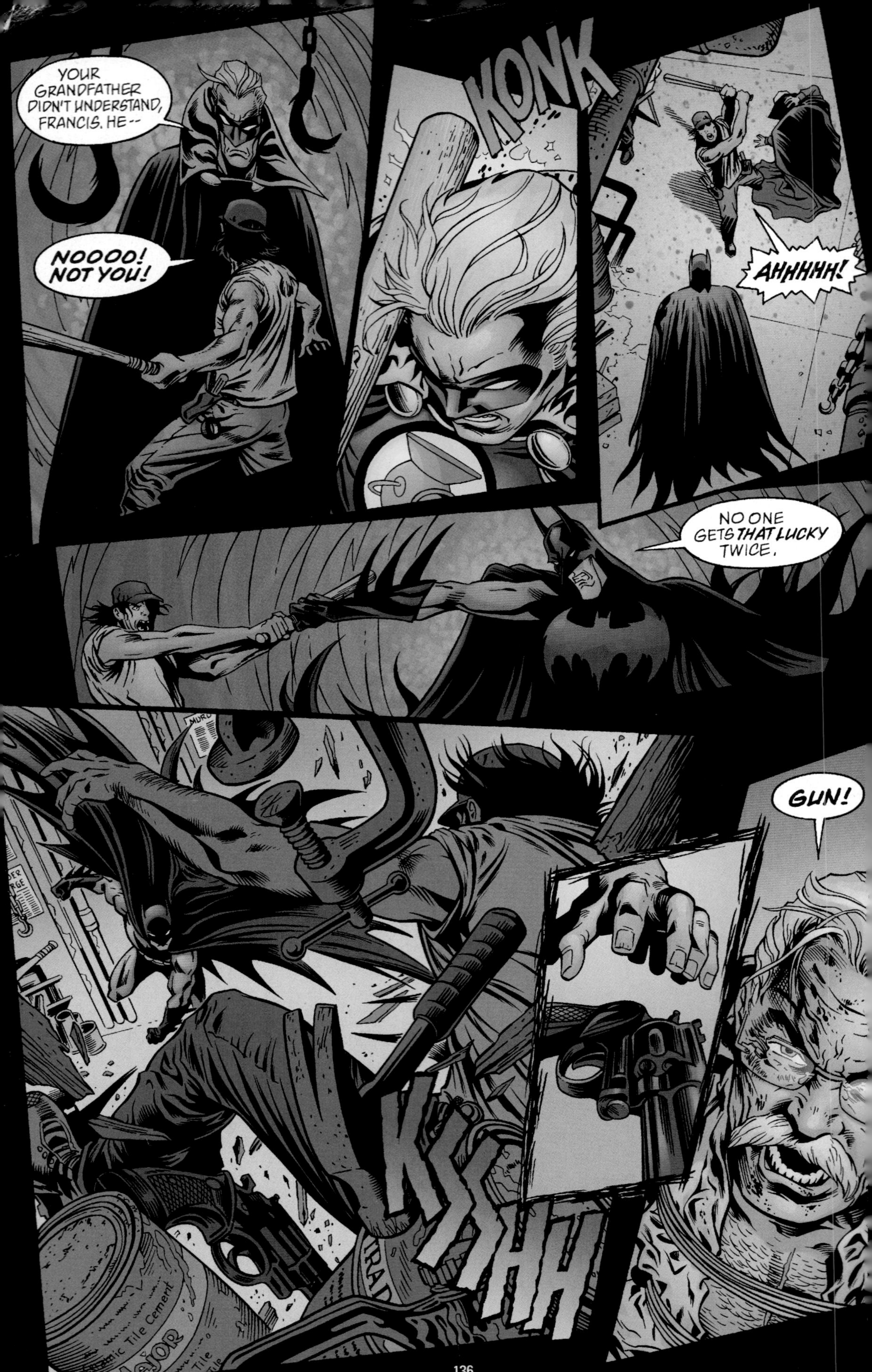
YOUR GRANDFATHER DIDN'T UNDERSTAND, FRANCIS. HE--
NOOOO! NOT YOU!
KONK
AHHHHH!
NO ONE GETS THAT LUCKY TWICE.
GUN!
Ceramic Tile Cement
MaJOR

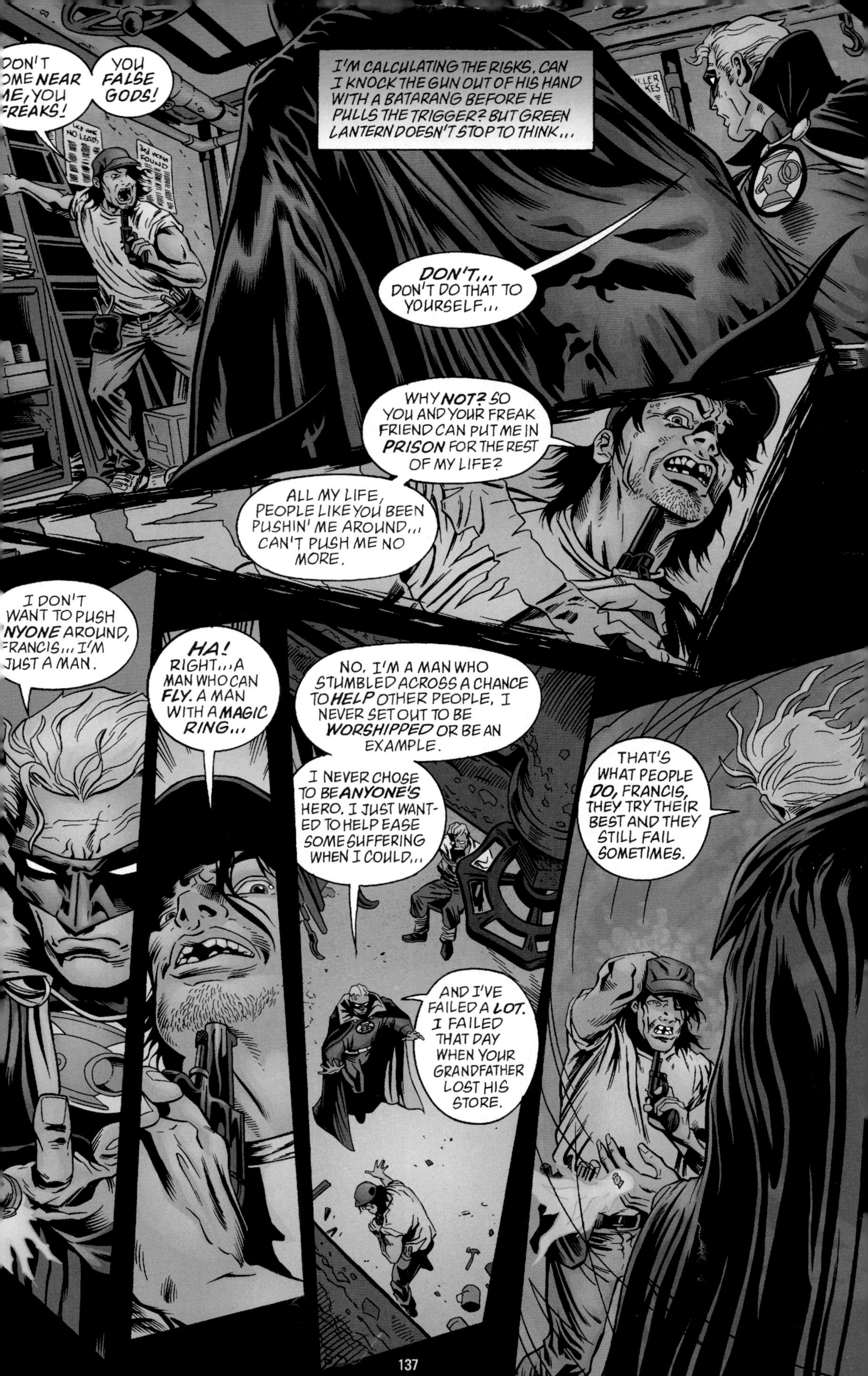
DON'T OME NEAR ME, YOU FREAKS!
YOU FALSE GODS!
I'M CALCULATING THE RISKS. CAN I KNOCK THE GUN OUT OF HIS HAND WITH A BATARANG BEFORE HE PULLS THE TRIGGER? BUT GREEN LANTERN DOESN'T STOP TO THINK...
DON'T... DON'T DO THAT TO YOURSELF...
WHY NOT? SO YOU AND YOUR FREAK FRIEND CAN PUT ME IN PRISON FOR THE REST OF MY LIFE?
ALL MY LIFE, PEOPLE LIKE YOU BEEN PUSHIN' ME AROUND... CAN'T PUSH ME NO MORE.
I DON'T WANT TO PUSH NYONE AROUND, FRANCIS... I'M JUST A MAN.
HA! RIGHT... A MAN WHO CAN FLY. A MAN WITH A MAGIC RING...
NO. I'M A MAN WHO STUMBLED ACROSS A CHANCE TO HELP OTHER PEOPLE. I NEVER SET OUT TO BE WORSHIPPED OR BE AN EXAMPLE.
I NEVER CHOSE TO BE ANYONE'S HERO. I JUST WANTED TO HELP EASE SOME SUFFERING WHEN I COULD...
AND I'VE FAILED A LOT. I FAILED THAT DAY WHEN YOUR GRANDFATHER LOST HIS STORE.
THAT'S WHAT PEOPLE DO, FRANCIS. THEY TRY THEIR BEST AND THEY STILL FAIL SOMETIMES.

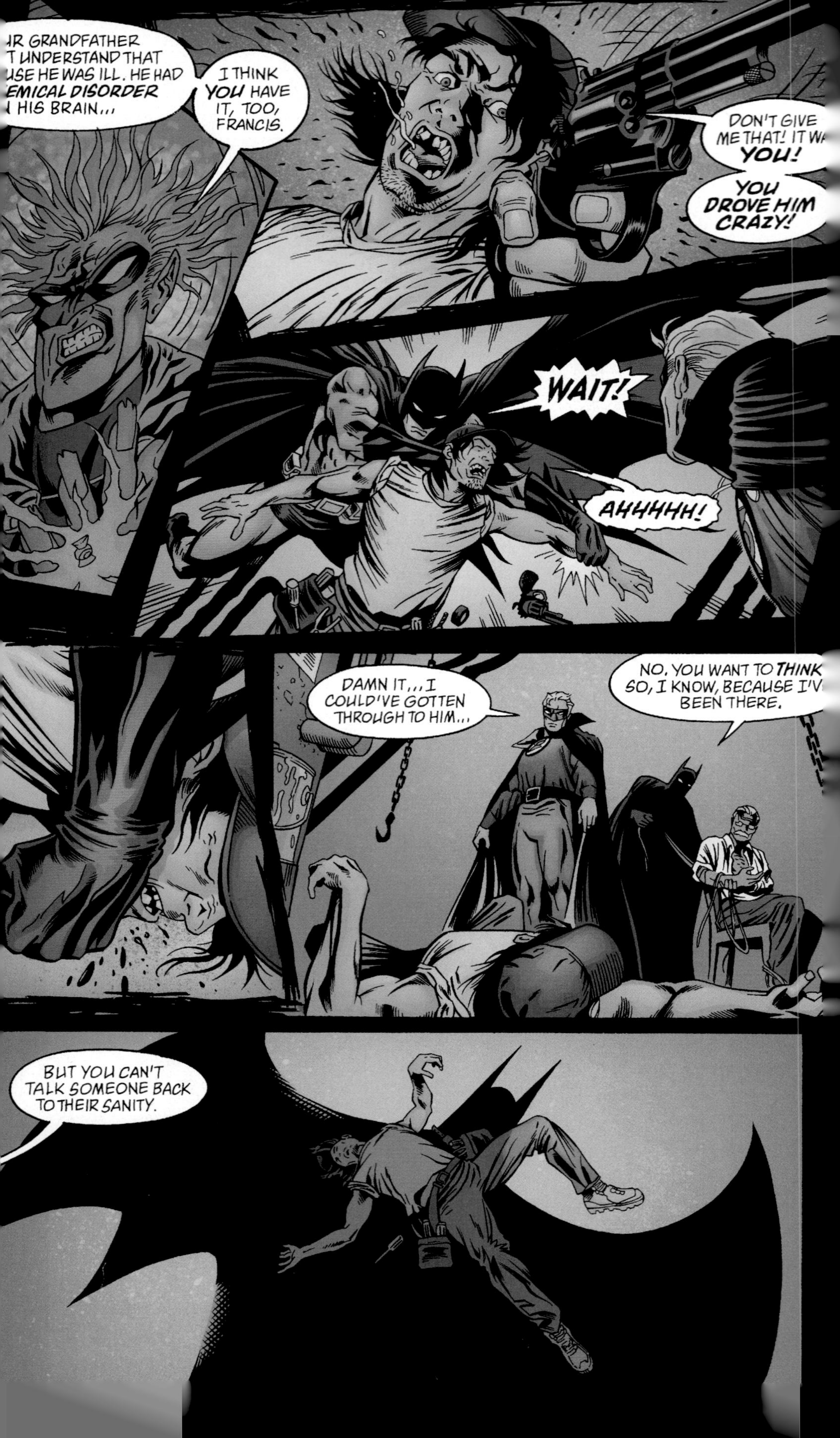

...R GRANDFATHER ...T UNDERSTAND THAT ...USE HE WAS ILL. HE HAD ...EMICAL DISORDER ...N HIS BRAIN...
I THINK YOU HAVE IT, TOO, FRANCIS.
DON'T GIVE ME THAT! IT WA... YOU!
YOU DROVE HIM CRAZY!
WAIT!
AHHHHH!
DAMN IT... I COULD'VE GOTTEN THROUGH TO HIM...
NO. YOU WANT TO THINK SO, I KNOW, BECAUSE I'V... BEEN THERE.
BUT YOU CAN'T TALK SOMEONE BACK TO THEIR SANITY.

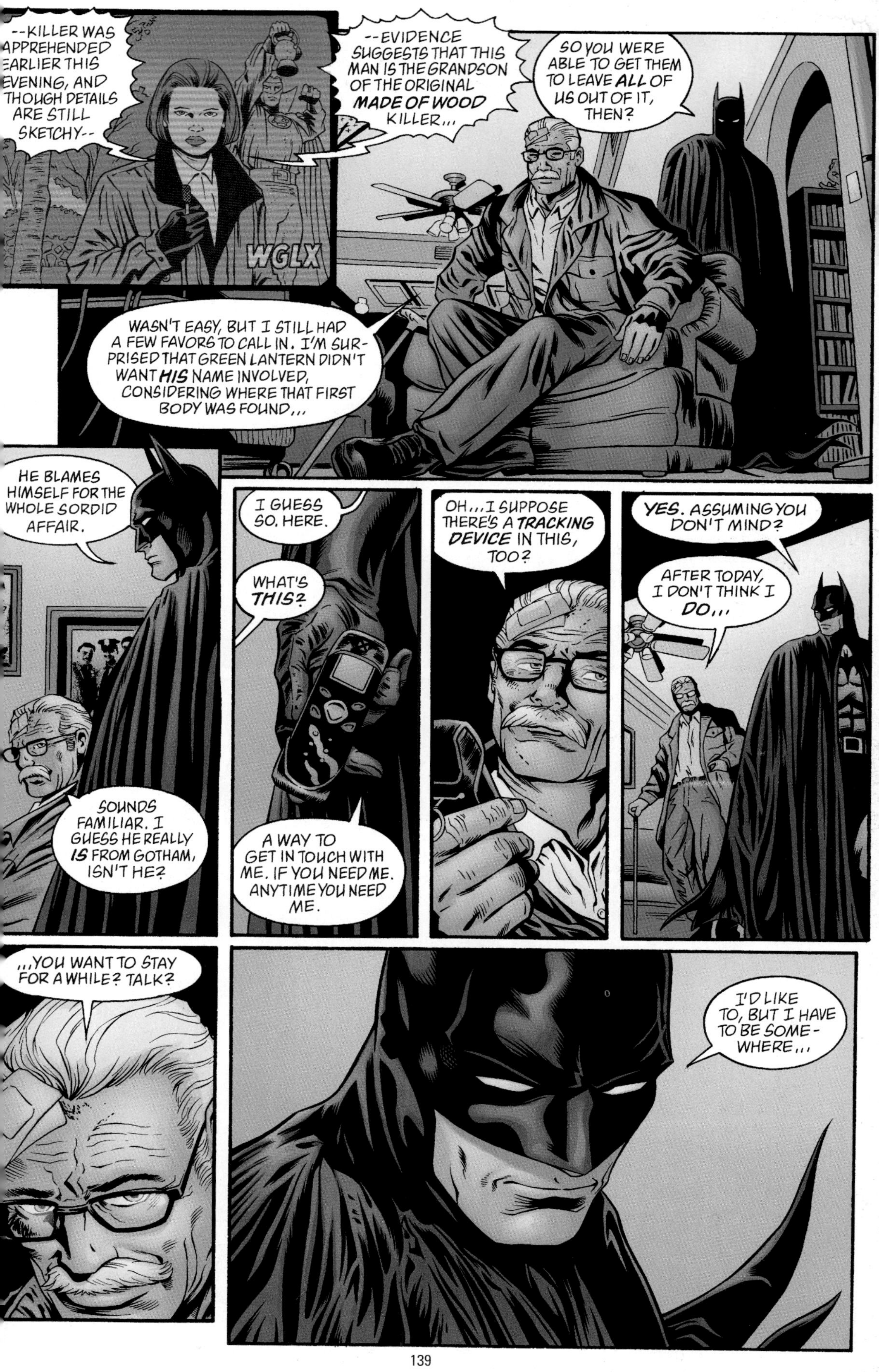
--KILLER WAS APPREHENDED EARLIER THIS EVENING, AND THOUGH DETAILS ARE STILL SKETCHY--
--EVIDENCE SUGGESTS THAT THIS MAN IS THE GRANDSON OF THE ORIGINAL MADE OF WOOD KILLER...
WGLX
SO YOU WERE ABLE TO GET THEM TO LEAVE ALL OF US OUT OF IT, THEN?
WASN'T EASY, BUT I STILL HAD A FEW FAVORS TO CALL IN. I'M SURPRISED THAT GREEN LANTERN DIDN'T WANT HIS NAME INVOLVED, CONSIDERING WHERE THAT FIRST BODY WAS FOUND...
HE BLAMES HIMSELF FOR THE WHOLE SORDID AFFAIR.
SOUNDS FAMILIAR. I GUESS HE REALLY IS FROM GOTHAM, ISN'T HE?
I GUESS SO. HERE.
WHAT'S THIS?
A WAY TO GET IN TOUCH WITH ME. IF YOU NEED ME. ANYTIME YOU NEED ME.
OH...I SUPPOSE THERE'S A TRACKING DEVICE IN THIS, TOO?
YES. ASSUMING YOU DON'T MIND?
AFTER TODAY, I DON'T THINK I DO...
...YOU WANT TO STAY FOR A WHILE? TALK?
I'D LIKE TO, BUT I HAVE TO BE SOMEWHERE...

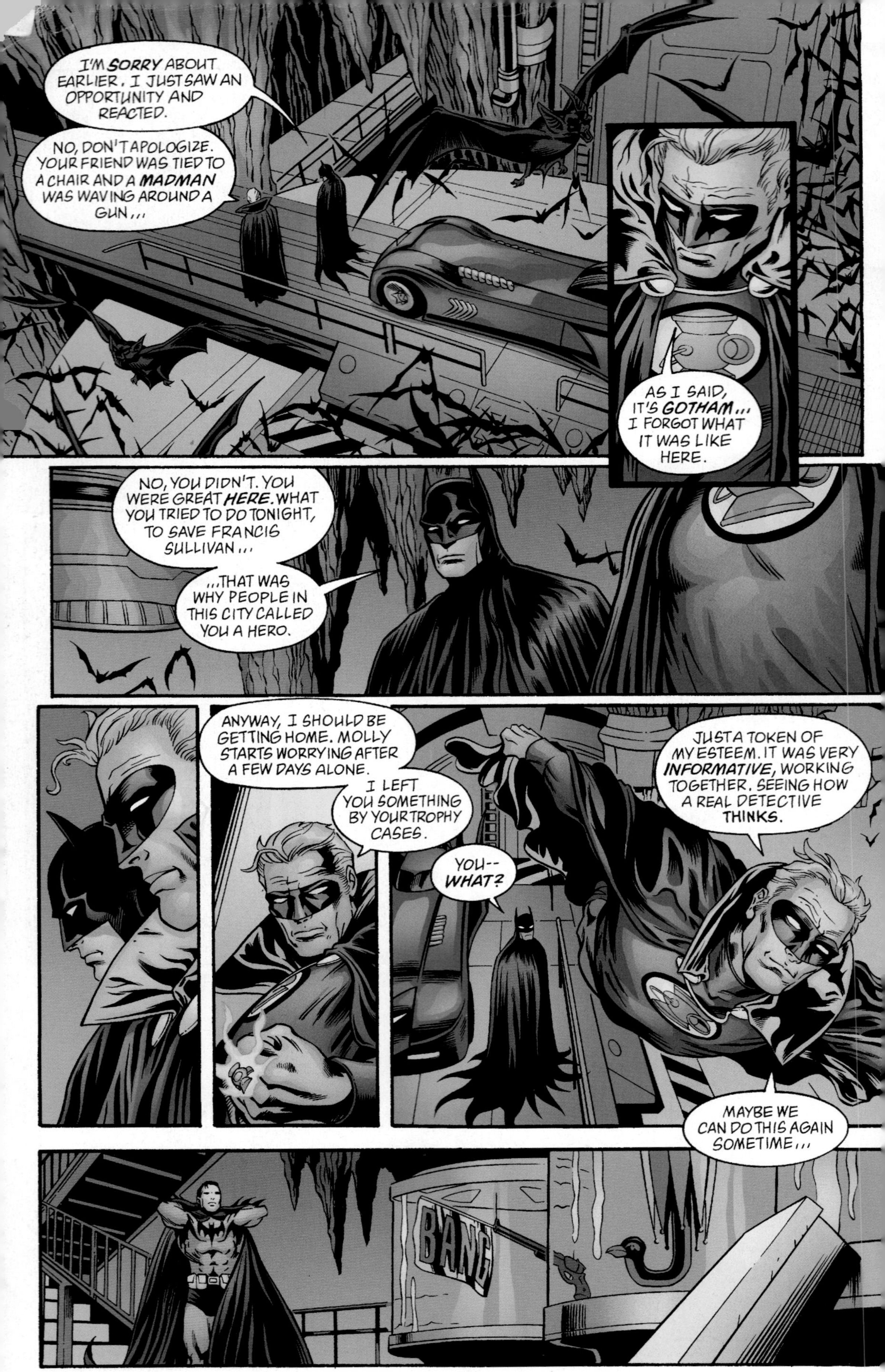

I'M SORRY ABOUT EARLIER. I JUST SAW AN OPPORTUNITY AND REACTED.
NO, DON'T APOLOGIZE. YOUR FRIEND WAS TIED TO A CHAIR AND A MADMAN WAS WAVING AROUND A GUN...
AS I SAID, IT'S GOTHAM... I FORGOT WHAT IT WAS LIKE HERE.
NO, YOU DIDN'T. YOU WERE GREAT HERE. WHAT YOU TRIED TO DO TONIGHT, TO SAVE FRANCIS SULLIVAN...
...THAT WAS WHY PEOPLE IN THIS CITY CALLED YOU A HERO.
ANYWAY, I SHOULD BE GETTING HOME. MOLLY STARTS WORRYING AFTER A FEW DAYS ALONE.
I LEFT YOU SOMETHING BY YOUR TROPHY CASES.
YOU-- WHAT?
JUST A TOKEN OF MY ESTEEM. IT WAS VERY INFORMATIVE, WORKING TOGETHER. SEEING HOW A REAL DETECTIVE THINKS.
MAYBE WE CAN DO THIS AGAIN SOMETIME...
BANG

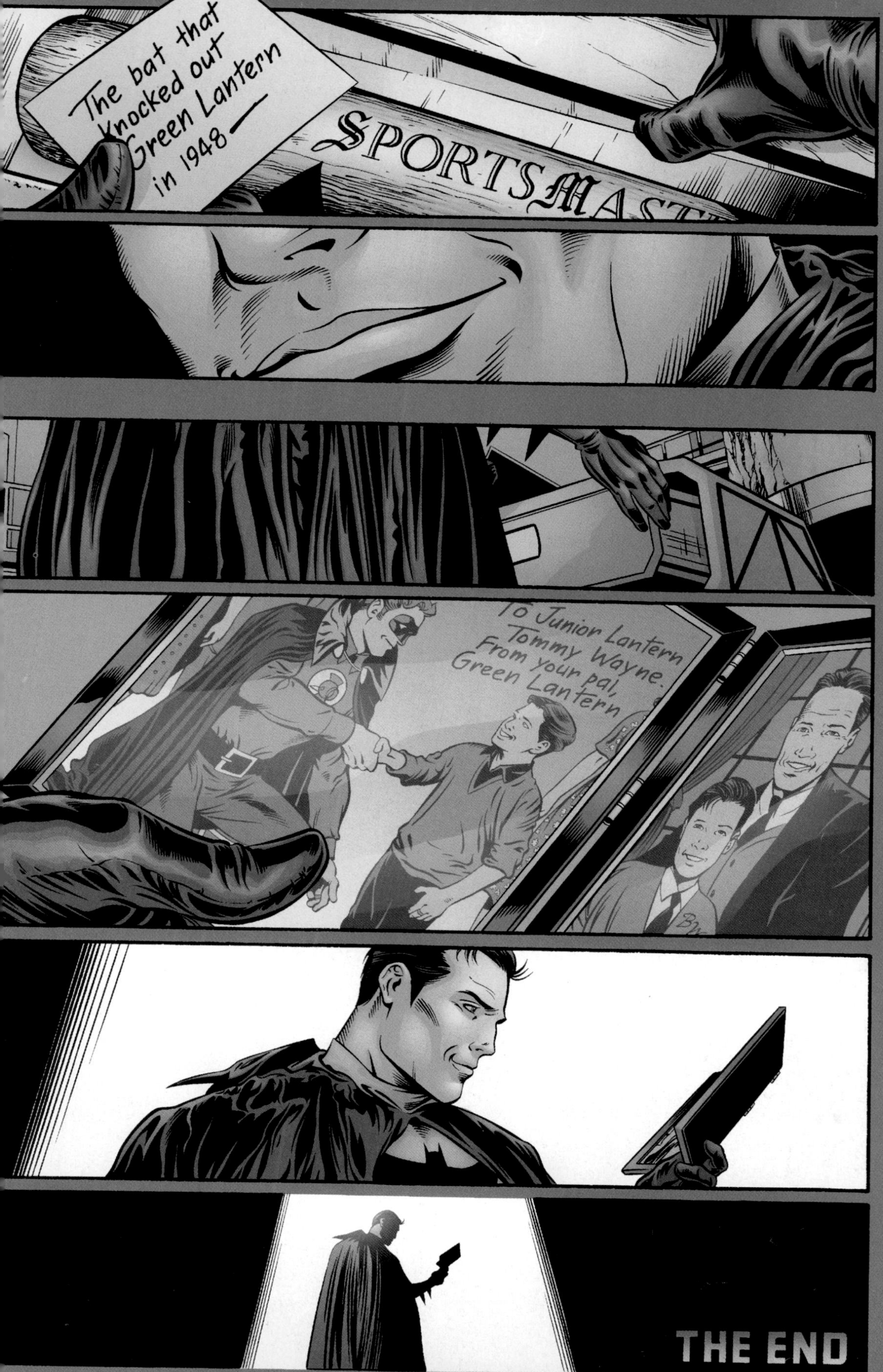

The bat that knocked out Green Lantern in 1948
SPORTSMAST
To Junior Lantern Tommy Wayne. From your pal, Green Lantern
THE END

Biographies

A one-time cartoonist, **ED BRUBAKER** has been working as a writer since the early 1990s, and in that time his work has won several awards, including both the Harvey and Eisner Awards for Best Writer in 2007, and has been translated around the world. His comics credits include BATMAN, CATWOMAN, GOTHAM CENTRAL and SLEEPER for DC/WildStorm and *Daredevil, Captain America* and *Criminal* for Marvel. He lives and works in Seattle, Washington with his wife, Melanie, and many pets.

Born in 1963 in the Year of the Rabbit, **DOUG MAHNKE** embarked on a love affair with comics at the age of five, having received a pile of *Spider-Man* issues from a rugby-playing college student named Mike who lived in his basement. A consistent interest in the medium, coupled with some art skill, landed Douga job drawing comics for Dark Horse at the age of 24 (the date is known precisely, as it occurred just two weeks before he wed his lovely bride). His first gig was illustrating a moody detective one-shot entitled *Homicide*, written by John Arcudi. The two went on to collaborate on Dark Horse's *The Mask* and their creator-owned series MAJOR BUMMER, originally published by DC. Since then Doug has worked on a wide variety of titles (including SUPERMAN: THE MAN OF STEEL, JLA, BATMAN, TEAM ZERO, SEVEN SOLDIERS: FRANKENSTEIN, BLACK ADAM: THE DARK AGE and STORMWATCH: P.H.D.) with such writers as Joe Kelly, Judd Winnick, Chuck Dixon, Grant Morrison, Christos Gage and Ed Brubaker, just to name a few. He resides in the midwest with his wife and six kids, one dog, and a bunny named Suzie.

PATRICK ZIRCHER has been drawing comics professionally for 15 years and insists that he's "just getting the hang of it." With over a hundred issues to his credit, his work has been featured in NIGHTWING, *Vampirella, Iron Man* and *Terror Inc.* The original Green Lantern is one of his favorite characters. Doiby Dickles is not. Patrick lives in Indiana with his wife, two children, and a black cat named Isis.

AARON SOWD has contributed to a wide variety of comics titles, including JLA, BATMAN: HARLEY QUINN, *The Uncanny X-Men, Weapon Zero* and his creator-owned comic *MasterMinds.* He has also created storyboards, conceptual designs and style guides for such films as *Transformers, Solaris, Austin Powers in Goldmember, Ultimate Avengers 2, God of War* and *Anastasia*, and his illustrations have appeared in *The New York Times, People, Time,* and *Playstation* magazines. Aaron teaches at the Art Center College of Design in Pasadena and lives by the beach in Venice, California, where he resents the fact that he has no free time to enjoy it.

MICS™

FROM THE CREATOR OF *300* & *SIN CITY*

FRANK MILLER

BATMAN: THE DARK KNIGHT RETURNS with KLAUS JANSON

BATMAN:
THE DARK KNIGHT
STRIKES AGAIN

BATMAN: YEAR ONE
DELUXE EDITION

th DAVID MAZZUCCHELLI

ALL-STAR BATMAN
& ROBIN, THE BOY
WONDER VOL. 1

RANK MILLER + JIM LEE

with JIM LEE

BATMAN: THE DARK KNIGHT RETURNS

FRANK MILLER

with KLAUS JANSON and LYNN VARLE

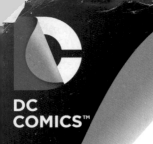

DC COMICS™

"Compelling drama. A great example c
the literary and artistic maturity of th
graphic novel format.
—SCHOOL LIBRARY JOURNA

FROM THE *NEW YORK TIMES* BESTSELLING WRITER:

ED BRUBAKER & GREG RUCKA

with MICHAEL LARK

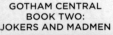

GOTHAM CENTRAL
BOOK TWO:
JOKERS AND MADMEN

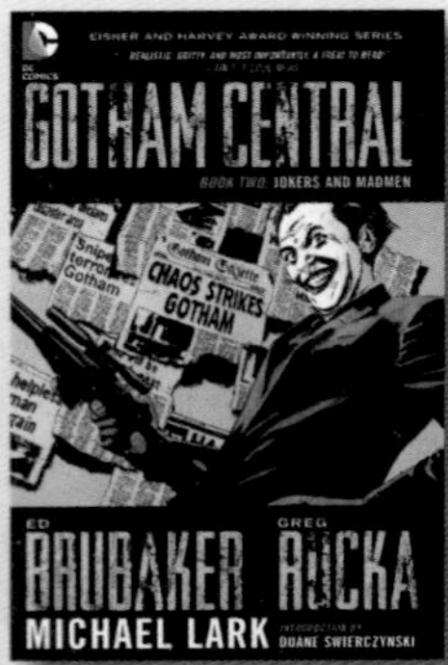
GOTHAM CENTRAL
BOOK TWO: JOKERS AND MADMEN
CHAOS STRIKES GOTHAM
ED BRUBAKER GREG RUCKA
MICHAEL LARK

GOTHAM CENTRAL
BOOK THREE:
ON THE FREAK BEAT

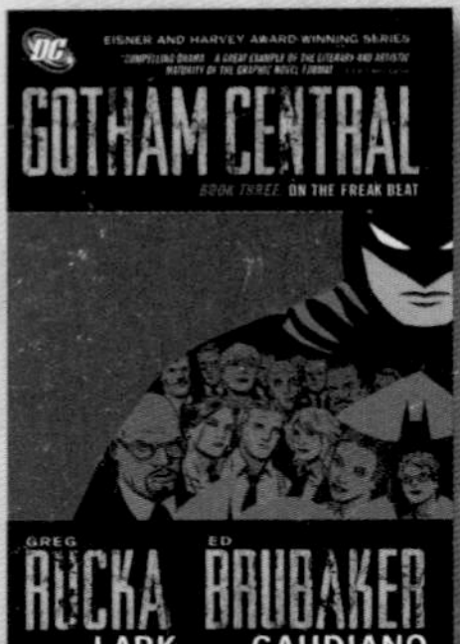
EISNER AND HARVEY AWARD-WINNING SERIES
GOTHAM CENTRAL
BOOK THREE: ON THE FREAK BEAT
GREG RUCKA ED BRUBAKER
MICHAEL LARK STEFANO GAUDIANO

GOTHAM CENTRAL
BOOK FOUR:
CORRIGAN

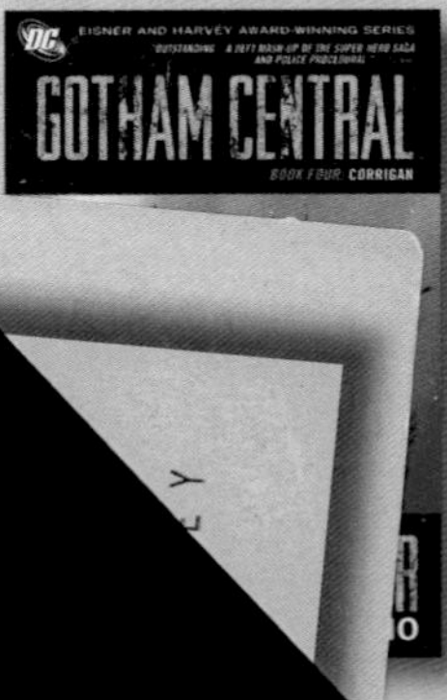
EISNER AND HARVEY AWARD-WINNING SERIES
GOTHAM CENTRAL
BOOK FOUR: CORRIGAN

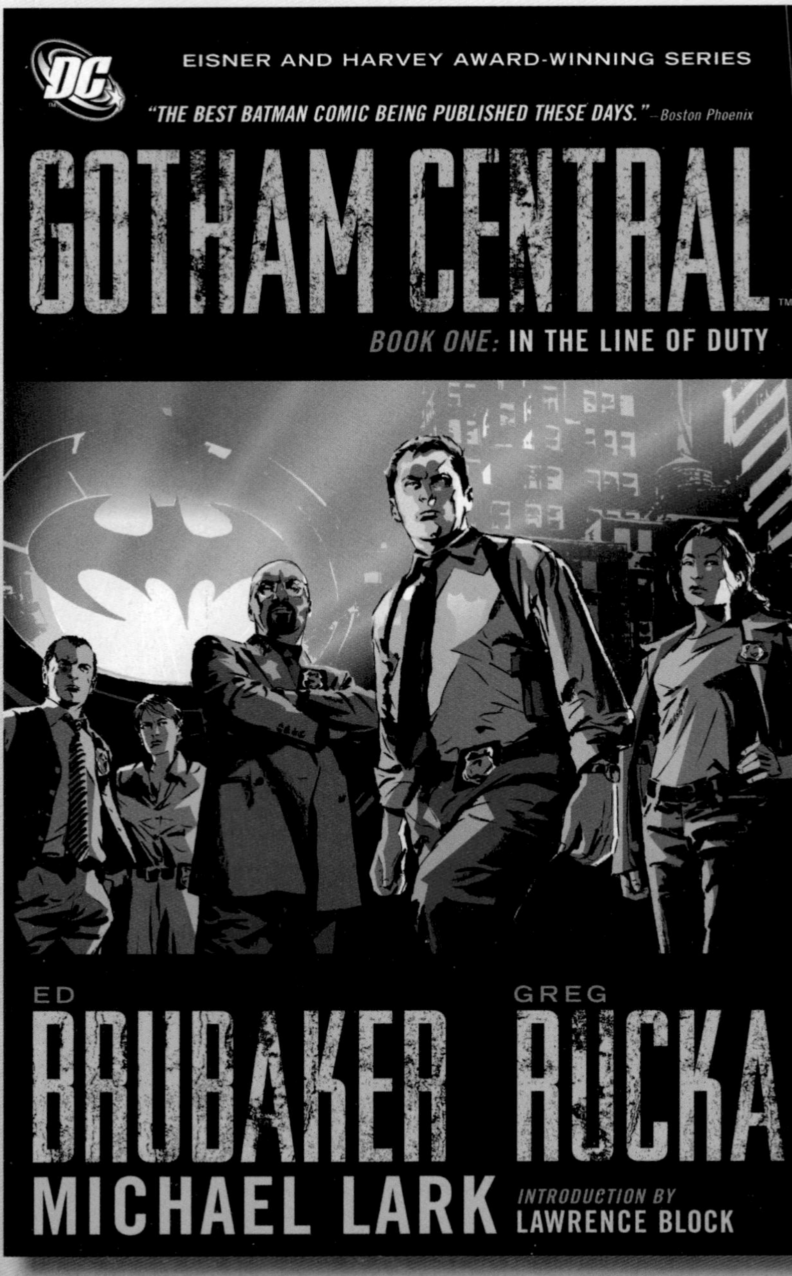
EISNER AND HARVEY AWARD-WINNING SERIES
"THE BEST BATMAN COMIC BEING PUBLISHED THESE DAYS." –Boston Phoenix
GOTHAM CENTRAL™
BOOK ONE: IN THE LINE OF DUTY
ED BRUBAKER GREG RUCKA
MICHAEL LARK
INTRODUCTION BY LAWRENCE BLOCK